Crime and Justice in a Mass Society

799-1B-72

CRIME
AND
JUSTICE
IN A
MASS
SOCIETY

Alexander B. Smith

Harriet Pollack

John Jay College of Criminal Justice
City University of New York

XEROX COLLEGE PUBLISHING

Waltham, Massachusetts / Toronto

CONSULTING EDITORS

Arthur Niederhoffer
Abraham S. Blumberg
John Jay College of Criminal Justice

To Jennie and Joe

Our criminal justice system has been characterized as archaic, bureaucratic, and inefficient. As a consequence each of its three main divisions—the police, the courts, and corrections—is under fierce pressure to change. This series of books on the criminal justice system assesses the problems, strengths and weaknesses, and the probable direction of change. The authors, all college professors, combine an academic background with practical experience in relevant fields. Each book will serve as a concise introduction and guide to a major area of criminal justice or law enforcement.

Foreword

Recently, the Crime Control Planning Agency of the City of New York began its planning document with the following:

> There is too much crime in New York City. There is too little justice and too little deterrence in our criminal justice system. . . .
>
> They [the citizens] now have a system for the administration of justice that is neither efficient enough to create a credible fear of punishment nor fair enough to command sincere respect for its values.

The same could be said of the other cities of the United States and, indeed, a good many observers are suggesting that in urban America the criminal justice system is close to the point of collapse. The citizen lives in increasing fear, crime statistics (whatever their validity) continue to climb, the police clearance rate for reported crimes declines, and the courts and penal institutions are overwhelmed by numbers.

What is wrong and how did it get that way? This nation took a system of criminal justice which developed over a long period of time in an essentially rural and homogeneous nation and transplanted it to a frontier society which consequently became heterogeneous and highly urbanized. The innate conservatism of the law and the relative inflexibility of the institutions which administer it have not adapted to the rapid changes which have taken place in American society, and the cracks and strains are now showing clearly enough for almost anyone to see. In fact, what was designed as an adversary system of justice has become an administered system—at least in urban America. Nevertheless, we continue to operate on the assumptions of the adversary system, with results that are satisfactory to few, if any, of the participants in the process—whether those who operate it or those who are its clients.

Almost everyone who is a part of or studies our present system sees the need for a fairly drastic overhaul of the machinery of justice, but there is little agreement on what kind of overhaul should take place. Before we can determine where we are and where we ought to go, we must ask a number of questions and attempt to answer them. For example, what is the nature of social control in this society? What is the relationship of criminal law to the total pattern of social control? How are our present institutions of criminal justice operating? What is the role of the police and what should it be? What is the function of our prisons? What should it be? How is a client of the criminal justice system treated as he goes through the process? Does the system operate as a rational, integrated whole or is it a series of unrelated institutions transferring the accused from one to the other? Or, to repeat my original question, where are we and how did we get here?

Professors Smith and Pollack do not answer all of these questions in this book. In fact, as in any good book, more questions are raised than are answered. On the other hand, a careful reading will convey to the reader much of the background and present conditions necessary for an informed opinion. This is a study of the legal history of this country, of the institutions which administer the law, and of the present state of the law in most of the important areas covered. Although the authors would never claim that they have written the last word on any of these difficult questions, they do provide an excellent beginning in asking them. Hopefully, this will lead to some answers.

DONALD H. RIDDLE
President
John Jay College of
April, 1971   *Criminal Justice*

Preface

This book is about criminal justice in the large cities of the United States. Our concern is with large cities because it is in urban America that our criminal justice system is perilously close to breakdown. Our smaller communities and rural areas may still be able to cope with the problems caused by law-breaking, but our big cities are in trouble. Most of the available data, moreover, comes from the large cities. In the 1970 election campaigns only the economic recession and the Viet Nam War took precedence over "law and order" as an issue of concern to the public. We are all against crime in the streets and for justice in the courts. But how we are to achieve these noteworthy goals is, of course, the unanswered question. There are at least as many suggested solutions as there are politicians running for office, and approaches run the gamut from the give-em-hell repressiveness of Vice President Agnew to the Lincolnian pleas for justice and mercy of former Attorney General Ramsey Clark.

We do not pretend to know the answers. In this book we have attempted only to put the *questions* into some kind of philosophical, political, and sociological context. We have not attempted to discuss all the problems, all the issues, all the suggested solutions, and all the relevant Supreme Court litigation. We have selected only those themes we considered especially important either for an understanding of the past, or as indicative of future trends. Perhaps the best we can do is to point out approaches which have not worked in the past, and which will surely not work in the future. These include simplistic appeals engineered by politicians for their rabble rousing qualities.

The problem of crime is highly complex, and we can be sure that it will yield only to painstaking, well thought out, well motivated efforts. There are no "quickie" penicillin shots for the cure of this social disease.

We would like to thank several of our colleagues who have helped in the writing of this book. Donald H. Riddle, the president of John Jay College has been sympathetic, encouraging, and helpful in providing space, moral support, and an atmosphere conducive to writing. Arthur Niederhoffer and Abraham S. Blumberg have been of great help in polishing the manuscript and correcting the inevitable errors that crept in. While we did not always accept their suggestions with enthusiasm (indeed some of our conferences made the corridors ring) they are the nicest gadflies in the business and we take pleasure in acknowledging them as good editors and—even more—good friends. Isidore Silver was kind enough to comment on the constitutional law section, and several of his suggestions were gratefully incorporated into the final version. Sylvia Rothberg was invaluable as our typist, accomplishing miracles of handwriting deciphering. Allean Easton was her usual helpful self. A special thanks to our students on whom we tried out many of our ideas, and from whom we have gained so much insight and knowledge, particularly Kenneth Dean, who helped with the research on the civil rights of prisoners. We, of course, accept responsibility for all those errors which defying our vigilance lurk unseen in the recesses of the manuscript.

ALEXANDER B. SMITH
HARRIET POLLACK

Contents

Crime and Justice in a Mass Society

Justice, Law, and The Courts

"Let right be done!"
From the English *Petition of Right*

"The prophecies of what the courts
will do in fact and nothing more
is what I mean by law."
Oliver Wendell Holmes, Jr., *The Path of
the Law* (1897)

"The final cause of the law is the
welfare of society."
Benjamin N. Cardozo, *The Nature of the
Judicial Process*

One can look at justice in two ways, either theoretically
or pragmatically. A theoretical inquiry into the nature of
justice must answer questions such as "Is justice absolute
or relative? Are there fixed principles of justice that tran-
scend time, place, and circumstance?" A pragmatic inquiry,
on the other hand, asks "Is this accused innocent or guilty?
Does the punishment given this defendant fit the crime he
has committed?" A successful criminal justice system must
attempt to deal with justice on both levels: the conduct
which a particular society labels as criminal must violate an
ethical system, and the accused who is judged guilty must
be the actual perpetrator of the alleged offense.

The society whose criminal justice system achieves
both these goals will have arrived at the millenium. Certainly
no such society exists.

In the United States today, we are painfully aware that
our criminal justice system is in trouble, that we are handling
crime and criminals badly. The torrent of criticism these
inadequacies has aroused suggests, however, that the ancient urge to "do justice" still persists.

When the victorious allies tried the leaders of the Hitler

regime at Nuremberg, the defendants were indicted on four counts: 1) The Common Plan or Conspiracy; 2) Crimes Against Peace; 3) War Crimes; and 4) Crimes Against Humanity. The fourth count included murder, extermination, enslavement, deportations, and other inhumane acts committed against civilian populations, before and during the war.[1] The Nazis' defense was that they were simply obeying the commands of their superiors, who in turn were enforcing the accredited, duly enacted statutes of the sovereign state of which they were all citizens. The prosecution's response was that however "legal" the statutes in question may have been, they were illegitimate and not to be obeyed because they had violated the fundamental tenets of decency and justice. The government of Germany, in other words, had had no "right" to enact such monstrous laws, and the defendants had had no "right" to obey them.

Presumably underlying the prosecution was the thought that somewhere immanent in the universe are rules for human conduct that are absolute and untransgressable, no matter how persuasive the circumstances or what the formal institutional justification to the contrary. These "rules"— whether called justice, natural law, higher law, or whatever— have eluded definition since the beginning of human society. Two thousand years before Christ, Hammurabi's code attempted to define socially impermissible conduct and prescribe punishment for it. Centuries later, the Ten Commandments which formed the nucleus of the Mosaic Code were given to mankind—allegedly by God himself. Later still, Plato defined the "just" state as one in which each individual was assigned a status and a code of conduct commensurate with his abilities. Thomas Aquinas taught that justice was embodied in natural law, that is, in that part of the mind of God which human beings could comprehend. Hobbes, Locke, and Kant all wrestled with the same problem: what are the ultimate standards for good and evil? Perhaps we can do no better than to agree with the British philosopher T. D. Weldon who said that while he couldn't define evil, when he saw a storm trooper beating up an old Jew, he knew that was wicked.*

There are in reality very few, if any, behavioral prohibitions which are universal. Though the deliberate killing of a human being, for example, is forbidden in almost all societies, Eskimos put their old and infirm people on ice floes to float away to their deaths when the community can no longer support them. The Greeks and others practiced infanticide, and Europeans in the name of protecting religion (that is, the moral code) and civilization perpetrated the horrors of the Crusades and the Spanish Inquisition. Incest, encouraged among Incan and Egyptian royalty, is taboo in the modern world, but many marital arrangements permitted by us are forbidden to certain North American Indian tribes. Western civilization permits only monogamy, but in parts of Africa polygyny is encouraged, and in Tibet polyandry is an acceptable way of life. The variety of property arrangements accepted as correct varies from the state capitalism of the Fascists, through the modified capitalism of the United States, to the democratic socialism of the Scandinavian countries and the state socialism of the Soviet Union and mainland China. In the United States we are permissive with regard to the consumption of alcohol, but highly restrictive of the use of opium derivatives and marijuana. Moslem society, on the other hand, prohibits the use of alcohol, but generally accepts the use of the drugs that we find so threatening. In America there is a noteworthy amount of freedom

---

*T. D. Weldon, *The Vocabulary of Politics* (London: Penguin Books, 1953), p. 43. The complete quote is: "But then you might have seen an S. A. man (or a lot of them) beating up a Jew and you might have said *'Das ist verbrecherisch'* (That is criminal). Your teacher would have said *'Durchaus nicht verbrecherisch. Eine ehrenwerte Tat'* (Not at all criminal, an honorable deed). And what could you say then? You might accept the correction in the same way as that in which in the United States you accept the correction 'We don't call them braces, we call them suspenders, and what you call suspenders, we call garters.' But if you did your friends would not have said 'You have learnt German very well.' They would have said, 'You are a liar and a hypocrite. You know it is wicked to behave like that, yet you are saying that it is praiseworthy. You are pretending in order to avoid trouble.' "

of expression, even for ideas which are politically heretical or sexually lewd; the Soviet Union insists upon political orthodoxy and considers pornography Western decadence. Spain, over the years, has continued to resist twentieth-century impulses toward sexual permissiveness, and strictly prohibits "obscene" literature.

That concepts of justice, and their external manifestations which we call law, vary in different cultures is unquestionable. It is fallacious, however, to conclude from this that there are no universal principles of right and wrong underlying the legal systems of most societies. It may be very difficult to define these universal principles of justice in terms of universal patterns of behavior. Nevertheless, there are few societies which do not sanctify and legitimize their actions through reference to a code of moral conduct which, in its basics, varies surprisingly little from ancient society to modern, and from country to country throughout the world today. In former times as well as now, even despotically ruled countries which may in fact have violated these basic principles of justice have been highly defensive about such actions, and have attempted either to hide or to so describe such actions as to legitimize them by making them compatible with these professed, if ignored, principles.

PRAGMATIC PROBLEMS

Justice in the mind of the layman is seldom conceived in terms of natural or higher law. His view is a pragmatic one: Is the outcome of a particular case "right"? On a mundane level practitioners of the criminal justice system must be concerned not only that their decisions be in accord with formal law but that they meet the expectations of the relevant community. For example, a judge who is insensitive to these expectations may find himself sharply criticized for what may seem to him a logical, strictly legal decision. Judge Nathan R. Sobel, one of the most respected judges of the New York State Supreme Court, was horrified at the storm of protest which arose when he ordered the severance from each other of the trials of two defendants who had been indicted for the murder of a young rabbinical student in Brooklyn in 1952. The crime occurred in a low-income, high-crime area populated mainly by Chassidic Jews, blacks, and Puerto Ricans where considerable hostility existed among the groups. The student in question, who was unknown to the two defendants, was walking through a park about 1 A.M. of a June night when he was sighted by two youths, Baldwin and Ferrick, who were skulking in some bushes some one hundred yards away holding an old .22 caliber rifle. Both had been drinking, and when Baldwin dared Ferrick to shoot the rabbi, the latter pulled the trigger. The rabbi fell mortally wounded, and was clinically dead before he hit the sidewalk. As a result of fine police work, the two youths were soon apprehended, and after indictment for murder, both were arraigned.[2]

A question immediately arose in the judge's mind as to the legal responsibility of Baldwin. A pre-pleading investigation was ordered to establish the facts of the killing which convinced him that, although Baldwin was morally guilty because he had urged Ferrick to pull the trigger, he was not legally responsible. Sobel then severed the action against Baldwin and subsequently dismissed the severed indictment. The Jewish community in Williamsburg reacted very strongly to the judge's handling of the case. Sobel was inundated with letters and telegrams. Community protest meetings were held at which speakers accused the judge of having succumbed to "pressures." Whatever the legal niceties of the decision, it obviously did not square with the community's sense of justice.

By way of contrast to the rabbi's case, an unusual disposition in a murder case in Brooklyn met with a surprising degree of community acceptance. One Bernard Lewis, a thirty-six-year-old maintenance man, became involved in an argument with his drunken wife while he was cutting up meat for stew. Using the same kitchen knife with which he had been preparing dinner, Lewis stabbed and killed his wife. He was subsequently arrested and indicted for the killing. Lewis was characterized in his probation report as a somewhat rigid individual who never drank to excess, had a

5

regular work record, and no previous criminal record. The deceased, a thirty-year-old mother of three, was a "fine girl" when sober but frequently became intoxicated, and on occasion, according to a social work agency's records, had left her small children at home unattended, remaining away from home for as long as three or four days. The defendant had frequently been notified at work of his wife's defection, and had often had to leave his job to go home to care for the children. The defendant pleaded guilty to Manslaughter I, and was referred to the Probation Department for a pre-sentence investigation. During the investigation, in an interview with the probation officer, the mother of the deceased declared that while she loved her deceased daughter, the latter was a "nuisance" when drunk, and although she (the mother) could not forgive the defendant, the children had no mother and needed a father. After due consideration, the judge placed the defendant on probation so that he could return home to care for his three children.[3] There was no comment by the community on the judge's sentence. The man returned to his children, adjusted very well on probation, and was discharged from supervision some years later.

An acceptable system of criminal justice obviously must take into account community expectations as well as formal law when disposing of cases. Not only judges, but policemen, prosecutors, probation officers, prison officials, and parole officers, if they are to avert criticism or even obstructionism on the part of the public, must make decisions which avoid offending community mores or expectations.* No matter how rigidly prescribed are the formal procedures of indicting, trying, and sentencing defendants, there remain substantial areas of discretion which prudent judicial and administrative officials normally use in accordance with the consensus of public opinion. In a very real sense then, justice may lie not so much in the mind of God as in the collective mind of the community.

---

*This is especially obvious with regard to parole boards. Consider the cases of Alger Hiss, Louis Wolfson, James Hoffa, and Morton Sobell, none of whom posed threats to the security or safety of the community, but all of whom were denied parole.

If it is true that, on a day-to-day basis, justice is prag-matically determined, is there any validity in the "higher law" notion of justice? Is there any relationship between what a community considers the right disposition of a case and the immutable principles of Judeo-Christian morality? On the lowest court levels on many occasions there is no such relationship. The internment during World War II of thousands of innocent Nisei and Issei who were, neither individually nor collectively, guilty of any crime whatsoever met with the hearty approval of both the local California community and California Attorney General Earl Warren (who later became Chief Justice of the United States). Similarly, the lower court decisions upholding the segrega-tion of school children along color lines were widely ap-proved locally. Certainly, racism and the imprisonment of innocent people are violative of higher law principles. Yet these decisions were right by contemporary community standards.

Communities, however, do not exist in a vacuum but are part of larger communities less affected by the idiosyn-cratic origins of particular cases. The people of the United States as a whole did not completely share the fear of Cali-fornians vis-à-vis the possibility of sabotage or invasion by the Japanese, nor were they as terrified of the implications of legally-mandated racial mixing in the schools as were those who lived below the Mason-Dixon line. In the relative absence of these special fears, the wider community con-sensus on the disposition of the cases tended to hew more closely to "natural law" principles. The U. S. Supreme Court, when faced with these questions, released and par-tially recompensed the Japanese,* declaring educational

Korematsu v. United States, 323 U.S. 214 (1944). The U.S. Supreme Court did, however, delay rehabilitation of the Japanese for three years until victory over Japan was in sight. Presumably the Court hesitated to challenge the local army commander's declaration of military necessity while the military outcome of the war was dubious. There is consider-able evidence, however, that the original Japanese internment was largely a result of local hysteria augmented by past economic rivalry between Japanese and whites on the West Coast. For a full discussion of the Japanese internment, see Alexander Leighton, *The Governing of Men* (New York: Octagon Books, 1964).

segregation to be unconstitutional.* To summarize, when the pragmatic justice rendered locally tends, for reasons peculiar to the locality, to wander too far from the principles of natural justice, the loser in the battle may appeal to the larger outside community in an attempt to redress the balance of forces against him.[4] On the simplest level the defendant may ask for a change of venue; on a more complex level, he may try to move from the state to the federal court system, or up the appellate court line to the United States Supreme Court. His ultimate goal is to present his case at the level where decision makers are most likely to be talking about the basic immutable principles underlying American society (which principles, presumably, will benefit his cause). To the extent that American society is based on such immutable principles, it will be Supreme Court justices, rather than local civil and criminal court judges, who will most likely be concerned with such principles.

Students of constitutional law might object that during much of American history, the decisions of the local courts were considered to be closer to the principles of natural justice than were those of the appellate courts, because the lower courts were more concerned with human rights than with property rights. The reverse was true of the higher courts. The United States Supreme Court, for example, from 1880 to 1937, invalidated virtually all state and local attempts to mitigate the lot of the working classes. It is of course true that during this period the higher courts were more concerned with property rights than with human rights. One could argue, however, that this was an era when the sanctity of property was widely held to be the most important of all personal rights since it was only through independence of means that the individual was able to protect himself from a slavish dependence on higher authority or other peo-

---

*Brown v. Board of Education, 347 U.S. 483 (1954). Since the mid-1930s the U.S. Supreme Court has given uniformly prompt and favorable rulings to school desegregation suits, which does not mean, of course, that educational desegregation in the United States has been anything like either prompt or satisfactory. For a good treatment of the *Brown* case, see Daniel Berman, *It Is So Ordered* (New York: Norton, 1966).

ple. It is only since 1937 that this philosophy has been replaced by a belief that the economy must be socially controlled for the benefit of all. Indeed, the basic reason for the bitterness of the conservative judges and their resistance to the validation of the New Deal program was that they sensed they were witnessing a major shift in the popular perception of natural justice, from laissez faire to welfare state. The United States Supreme Court is frequently considered to function as a legitimizer of the resolution of group conflicts precisely because the Court tends, through its legalistic discussion of due process, to base its decisions on its (and hopefully society's) notion of natural justice.

In the American system, pragmatic justice and natural justice, if they do not coincide at the lowest level, may become reconciled at the highest court levels. This is not to say, of course, that such reconciliation is always, or even frequently, accomplished. It is a utopian goal, not a reality, that man-made and natural law coincide.

ENGLISH ROOTS OF AMERICAN LAW

When the English colonists first came to North America they brought with them, in addition to their material possessions, a cultural heritage not the least part of which was English law, especially the Common Law. The development of the Common Law started under the Norman and Angevin kings during the eleventh and twelfth centuries. It replaced earlier tribal and feudal law in which justice had been in the hands of popular assemblies known as folk-moots. As feudalism developed, folk-moots evolved eventually into shire-moots, local courts whose membership included the elite of feudal society: large landowners, bishops, lords, and shire-reeves. The first step in the nationalization of these courts was taken when William the Conqueror attempted to consolidate his power by sending his own representatives to the local shire-moots. William also separated lay from ecclesiastical courts, so that two distinct legal systems emerged: state law and canon law. State law came to be called Common Law, was judge-made (as opposed to king-made, or parliament-made), and was common to all England in the same way that canon law (church law) was common to all Christendom. The law was also "common" because it had been derived by the royal justices from the customary practices of the realm.

Ultimately, three great courts of common law developed: the Court of Common Pleas, which heard minor cases where the king's presence was not required; the Court of Exchequer, for tax and fiscal cases; and the Court of King's Bench, for important cases where the presence of the king was mandatory. By the time of Henry II the administration of justice in England had been centralized, and it was the king's peace, rather than the local lord's peace, that was preserved.

> The king was now a territorial king, and his peace extended throughout the land. The king was now the source of law. He had jurisdiction in every case. The State, and not the family or the lord, was now the proper prosecutor in every case.[5]

It was during the same period that crime ceased to be a tort, that is, a dispute between private individuals which could be resolved by the direct action of the aggrieved party, and became instead an offense against the state to be resolved only by stated procedures involving the courts and other state officials.

The Common Law is thought to have developed over approximately four centuries from about 1100 to 1500 A.D. During this period, judges, in deciding cases brought before them, relied heavily on decisions made by other judges in handling similar earlier cases. This heavy reliance on precedent is known as the doctrine of *stare decisis*. The Common Law developed a pragmatic orientation: decisions were based on the facts of a case rather than on a generalized statement of principle. It also rested solidly on centuries of local practice apparently sanctified into acceptability by time. The Common Law, however, suffered from two basic flaws: it tended toward rigidity, since new sets of facts were difficult to handle under the old precepts; and it could not handle satisfactorily cases where damage inflicted by a wrongdoer could not be compensated by money. These two defects of the Common Law led to the growth of Equity, a parallel system of judge-made law which originated in the appeals of litigants to the royal chancellor (the keeper of the king's conscience) for justice. It was in the courts of Equity that such devices as the injunction, to prevent the commission of a wrong rather than compensate for it later on, originated. The trust, wherein one may manage the property of another for the benefit of a third, also is a product of the system of Equity. Thus by the end of the fifteenth century a fairly comprehensive system of law had developed in England based in large part on the decisions of generations of judges in the Crown's courts of Law and Equity.

The English settlers of the seventeenth century brought with them the courts of Law and Equity with which they were familiar. The Common Law, by that time fully developed, formed the underlying bedrock on which the system of colonial law was based. It was, however, supplemented and modified by the royal charters issued to the governing body of each colony and, later on, by the edicts of the royal governors and the statutes enacted by the colonial legislatures. However, most law in the colonies, just as in England, continued to be made by the courts rather than by either the executive (king or royal governor) or the legislature (colonial or Parliament).

THE AMERICAN REVOLUTION, NATURAL RIGHTS, AND JUDICIAL REVIEW

Every modern society has many lawbreakers, most of whom (if they are not too numerous) are relatively easily handled by the police because even while breaking the law they do not challenge its legitimacy. A burglar, while he may wish fervently that he had not been caught, will not plead that the law which defines burglary as a crime is unreasonable or morally wrong. More troublesome to society

11

are those who break the law because they feel the law is morally improper. Consider, for example, the thousands who violated the South's segregation laws in the civil rights demonstrations led by Martin Luther King. Of such disbelievers in the law's legitimacy political heretics and ultimately revolutionaries are made. The stability of American government over almost two hundred years is, however, testimony to the existence of a fair degree of consensus as to the legitimacy of our form of government.

Probably the best single statement of the political beliefs underlying this sense of legitimacy is still the Declaration of Independence. Jefferson's statements then, as now, are highly acceptable to most Americans, and indeed seem to be only common sense.

> We hold these truths to be self-evident, that all men are created equal, that they are endowed by their Creator with certain unalienable Rights, that among these are Life, Liberty and the pursuit of Happiness. — That to secure these rights, Governments are instituted among Men, deriving their just powers from the consent of the governed, — That whenever any Form of Government becomes destructive of these ends, it is the Right of the People to alter or abolish it.

John Adams, stung by the acclaim his rival Jefferson received for writing the Declaration, remarked resentfully that he did not understand why Jefferson was so widely praised, since he simply repeated in the Declaration the things that everyone was saying anyway. Historically, this appears to have been true, but why? How did it happen that the principles of the Declaration, being, of course, almost a paraphrase of Locke's *Second Treatise on Civil Government,* were so widely known and accepted? Locke's treatise was an attempt to justify the Glorious Revolution in England wherein Parliament removed James II from the throne and installed his daughter Mary and her consort William as king and queen of England. Locke attempted to explain why this drastic departure from the normal accession pattern should be accepted, and he justified the parliamentary action on the basis of his theory of social contract.

In the state of nature, men, according to Locke, were created by God—free, equal, independent, and with inherent inalienable rights to life, liberty, and property. As a concomitant of these rights each individual had the right of self-protection against those who would infringe on his personal liberties. While most men, in the Lockean view, were basically good, content to live and let live, some would be likely to prey on their fellows, who in turn would have to be constantly on guard against such wrongdoings. To avoid this brutish existence, men joined together to form governments to which they surrendered their rights of self-protection; in return, they received governmental protection of their lives, liberty, and property. As in any proper contract there are benefits and considerations on both sides: men give up their rights to protect themselves and receive protection in return. Governments give protection and receive loyalty and obedience in return. Government, in its control over men, cannot exceed the stated aims of the contract, however. Once it controls men more than is necessary for the protection of the mutual welfare it becomes illegitimate and no longer deserving of loyalty or obedience.

Locke, of course, had no notion of when or how the state of nature existed. Nor did he specify the mechanism by which the social contract was entered into. Like other Enlightenment thinkers, Locke derived this theory inductively, that is, by reasoning how it ought to have been. Although his theory reflected the desire of the rising mercantile middle class in England to have done with the absolutist, divine-right Stuart kings, it was enthusiastically, if perhaps unconsciously, adopted by the American colonists with whose experience and aspirations it fitted remarkably well. After all, could there have been anything closer to the state of nature than the New England shore that greeted the first Pilgrim settlers? To the men who carved a society out of a wilderness through their unaided individual efforts, the fruits of this society seemed surely to belong to themselves and not to a sovereign over whom they exercised no control. To a society that practiced, at least initially, equality of opportunity, it was only self-evident to preach that all men were created equal.

Thus the Declaration of Independence became the blueprint for American notions of governmental legitimacy: government must be representative, that is, based on the consent of the governed, but the majorities thus represented must be restricted in the exercise of their power so that basic individual freedoms are not impaired. These sentiments were not only noble and utopian, they were, unfortunately, mutually contradictory, since to preserve minority rights of necessity impaired the immediate desires of the majority; and to enforce the will of the majority required, at least for the moment, that the minority forego its protections. American history has been from this vantage point a balancing act, an attempt to fix the point at which majorities prevail and minorities yield.

The political embodiment of the Declaration of Independence was the government created by the Articles of Confederation. Power lay in the hands of the popularly elected state legislatures, a radical state of affairs in the highly class-conscious world of the eighteenth century. When the weak federal government proved unable to maintain the climate of order and stability necessary for the growth of commerce and industry, the representatives of the middle and upper classes met at Philadelphia to create a new central government. The Constitution which was the fruit of that convention was essentially a counterrevolutionary document one of whose main purposes was to prevent the formation in a short period of time of popular majorities on any single issue. The purpose of fragmenting power among the executive, legislative, and judicial branches of the federal government, and between the states and national government, was to insure that no wave of popular sentiment could infringe the rights of property as some debtor-controlled state legislatures had already done. The Bill of Rights was not part of the original Constitution, and was added by those more interested in personal than property rights as the price of ratification. Thus the Consti-

tution with its Bill of Rights emerges as a plan for a central
government with ambiguous and, as it turned out, extensive
powers, but with distinct limitations on majority domination
of the rights of either persons or property.

The founding fathers meeting in Philadelphia in 1787
created a form of government which was, at the time, struc-
turally unique. The importance they attached to the legislative branch is reflected by the fact that fully one-half of the
text of our Constitution is taken by Article I which deals with
the structure and powers of Congress. Article II, on the
presidency, was perhaps the most difficult for them to draft
since no one seemed to have a clear idea what role an
executive who was neither a hereditary monarch nor a
popularly elected governor ought to play, or indeed, how
he was to be chosen. However, it was in Article III, establishing a Supreme Court, that the founding fathers created a
really new institution: a court that could sit in judgment on
the actions of both legislature and executive. This power—
judicial review—is nowhere spelled out in the text of the
Constitution, which simply gives the Court the power to hear
all cases in law and equity arising under the laws, treaties,
and Constitution of the United States; but it was assumed
for the Court by Chief Justice John Marshall in the famous
case of *Marbury v. Madison:*

> If an act of the legislature, repugnant to the Constitution is void,
> does it, notwithstanding its validity, bind the courts and oblige
> them to give it effect? This . . . would seem, at first view, an
> absurdity too gross to be insisted on. . . . It is emphatically the
> province and duty of the judicial department to say what the
> law is. . . . So if a law be in opposition to the Constitution; if both
> the law and the Constitution apply to a particular case, so that
> the court must either decide the case conformably to the law,
> disregarding the Constitution, or conformably to the Consti-
> tution, disregarding the law; the court must determine which of
> these conflicting rules governs the case. This is the very es-
> sence of judicial duty.[6]

Scholars have long argued the question of whether the
founding fathers intended for the Supreme Court to have
the power to sit in judgment on its co-equal legislative and

executive branches. Neither the Constitution, nor the Federalist Papers, nor any official documents of the times indicate unequivocally that it was intended for the Supreme Court to have this power. On the other hand, that part of the *Marbury v. Madison* decision which enunciated judicial review excited very little opposition even among Jeffersonians. Contemporary evidence seems to indicate that the notion of judicial review was well understood and expected of the Supreme Court. By 1803, state high courts had on previous occasions sat in judgment on the actions of their state legislatures, and, during colonial times, disputes over whether actions of a colonial legislature violated the colony's charter had been referred to the Privy Council in England for resolution. On balance, the preponderance of historical evidence tends to favor Marshall's interpretation of the powers of the Court, and the argument today has become almost totally irrelevant in view of the firm establishment of judicial review as an accepted practice.

However, there is still an ongoing debate today as to how activist the Court ought to be. Those who favor judicial self-restraint, perhaps influenced by lingering doubts as to the legitimacy of judicial review, argue that the Court is essentially an anti-democratic institution inasmuch as it is elitist (drawn from the upper socioeconomic groups), unrepresentative (not elected), and not responsible to the public (justices appointed for life). For all these reasons, they conclude the Court ought to confine its activities to the bare minimum required for it to act as umpire of the federal system. The Court should avoid, wherever possible, involvement in disputes that can be handled by the popularly elected branches of government.

The judicial activists, on the other hand, claim that an uninhibited, fully active court is necessary to maintain a balance within the system between the right of the majority to govern and the right of minorities to preserve their inalienable rights from infringement by the governing majority. Democracy, the activists reason, is not simply majority rule. Individual rights are an important part of the question, and in a government where both the legislature and the executive are essentially instruments of the majority, it is essential that one branch respond to the needs of those who cannot succeed in influencing either president or Congress. Were the Court to be unduly modest the democratic balance would be upset.

Like the argument over the historical validity of the Court's assumption of the power of judicial review, the argument over whether the justices should be restrained or activist cannot be resolved. It is clear, however, that whichever course of action the Supreme Court chooses in a particular controversy, it of necessity influences the outcome of that controversy. Whether it chooses to intervene or modestly declines to participate, the outcome of the dispute will be affected. For the Court there is no neutral middle ground. Once it is agreed that the Court could, if it would, intervene, failure to do so is as much a decision as direct intervention. Most partisans in the judicial activism–judicial restraint controversy choose sides according to their preference for certain substantive results in a current dispute. While it is perfectly proper to advocate that the Court not intervene in a given situation because one hopes to preserve the ruling of the lower court, there is no moral superiority in the non-intervention position. It is, in a negative way, as activist as a more aggressive stance on the part of opponents of the status quo. The ongoing argument over whether the Supreme Court ought to be more or less active generally resolves itself into a question of whose ox is being gored.

STATE AND FEDERAL JUDICIAL SYSTEMS

The United States has fifty-one court systems: fifty state and one federal. Typically, most court systems operate on three levels: courts of original jurisdiction (trial courts); intermediate appellate courts; and final appellate courts. Unfortunately for students and laymen, there is no uniform terminology for the designation of these courts. In most states, and in the federal system, the highest appellate court is called the Supreme Court, and the intermediate appellate court is called the Court of Appeals. In New York State however, the lowest state-wide court of general jurisdiction is the Supreme Court, and the final appellate court is called the Court of Appeals. Despite the lack of uniformity in terminology, however, there are widespread uniformities of practice in both state and federal systems.

Most state courts of general jurisdiction are called superior or county courts. It is in these courts that important civil and criminal actions are initially heard, that is, suits involving large sums of money and felonies. They also hear, on appeal, minor cases which originated in local magistrates' courts or with justices of the peace. The intermediate courts of appeal hear cases appealed from the county, superior, or other courts of original jurisdiction. Above this level appeal may be had to the highest court of the state, although such appeal may be of right (not at the discretion of the court) only if certain procedural or other requirements are met. State judges are generally elected rather than appointed, usually for seven to fourteen years.

The federal court system parallels that of the states. The lowest federal court of general jurisdiction is the District Court, of which there were ninety-three in 1969, handling all criminal cases arising under federal law and civil suits in excess of $10 thousand. Cases from the District Courts are appealed to the federal Courts of Appeal, of which there were eleven in 1969, ten for the states and one for the District of Columbia. An exception to this appellate jurisdiction is that the decisions of certain specially constituted federal district courts, known as three-judge courts, are appealed directly to the Supreme Court, bypassing the Courts of Appeal. These three-judge district courts are convened on an ad hoc basis to consider important cases usually involving constitutional principles, and are comprised of two district judges and one judge from the Court of Appeals. All federal judges are appointed for life.*

---

*An exception are those judges appointed to legislative courts such as the U.S. Court of Claims, the U.S. Customs Court, and the U.S. Court of Customs and Patent Appeals.

The highest court in the federal hierarchy is the United States Supreme Court, whose docket encompasses a small number of cases, arising under a constitutionally prescribed original jurisdiction, which must be heard, and a very much larger number of cases on appeal which may be heard. The great bulk of the Court's agenda comes to it on appeal from the lower state and federal courts. Technically, there are two methods by which cases may be appealed to the United States Supreme Court: by appeal or by writ of *certiorari.* Cases come on appeal generally when they involve: federal courts which have declared state laws unconstitutional; state courts which have declared federal laws unconstitutional; or two federal Courts of Appeal which have made conflicting decisions on the points of law. All other cases come on writ of *certiorari*, that is, a petition from the appellant to the Supreme Court for an order from the high court that the lower court, which had previous jurisdiction over the case, send up the records of the case for review. Although technically the Supreme Court is required to hear all cases which come up on appeal, in practice it dismisses those cases it does not wish to consider with the brief notation, "Dismissed for want of a substantial federal question." Petitions for *certiorari* are granted at the option of the Supreme Court. The net effect, thus, is to make the appellate caseload of the Court almost entirely that of the Court's own choosing. The Court tends to select for review those cases which present questions of national importance. All cases in the federal courts must arise under the laws, treaties, or Constitution of the United States; must allege the infringement of a federal right; or must present problems of diversity of citizenships between litigants, that is, must involve actions between citizens of different states, or between citizens and foreigners.

The state and federal systems overlap. It is possible for a given civil or criminal case to be handled by either system or by both. The overlap affects the actions of both public officials and litigants. On the whole, the relationship between state and federal law enforcement officials is one of somewhat distant politeness. Most cases are handled exclusively

19

by one jurisdiction or the other. In those cases which are handled simultaneously at both levels, problems arise on occasion either because of over-competitiveness or, even worse, over-cooperativeness.

The Weinberger kidnapping case was one which created hostility between the local police and the FBI. The Weinberger infant was kidnapped from his carriage in front of his parents' Long Island home in July 1956. Seven days later (in accordance with the traditional presumption that the victim might, after one week, have been transported across state lines in violation of federal law) the FBI entered the case.[7] From an analysis of handwriting samples taken from the ransom note, it was determined that one Angelo LaMarca was the likely kidnapper. Federal agents accompanied by Nassau County detectives thereupon arrested LaMarca. The baby was found dead and subsequent investigation disclosed that the child had never left New York State. Since no federal law had been violated, the suspect was turned over to county officials who succeeded in convicting LaMarca of the crime. He was electrocuted two years later. Despite the successful outcome of the case in terms of apprehending and punishing the criminal, strained relations developed between Nassau County officials and the FBI because the local authorities felt that the federal agents had unfairly taken all the credit for the results.

Not all such parallel handling arouses federal-local antagonism, of course. In November 1962, Roberto Santiesban, a Cuban, and two of his compatriots residing in the United States were arrested in New York City by the FBI and charged with conspiring to blow up department stores, utilities, and other installations around New York Harbor.[8] Because the attempted bombing involved delicate questions of international relations, the FBI had not called in the New York City police (who had concurrent jurisdiction) during the original investigation, but asked their help only later, in the disposal of the explosives. Conspiracy charges were dropped against the three Cubans who, along with a fourth Cuban arrested on a separate charge, were exchanged for twenty-three Americans held in Cuba on political charges. In this case the New York City authorities made no objection to the FBI's actions, because it was patent that important national interests were involved rather than the handling of local criminals.

Sometimes over-cooperativeness, rather than over-competitiveness, becomes a problem, and relations between the state and federal agents become too close for legality. Until quite recently, it was a fairly common practice for state police to illegally seize evidence of a federal crime and turn it over to the federal authorities, who were then permitted to use it against the accused. While the rules of procedure in federal court did not permit the introduction of evidence illegally obtained by federal agents, under the terms of the notorious "silver platter" doctrine, such evidence could be used if obtained by non-federal agents. State officials working on a state case that was also of interest to federal agents were thus permitted to commit illegal acts in the name of "law enforcement." In 1960, however, the United States Supreme Court put an end to this practice by excluding from federal court all illegally seized evidence.*

Private litigants, too, are affected by the bifurcated state-federal structure. It is, for example, a common practice among attorneys handling civil suits which procedurally could be heard in either state or federal court, to shop for the court that will provide the most favorable forum for the client's interests. In the criminal field, defense attorneys, by use of the appropriate writ, will sometimes shift a case from the state court system, where appeals have been decided unfavorably to the client, to the federal system in the hope

---

*Elkins v. United States, 364 U.S. 206 (1960). It should be noted that the Fourth Amendment prohibition against illegal search and seizure applies only to government officials, both state and federal. In 1921, in *Burdeau v. McDowell,* 256 U.S. 465, the U.S. Supreme Court (Holmes and Brandeis dissenting) ruled that stolen, incriminating evidence might be used in federal courts if the evidence had been seized by private parties and government officials had played no part in the theft. No further Supreme Court review of this question has occurred since 1921. State and lower federal courts have reaffirmed the *Burdeau* doctrine over the years.

that a federal judge will be more sympathetic to the client's cause. When Dr. Samuel Sheppard contended vainly in the Ohio courts that he had been unable to receive a fair trial because of prejudicial pre-trial publicity engendered by a Cleveland newspaper, his attorneys were able to appeal to the federal courts on the ground that Sheppard's due process rights had been infringed. Sheppard's appeal went up the federal-judicial ladder, and ultimately succeeded when the Supreme Court ordered that he be released from custody unless the State of Ohio retried him within a reasonable time.[9] On retrial in 1966, he was acquitted, twelve years after the murder.

The NAACP Legal and Education Fund recently used a petition for a writ of *habeas corpus* to the United States District Court for the Eastern District of New York as a means of terminating a New York State addiction program that had been severely criticized, but upheld as constitutionally permissible by the New York State appellate courts. Under the program, criminal addicts were confined to a state institution, ostensibly for rehabilitation, for periods longer than the maximum penal sentence for the crime for which they were convicted. It was the contention of the Legal Defense Fund, on behalf of one Edward Johnson, that the addiction treatment program on Riker's Island, New York City, was almost entirely punitive and not rehabilitative, and therefore the lengthened sentence was a violation of the defendant's due process rights. Since the New York State Court of Appeals had recently held in regard to Rudolf Blunt, a similarly situated appellant, that the program, although inadequate, was not a violation of due process rights, the Federal District Court agreed to consider Johnson's case on the merits. When the New York State Narcotics Addiction Control Commission officials were informed of the federal court's intention, they sent word that the program was being terminated, and that they had no objection to Johnson's release from custody.[10] In both the *Sheppard* and *Johnson* cases, federal court action released defendants who had been denied relief in the state courts.

The dual state-federal judicial structure of the United States can also, on occasion, act like twin millstones grinding a hapless defendant between them. As of the present writing, a man tried and convicted in federal court for an offense such as robbery of a federally insured bank (a violation of both state and federal law) can be retried and reconvicted in the state court for the same offense.[11] It is only recently, moreover, that the Supreme Court has ruled that testimony compelled under a grant of immunity by one jurisdiction may not be used by the other to try and convict a defendant.[12] The Court has also only recently ruled that evidence illegally seized by law enforcement officers of a state cannot be used for prosecuting purposes in the federal court, and vice versa.[13]

Judicial review of state and federal practices has not only affected the substance of our criminal justice systems, but has tended to make them more uniform. Increasingly, the substantive and procedural guarantees of the Bill of Rights (originally conceived as applicable to the federal government only) have, through the due process clause of the Fourteenth Amendment, been made applicable to the states also. This evolving national standard concerns not only the courts, of course, but police, prosecutors, and corrections officials as well. Even local and state legislatures are bound by the evolving national standard of what a fair law is, and what kinds of activities can be labeled crimes. Whether for good or for ill, the days when Connecticut could make the use of a contraceptive a crime, or Massachusetts declare *Fanny Hill* obscene, or any state convict a felon unrepresented by counsel in court, are gone. Whether this tendency will become oppressive because of the overcentralization of judicial law-making in Washington remains to be seen. Local option and local flexibility has been curtailed at least in those instances where a determined litigant (especially one supported by appropriate interest groups) is able and willing to carry his case to the highest level. This nationalizing thrust tends to lessen the disparities among the fifty-one systems of criminal justice in this country; and,

23

in the process of removing controversies from local forums to the federal arena, parochial standards for the dispensing of justice have tended to give way to more broadly based conceptual notions of justice.

Selected Readings

Berman, Daniel. *It Is So Ordered.* New York: Norton, 1966.

Chambliss, William J. *Crime and the Legal Process.* New York: McGraw-Hill, 1969.

Clark, Ramsey. *Crime in America.* New York: Simon and Schuster, 1970.

Hall, Jerome. *Theft, Law and Society.* 2nd ed. Indianapolis: Bobbs-Merrill, 1952.

Harris, Richard. *Justice: The Crisis of Law, Order and Freedom in America.* New York: Dutton, 1970.

Krislov, Samuel. *The Supreme Court in the Political Process.* New York: Macmillan, 1965.

Leighton, Alexander. *The Governing of Men.* New York: Octagon Books, 1964.

Mitford, Jessica. *The Trial of Dr. Spock.* New York: Knopf, 1969.

President's Commission on Law Enforcement and Administration of Justice. *Task Force Report: The Courts.* Washington, D.C.: U.S. Government Printing Office, 1967.

Quinney, Richard, ed. *Crime and Justice in Society.* Boston: Little, Brown, 1969.

Schattschneider, E. E. *The Semi-Sovereign People.* New York: Holt, Rinehart and Winston, 1960.

Weldon, T. D. *The Vocabulary of Politics.* London: Penguin Books, 1953.

Notes

[1] *New York Times,* October 19, 1945, pp. 1, 11–14.

[2] *New York Times,* June 28, 1952, p. 10; July 19, 1952, p. 1.

[3] *New York Times,* December 25, 1958, p. 2.

[4] For an interesting exposition of the relationship of the widening of conflict to decision making, see E. E. Schattschneider, *The Semi-Sovereign People* (New York: Holt, Rinehart and Winston, 1960), Chapter 1.

5 Clarence Ray Jeffrey, "The Development of Crime in Early English Society," as quoted in William J. Chambliss, *Crime and the Legal Process* (New York: McGraw-Hill, 1969), p. 27.

6 *Marbury v. Madison,* 1 Cranch 137 (1803), at 177–178.

7 *New York Times,* July 5, 1956, p. 27; July 12, 1956, p. 12.

8 *New York Times,* November 18, 1962, p. 1; November 22, 1962, p. 9.

9 *Sheppard v. Maxwell,* 384 U.S. 333 (1966).

10 See *New York Times,* October 15, 1968, p. 94, for details on *People ex rel. Rudolph Blunt v. Narcotics Addiction Control Commission.* For *Edward Johnson v. Warden, Riker's Island Prison,* see Michael Meltzner, "A Defense Attorney's View of the Future of Correction," scheduled for publication in *Crime and Delinquency,* July 1971.

11 *Bartkus v. Illinois,* 359 U.S. 121 (1959); *Abbate v. United States,* 359 U.S. 187 (1959). See also discussion, Chapter 9.

12 *Murphy v. Waterfront Commission,* 378 U.S. 52 (1964).

13 *Rea v. United States,* 350 U.S. 214 (1956).

2

Crime: Parameters and Perceptions

"Crime is . . . necessary; it is bound up
with the fundamental conditions of all
social life, and by that very fact it
is useful, because these conditions of
which it is a part are themselves
indispensible to the normal evolution of
morality and law."

Emile Durkheim, *Rules of Sociological
Method*

Crime, like good and evil, is hard to define. Lawyers,
judges, and policemen, when questioned, will call a crime
that which is contrary to the penal code. Nevertheless, the
basic question remains: What is the hallmark of conduct
that causes it to be forbidden by the penal code?

While most people would agree that a killing committed
in the course of robbery is unquestionably illegal behavior,
there is no such consensus on whether smoking marijuana
should be considered a crime. The Index Crimes listed in
the Uniform Crime Reports of the FBI (willful homicide,
forcible rape, robbery, aggravated assault, burglary, larceny
[fifty dollars or over], and motor vehicle theft) are generally
conceded to be wrong both morally and legally. The case
for Sabbath blue laws is not so clear-cut, however. In 1949,
one Sam Friedman, the proprietor of a kosher butcher shop
on Manhattan's Lower East Side was tried for violating the
New York State Sunday closing law by selling fresh meat
on Sunday. On the stand Mr. Friedman denied vehemently
that he had previously been convicted of a crime. On cross-
examination, when reminded by the district attorney that he
had previously been convicted and fined for the identical
offense for which he was currently being tried, that is, Sabbath breaking, Friedman responded: "That's a *crime*?"

Clearly, Mr. Friedman did not see eye-to-eye with the legislators in Albany as to the standards for defining criminal conduct.[1]

Criminal behavior, according to a widely used criminology textbook, is "behavior in violation of criminal law."[2] The selection of certain modes of behavior for inclusion in the criminal law makes it possible to punish offenders; but to give that punishment legitimacy in the eyes of society, it is necessary for the conduct proscribed to be contrary to the ethos of that society. Some acts are more clearly in violation of the prevailing mores than others, thus the agreement on the criminality of the acts listed in FBI Uniform Crime Reports. These Index Crimes are considered *mala in se* (evil in themselves) and have been forbidden in many societies, and in many eras of history. Some indeed are among the prohibitions of the Ten Commandments. In most countries murder, robbery, arson, and rape are considered wrong and punishable. Whatever problems of enforcement these offenses may create, the laws prohibiting them are, at least, non-controversial. While many accused murderers and rapists have had partisan groups protesting the innocence of the particular accused person, no group has ever protested the illegitimacy of the statutes under which these defendants were prosecuted. The trials of the Scottsboro Boys, Sacco and Vanzetti, Tom Mooney, Dr. Sam Sheppard, and Dr. Carl A. Coppolino were controversial because of doubt as to the guilt or innocence of the defendants, or as to the propriety or impropriety of the arrest and trial procedures. At no time, however, was any question raised of the wrongfulness of the act charged. All agreed that the act was wrong.

By way of contrast, the history of prosecutions for other offenses which are termed *mala prohibita* (evil because forbidden) is replete with impassioned argument over whether the act, even if committed by the accused, was wrong to begin with. These offenses have been defined generally by "morals" legislation and relate to acts such as gambling, drug use, obscenity, and prostitution. In more controversial cases, however, prosecutions for such offenses have been

27

legitimized by demonstrating that the prohibited act was not only illegal but inherently evil. The struggle to reform birth control and abortion laws in the United States is an interesting case study of the relationship of public notions of morality to the content of the law, and demonstrates the greater permanence and stability of proscriptions based on *mala in se* concepts as compared to those based on acts merely *mala prohibita.*

For fifty years reformers attempted to nullify the Connecticut anti-birth control statute which made it a crime to use a contraceptive, and made a criminal accessory of anyone prescribing or counseling such use. Although the law originally had been placed on the books in 1878 by Protestant zealots influenced by Anthony Comstock, the attempts to invalidate the law were led in the twentieth century by Protestants and Jews and opposed by the Catholic Church. Reformers contended that the state was acting arbitrarily in forbidding the use of contraceptives, since no demonstrable, measurable, objective harm could be found to result from such use. Since there was in fact no harm to the practice of contraception, the state had no legitimate interest in prohibiting it. Catholic response was that birth control was not wrong simply because Catholics said that it was wrong; it was wrong in the same way that lying and stealing were wrong. Birth control was akin to murder or suicide, and deprived society of members it ought to have. In short, contraception was not *malum prohibitum,* but *malum in se.* After half a century of struggle, the Connecticut statute was invalidated by the U.S. Supreme Court in 1965.[3] The decision was received with great public equanimity, probably reflecting a widespread agreement that contraception, while it may have been forbidden by law, was not basically immoral.

By way of contrast, the Catholic Church had far more widespread public support for its leadership of the campaign to prevent the liberalization of state abortion laws. While reformers contended that to deny abortion relief, especially to victims of rape or incest, or in cases where the fetus might be abnormal, was unreasonable and arbitrary on the part of the state, the opposition argued that the prohibition on abortions was merely a reflection in statute form of the natural-law prohibition on the taking of life: the fetus, like the mother, had rights to life and health, and the state was doing no more in its anti-abortion law than to recognize these rights. Attempts to modify state abortion laws have recently achieved some substantial success, notably in New York State, but the fight has been a very hard one. The opposition to reform has been far less parochial and partisan than in the birth control struggle. Whereas the opponents of contraception were, for the most part, rather doctrinaire orthodox Catholics, opponents of abortion reform cover a much wider spectrum of political and ethical thought. The uneasiness of the public over the concept of "abortion on demand" is a reflection of the extent to which many people believe that abortion is indeed *malum in se* rather than *malum prohibitum*.

DEVIANCE: CONSIDERATIONS AND CONCEPTS

To the audience in the courtroom and to the public at large, the prisoner in the dock is a deviant. Deviance, from the onlooker's point of view, is defined in terms of the consensus of the group, a consensus defined in terms of the values of the group. Deviant conduct, then, is always conduct different from that of most members of the group.[4] Not all different conduct, however, is deviant. One may sport red hair and be left-handed, and thereby differ from the public at large which is mainly right-handed and brunette; but redheaded southpaws are not labelled deviant. Mere statistical variation, then, does not determine deviance. If merely being different is not deviant, can deviance perhaps be defined in terms of being pathologically different? This definition, while it commands wide acceptance, defines deviance not so much in terms of the act that is committed as in terms of the reaction of the group to that act. In Puritan New England, for example, blasphemy was a crime against the state; such utterances today might be considered, at worst, tasteless, but hardly illegal. Flogging, once the standard method of punishing criminals, is now in disrepute throughout the United States, and even where it exists, is probably unconstitutional. Conduct once considered acceptable falls from public favor and ultimately comes to be considered deviant — or vice versa.

The reactions of the dominant groups in society to the rightness or wrongness of specific acts vary most widely, of course, as to acts which are *mala prohibita,* but there are occasionally wide societal differences in relation to acts which are *mala in se,* such as the permissiveness in ancient Greece and China toward infanticide and the socially approved starvation of old people by the Eskimos. An interesting comparison can be made between changing patterns of societal attitudes toward the use of drugs on one hand, and the consumption of alcohol on the other. In handling problems arising from the use of marijuana, heroin, and whiskey, American society has displayed a wide range of reactions, from a harsh, extremely punitive stance to permissiveness and sympathetic understanding of the pathological needs of the user.

Nineteenth-century America displayed an indifferent attitude toward the consumption of opium and opium derivates. The use of such drugs was mildly disapproved for vaguely medical reasons, but on the whole was a matter of indifference to the public. In *The Sign of the Four,* Dr. Watson chides his friend Sherlock Holmes for using the "filthy stuff" because it will ruin his health, but Holmes scoffs at his friend's objections and proceeds with his cocaine injection. The dividing line between permissive (if somewhat disapproving) and punitive attitudes toward drug use was probably the passage by Congress of the Harrison Act in 1914. Ostensibly a revenue measure, the act provided for the payment of a nominal excise tax on narcotics, the use of special forms when drugs were transferred, and the registration of all persons and firms handling drugs. The act also stated that:

Nothing contained in this chapter shall apply to the dispensing or distribution of any of the drugs . . . to a patient by a physician, dentist, or veterinary surgeon registered . . . in the course of his professional practice only.[5]

The statute however, did not define the meaning of legitimate medical practice with respect to addicts, and several doctors who prescribed drugs regularly for addict patients shortly found themselves in trouble with the federal authorities. In two cases, decided in 1919 and 1922,[6] the Supreme Court ruled that drugs could not legally be dispensed to keep addicts comfortable by maintaining their customary use. In the *Webb* case, the physician in question had issued thousands of prescriptions which he sold for fifty cents apiece to addicts; in the *Behrman* case, the physician had issued a prescription for a large quantity of narcotics to be used at the addict's discretion. In both cases, although the actions of the doctors were questionable in terms of legitimate medical practice, the prosecution proceeded on the assumption that such prescriptions were made in good faith for the treatment of addiction. The net result was to obscure the distinction between the honest physician, trying to relieve the addict's withdrawal distress, and the unethical practitioner who indiscriminately sold narcotics prescriptions for personal profit.

The issue was joined in 1925 in the *Lindner* case[7] where a reputable Seattle practitioner provided four small narcotics tablets to ease the withdrawal symptoms of an addict who subsequently turned out to be a federal agent posing as a patient. Dr. Lindner was convicted under the Harrison Act, and after extensive litigation (said to have cost Lindner $30 thousand) achieved Supreme Court review of his case. The court unanimously reversed the doctor's conviction, on the ground that addicts were diseased persons, and proper subjects for bona fide medical treatment. Although this decision would appear to have opened the way for treatment by reputable physicians of addicts and the diseases incident to their addiction, the effect of the earlier decisions, together with the vigorous enforcement policies of the Federal Bureau of Narcotics, has apparently had an effect sufficiently intimidating to cause physicians to be unwilling to prescribe narcotics for addicts under any circumstances. As the rights of the doctor under federal law remain ambiguous, no doctor has been willing to risk his livelihood and his professional reputation in a case testing the validity of the Federal Bureau of Narcotics' rigorous interpretation of the Harrison Act.

The net result of current federal and state regulations is that addicts have no legal access to drugs. Far from curing the addiction problem, the rate of addiction is thought to have increased in recent years, despite the fact that:

> The average sentence of the Federal offender against these statutes has increased by more than 300 per cent within the last decade, and with the denial of probation and parole many narcotics violators are now being punished more severely than the average murderer.[8]

Worse than the growing number of addicts is the tremendous social problem of their criminal activities, a concomitant of their inability to obtain drugs legally. Thus the punitive restrictive attitudes encompassed in federal and state law enforcement have accomplished little, if anything, more than the earlier (pre-1914) permissive attitudes toward drugs. Many authorities go so far as to consider present punitive programs counterproductive in that they aggravate rather than relieve the problem. Most interesting of all, perhaps, is that the change from permissiveness to punitiveness in the drug field was unaccompanied by any scientific demonstration of a correlation between drug use and antisocial conduct. To this day there is no unanimity of professional opinion on how drug use affects the individual, either physically, psychologically, or socially. There is little evidence that drug use (at least in relation to marijuana and heroin), in and of itself, leads to criminal conduct.

In contrast to the dearth of scientific evidence linking drug use per se directly to crime (excluding, of course, crime committed by addicts in order to obtain drugs), there is voluminous evidence linking the consumption of alcohol to all kinds of antisocial conduct. The President's Commission on Law Enforcement and the Administration of Justice states that "two million arrests in 1965 — one of every three arrests in America — were for the offense of public drunkenness."[9] While some of these arrests were, no doubt, merely for the offense of being intoxicated in public, others involved assaults, boisterous conduct, and committing public nuisances. In addition to arrests for drunkenness, alcohol is involved in an undetermined number of detentions for murder, rape, vagrancy, loitering, disorderly conduct, and non-support of families. Accident statistics also indicate that a high proportion of drivers involved in both fatal and non-fatal motor vehicle accidents, had been drinking shortly before. More recently, statistics show the same to be true for crashes involving non-commercial aircraft.

Twentieth-century public attitudes toward consumption of alcoholic beverages, in contrast to attitudes toward drug use, have, however, changed from punitive to permissive. The early part of the century saw the full flowering of the nineteenth-century temperance movement whose underlying philosophy was that the use of alcohol was morally evil. The ultimate victory of the WCTU and its allies was, of course, the Eighteenth Amendment and the ill fated era of Prohibition. With the collapse in 1933 of the "noble experiment," public attitudes toward social drinking softened markedly among almost all social groups. Such drinking today is a widely accepted part of our social mores, and the readily apparent abuses of such drinking, which take the form of antisocial and even criminal conduct, tend to be treated therapeutically rather than punitively. Excessive drinking and alcoholism are looked upon most commonly today as diseases or personality disorders rather than as the results of moral weakness, or as illegal conduct.

The contrast between public attitudes toward the use of marijuana or heroin and the consumption of alcohol is marked. One can only speculate as to why the public is tolerant toward drinking, which is known to produce antisocial conduct, but is almost rabidly intolerant of marijuana and heroin use, which is far less obviously connected to

aggressive antisocial behavior. While possibly 60 to 70 percent of those imprisoned in our metropolitan jails are there
because of drug-related offenses, almost all of this crime
stems from the need to procure either the drugs or the money
for the drugs. Very little criminal conduct occurs as a direct
result of the taking of marijuana or heroin as distinguished
from the criminality associated with drunkenness.

The contradictory and irrational quality of these attitudes
may, however, be seeping into the public consciousness* to
the extent that, in many jurisdictions, a new look is being
taken at the drug abuse statutes. In New York, which followed California and a few other states, a series of laws
has been passed aimed at establishing a comprehensive
program of treatment, rehabilitation, and after-care for narcotics addicts.[10] The aim of the program is to place addicts,
even those who have committed minor criminal acts, in a
non-punitive, rehabilitative setting where they can receive
individual and group treatment and be helped to return to
the community. In some cases, some individuals may be
put on methadone to help them during certain critical periods
of the treatment process. In New York, as in other states,
the program is in its early stages, too new for evaluation.

Another type of deviant conduct viewed more sympathetically and less punitively in recent times by the general public is homosexuality. The law in Western society has
until recently considered sodomy a crime against nature,
and homosexual behavior a serious perversion. Moreover,
judges and legislators have labored under the impression
that such proscribed forms of sexual behavior are comparatively rare. Present-day research has cast doubt upon these

---

*President Richard Nixon, elected on a law-and-order platform which
included promises of severe punishment for violators of all drug laws,
admitted a year later that the problem was more complex than he had
at first assumed. He said that he once thought "the answer was more
penalties for drug offenses. I thought that the answer was simply enforce the law and that will stop people from the use of drugs. But it
is not," he said. "When you are talking about 13-year-olds and 14-year-
olds and 15-year-olds, the answer is not more penalties. The answer
is information. The answer is understanding." *New York Times*,
December 4, 1969, p. 37:5.

premises. The Kinsey Report,[11] which contains an analysis of the incidence and frequency of orgasm through six sexual outlets (masturbation, nocturnal emissions, heterosexual petting, heterosexual intercourse, homosexual outlets, and animal outlets), indicates that at some period in their lifetimes more than one-third of American males have experienced homosexual activities resulting in orgasm. In spite of the implications of this report, attitudes in the United States toward homosexual behavior have remained on the whole disapproving and highly punitive until comparatively recently.

In England on the other hand, a more reasonable approach in the handling of such sexual offenses has evolved. In 1957, the Wolfenden Report was published, indicating a general measure of agreement on two propositions: first, that there exists in certain persons a homosexual propensity that varies quantitatively according to the individual, and second, that this propensity can affect behavior in a variety of ways, some of which are not overtly sexual.

> Although homosexual behavior in some cases may result from disease, the evidence placed before us has not established to our satisfaction the proposition that homosexuality is a disease. This does not mean, however, that it is not susceptible to treatment.... [Psychiatrists] deal regularly with problems of personality which are not regarded as diseases. It seems to us that the academic question whether homosexuality is a disease is of much less importance than the practical question of the extent to which, and the ways in which, treatment can help those in whom the condition exists.
>
> In this connection, it is important to consider what the objectives of this help should be. It seems to us that these may be one or more of the following. First, a change in the direction of the sexual preference; secondly, a better adaptation to life in general; and thirdly, greater continence or self-control.[12]

In 1967, ten years after the publication of the Wolfenden Report, and after protracted and heated parliamentary debate, the laws relating to homosexual offenses in England were finally repealed so as to legalize homosexual relations in private between consenting adults.[13]

Similar attempts at restructuring the law have occurred (though less successfully) in the United States within the past ten years. In New York State, for example, the recent revision of the Penal Code was the occasion for a concerted effort to remove from the code those provisions making unorthodox private sexual conduct a crime. Although these efforts were unsuccessful, they were on the whole greeted sympathetically, and as a matter of New York police practice, it is almost unheard of for homosexual relations in private between consenting adults to form the basis for a prosecution. Typical of present-day attitudes is a comment in an *Albany Law Review* article on legislation regulating deviant sexual behavior:

> It is believed that the proscription of deviate sexual behavior between consenting adults is not within the proper scope of legislative endeavor. The fact that such acts are considered by many to be immoral does not prove sufficient reason for state regulation. In addition, the various harms resulting from their criminal sanctions far out-weigh their questionable deterrent effects.[14]

A concomitant of the "disease view" of homosexuality is psychological treatment of homosexuals. An interesting experiment of this nature was the group therapy program carried out from 1953 to 1957 at the Brooklyn Association for the Rehabilitation of Offenders' Civic Center Clinic in Brooklyn, New York. The BARO Clinic was, at the time, the only full-time licensed, privately-endowed, mental hygiene clinic devoted exclusively to the psychiatric treatment of adult offenders. In 1954, a group therapy program for offenders was established, designed to treat individuals referred by various criminal courts, agencies, and other sources. While at first the therapy groups included homosexuals as well as other kinds of offenders, later, at the request of homosexual patients, separate groups were organized for homosexuals. After several years of work with male homosexual offenders, the therapists conducting the sessions came to the conclusion that while it was probably not possible to change the sexual proclivities of most patients, it was possible to make the homosexual a more comfortable and law-abiding member of society. If his sexual problems could not be solved, at least the homosexual could be helped to accept his condition, and to lead a reasonably satisfying, law-abiding life in other areas of his day-to-day existence.[15]

CRIMINAL LAW: THEORIES OF ORIGIN

The criminal law, thus, seems to relate to two kinds of proscribed conduct: those acts which are *mala in se* and those acts which are *mala prohibita*. The offenses we call *mala in se* are related to our notions of natural law; the *mala prohibita* reflect social consensus but in narrower terms, more closely related to time, place, and circumstance. How are these two types of social consensus translated into legislative, judicial, and administrative action?

Several theories have been advanced to explain how our criminal law evolved. A purely historical approach suggests that criminal law developed from the private law characteristic of the far simpler social systems (*Gemeinschaft*)* prevailing before the Middle Ages. Law in those systems was private law, that is, it prescribed redress for torts (private wrongs committed by one individual against another). Attacks, assaults, and stealing were originally thought to be offenses which concerned only the perpetrator and his victim, and redress was usually arranged in terms of compensation to the victim, his family, or his clan. Subsequently, as social organization became more complex in the later feudal era (*Gesellschaft*),** offenses of this nature became offenses against the state: wrongdoers became disturbers,

---

*A concept developed by Ferdinand Tönnies, defined as "A society in which people feel they belong together because they are of the same kind." For a full discussion, see Leonard Broom and Philip Selznick, *Sociology*, 3rd ed. (New York: Harper and Row, 1963), p. 47.

**In sociology, the typology constructed by Ferdinand Tönnies— *Gemeinschaft* and *Gesellschaft*—illustrates this point. *Gemeinschaft* was used by Tönnies to typify group relationships which developed unconsciously or subconsciously and which were familistic in nature, whereas *Gesellschaft* was used by him to indicate group relationships entered into deliberately to achieve recognized ends." Alvin L. Bertrand, *Basic Sociology* (New York: Appleton-Century-Crofts, 1967), p. 50.

not of the victim's peace, but of the king's peace. Crime, and the punishment therefor, became matters of public rather than private concern. According to the classical historical theory criminal law thus developed directly from the laws relating to private torts, and changed, as our social system changed, into a system of public law. However, not all wrongs in primitive society were torts; some, such as sacrilege and treason, were always crimes against the group. Furthermore, even to say of torts that they developed into crimes is not to explain the pattern of development.

Another theory of the origin of criminal law is that it represents the considered, orderly thinking of society as to what regulations are necessary to maintain order. Just as John Locke hypothesized that governments came into being to insure order, tranquility, and the inalienable private rights of individuals, so one may theorize that the substance of our criminal law resulted from the intellectual assessment of social problems, and considered judgment as to the best remedies possible. Few practitioners familiar with criminal law and its idiosyncracies, contradictions, and irrationalities could accept this theory except perhaps in very general terms.

A more promising theory is that criminal law is a crystallization of the mores of a society, that is, that normative behavior upon which society places a high evaluation. Sabbath blue laws and those laws relating to gambling, prostitution, obscenity and pornography, alcohol and drug use are all reflections of public opinion regarding such modes of conduct at the time the legislation was placed on the books. American legislatures are notorious for their failure to repeal outmoded morals legislation, and therefore, as social attitudes towards these practices change, it is left to the judiciary, and even to the police and prosecutors, to modify the stated law in accordance with the changing consensus of society. Such modification is achieved through "interpretation" by the courts and through either selective enforcement or non-enforcement by police and prosecutors.

This changing social consensus is frequently given

form, direction, and impetus by interest groups which promote a particular point of view regarding desirable social goals. Such groups operate essentially as educational institutions, that is, through mass media and other instruments of social communication. They educate the public as to the "rightness" of their views and urge public support for them. Thus, as the public comes to accept the innocuousness of private homosexual behavior between consenting adults, less and less pressure is placed on police and prosecutors to take action against such conduct, and judges are freer to impose minimal or suspended sentences. Ultimately, if and when public opinion becomes sufficiently mobilized, the legislature may be moved to take action to modify or repeal the formal statute. In some areas of legislation, such as obscenity and birth control, pressure groups have been markedly successful in bringing "test cases" to court to afford the judiciary an opportunity to reinterpret old statutes in the light of more modern standards.

The operations of interest groups are extremely complex and subtle, and extend for example, to efforts to influence the curricula of law schools and the training of lawyers. New emphases on labor law, poverty law, and criminal law in the law schools have been the product in the first instance, at least, of the persuasive efforts of interest groups concerned with social problems such as the improvement of the position of the working man, the rights of the poor, and the equalization of the treatment of defendants in our criminal justice system. Critics of our legal system, and especially of our criminal law, sometimes charge that the more politically powerful middle- and upper-class groups are able to define law in terms that regulate the conduct of the lower classes but leave them free to act in ways often just as reprehensible. From this point of view, the nature of criminal law and the enforcement processes are dependent upon the outcomes of struggles between various social classes (rich–poor, landlord–tenant, urban–rural, debtor–creditor, propertied–property-less) for power. Those groups which win the political struggle get to decide what are and who commits crimes. Who is a criminal, and what is a crime are, in this view of the matter, a function of the social stratification system. While this is at least partially true, the interests of the disadvantaged have been championed by interest groups which have attempted to redress the balance. For example, by the successful fight for countervailing rights, the rights of property have been modified to permit the recognition of the rights to collective bargaining, safe and healthful working conditions, minimum wages, controlled rents, and equal opportunity employment.

Thus upon examination, crime, far from being the exact mode of forbidden conduct it superficially seems to be, is really a highly philosophical concept, reflecting nothing less than a Weltanschauung (world outlook) as to the kind of society we ought to live in. The definition of crime in the first instance is found on the statute books, but it is highly modified, sometimes to the point of extinction, by both administrative (police and prosecutorial) action and by judicial interpretation. Moreover, the modes of conduct proscribed by the formal law have found their way there from a variety of sources: either as vestigial historical remains, or as a result of a rational effort at problem solving, or as a crystallization of widely held notions of natural law or, on a less lofty plane, of notions of proper social conduct. Criminal law, like all law, is in a state of flux, reflecting the movements of a dynamic society. Much of this movement is channeled and focused through the mechanism of ad hoc or ongoing interest groups which educate or inform the general public in the process of serving their own causes.

Selected Readings

Becker, Howard S. *Outsiders: Studies in the Sociology of Deviance.* New York: Free Press, 1963.

Chambliss, William J. *Crime and the Legal Process.* New York: McGraw-Hill, 1969.

Cipes, Robert M. *The Crime War.* New York: New American Library, 1968.

Committee on Homosexual Offenses and Prostitution. *Wolfenden Report,* Command Paper 247. London: Her Majesty's Stationery Office, September 1957.

Erikson, Kai T. *Wayward Puritans.* New York: Wiley, 1966.

Ferri, Enrico. *Criminal Sociology.* New York: Appleton, 1896.

Lindesmith, Alfred R. *The Addict and the Law.* New York: Vintage Books, 1967.

President's Commission on Law Enforcement and Administration of Justice. *Task Force Report: Drunkenness.* Washington, D.C.: U.S. Government Printing Office, 1967.

Quinney, Richard, ed. *Crime and Justice in Society.* Boston: Little, Brown, 1969.

Schur, Edwin M. *Crimes Without Victims.* Englewood Cliffs, N.J.: Prentice-Hall, 1965.

Sutherland, Edwin H., and Cressey, Donald R. *Principles of Criminology.* 8th ed. Philadelphia: Lippincott, 1970.

Notes

[1] *People v. Friedman,* 302 N.Y. 75 (1950), as quoted in Leo Pfeffer, *Church, State and Freedom,* rev. ed. (Boston: Beacon Press, 1967), pp. 283–284.

[2] E. H. Sutherland and D. R. Cressey, *Principles of Criminology,* 8th ed. (Philadelphia: Lippincott, 1970), p. 4.

[3] *Griswold v. Connecticut,* 381 U.S. 479 (1965).

[4] For an extended discussion of the concept of the "outsider," see Howard S. Becker, *Outsiders* (New York: Free Press, 1963).

[5] Harrison Act, 1914. For a more complete discussion of the development of federal policy toward drug use, see Alfred R. Lindesmith, "Federal Law and Drug Addiction," in William J. Chambliss, *Crime and the Legal Process* (New York: McGraw-Hill, 1969), pp. 63–73; and Edwin M. Schur, *Crimes Without Victims* (Englewood Cliffs, N.J.: Prentice-Hall, 1965), pp. 120–168.

[6] *Webb v. United States,* 249 U.S. 96 (1919); *United States v. Behrman,* 258 U.S. 280 (1922).

[7] *Lindner v. United States,* 268 U.S. 5 (1925).

[8] Lindesmith, p. 63.

[9] President's Commission on Law Enforcement and Administration of Justice, *Task Force Report: Drunkenness* (Washington, D.C.: U.S. Government Printing Office, 1967), p. 1.

[10] Metcalf-Volker Bill (Article 9 of the Mental Hygiene Law, New York State), Chapter 192 of the Laws of 1966, as amended to November 1968.

[11] Alfred C. Kinsey, Wendell B. Pomeroy, and Clyde E. Martin, *Sexual Behavior in the Human Male* (Philadelphia: W. B. Saunders, 1948).

[12] Committee on Homosexual Offenses and Prostitution, *Wolfenden Report,* Command Paper 247 (London: Her Majesty's Stationery Office, September 1957), p. 66.

[13] *New York Times,* July 5, 1967, p. 1.

[14] R. M. Fritts and F. V. Smith, "Deviate Sexual Behavior: The Desirability of Legislative Proscription," *Albany Law Review* 30 (1966): 304.

[15] For fuller discussion, see Alexander B. Smith and Alexander Bassin, "Group Therapy with Homosexuals," *Journal of Social Therapy* 5, no. 3 (1959): 225–232.

Criminals: Status Groups and Differential Handling

3

Superficially, the neatly bound volumes of statutes in the law libraries may seem to be rocks of stability and objectivity in a bewildering, rapidly changing world. The heavy books with their precise, stilted language, describing seemingly every contingency, every mode of proscribed conduct imaginable, seem the very essence of certainty and immutability. The appearance is deceptive. In the long run, societal perceptions of natural law and the changing standards of approved conduct will affect the substance of the law. In more immediate terms, the content of the law will change with the enactment of new laws, repeal of old laws, and shifting judicial interpretations in cases adjudicated under the penal code.

It is not only the formal substance of the law that varies, however. Were it fixed (and it is of course fixed during relatively short periods of time) an additional variable would exist in the way the law is applied to those over whom it has jurisdiction. Is the law really the same law for rich and poor, black and white, child and adult, blue-collar and white-collar, homosexual and heterosexual, rational and insane, normal and retarded? The impact of the law is obviously not the same, and few people would argue that it should be. The five-year-old who unthinkingly locks a playmate in an abandoned refrigerator ought not to be treated in the same manner as the hold-up man whose gagged victim suffocates. The mental incompetent cannot be questioned in the same manner as the normal suspect; the results of the interrogation as well as the evaluation of the intent of his conduct must make allowance for his mental capacity.

Most people would nevertheless indignantly reject the notion that social position, education, affluence, or political connections warrant specially favorable treatment at the hands of the law. In reality however, the law works differently not only for the child, the mentally incompetent, and the insane, but also, to some extent, for those whose status is other than white and middle or upper class. On the whole the poor, alcoholics, hippies, addicts, homosexuals, non-whites, and political radicals are frequently treated more severely for the same kinds of conduct than white, middle-class, conventional defendants would be.

DIFFERENTIAL HANDLING: RICH AND POOR

Case 1. Tobacco heiress Doris Duke, while intoxicated, drove her car along a private road on her Rhode Island estate, hitting and crushing to death against a wall a male employee, one Tirella, reputedly her lover. The police refrained from interrogating her for three days until she recovered her composure. At that time she was questioned at home. No indictment was handed down.[1]

Case 2. In an affluent, upstate New York, suburban community residents reported being annoyed by a peeping Tom. The police knew the culprit to be one of the town's leading citizens. The complaint was handled by calling the suspect's wife and asking her to take care of the matter.[2]

Case 3. Mrs. Anne Woodward, a Long Island socialite, was allegedly awakened from sleep at about three A.M. on October 30, 1955. She claimed that she was frightened, grabbed the family shotgun, and on seeing a shadow nearby, let go with both barrels, hitting and fatally wounding her husband. She was handled very gently by the police. On November 22, 1955, she voluntarily left the hospital for the questioning at Nassau County Police Headquarters. On November 26, 1955, the Grand Jury cleared her, after she and thirty-one witnesses testified.[3]

Case 4. On April 6, 1966, the Reverend Harold L. Elliott of North Babylon Center, Long Island, was arrested on a charge of luring a seven-year-old girl into a station wagon and committing sodomy in the presence of a nine-year-old girl. The police reported that, in the one year Elliott had been in charge of his church on Long Island, he was involved in at least forty to fifty similar cases in Nassau and Suffolk counties. The Reverend Elliott had previously been arrested in Elizabeth, West Virginia, on March 26, 1964, charged by a fifteen- and a sixteen-year-old girl with indecent exposure. He posted a small bond which he forfeited, and then moved to Levole, Maryland, with a new church position. There, less than a year later, on February 16, 1965, he was again arrested for indecent exposure, this time on complaint of a number of twelve- and thirteen-year-old girls. These charges were dropped with the understanding that Elliott would undergo psychiatric treatment.

Elliott was indicted in Nassau County on seven counts of sodomy. The court ordered a succession of psychiatric examinations, after which Elliott was found sane. Finally, he was permitted to plead guilty to one count of Sodomy, First Degree by Nassau County Judge Martin Kolbrener. Although the district attorney asked that a life sentence be imposed, Judge Kolbrener gave Elliott a five- to ten-year suspended sentence, on condition that the latter commit himself to a state hospital until certified as cured. Elliott was thereupon admitted to Central Islip State Hospital. The newspaper commented that the sentence imposed was very lenient.[4]

All of the above cases have one thing in common: the treatment of the offenders was extraordinary in that it differed markedly from treatment given to ordinary suspects. It is inconceivable, for example, that a lower-class or lower-middle-class woman involved in a vehicular case would have been accorded the courtesy of three days respite from questioning in order that she might regain her composure. Most peeping Toms are arrested, questioned, publicly arraigned, plead guilty to a minor charge, and are given a short sentence or probation. Householders who fatally wound alleged intruders are, normally, rigorously and promptly questioned by the police. Sex offenders who are not upper-middle-class clergymen of established religious denominations are seldom treated gently and sympathetically. In short, to state the matter baldly, every criminal justice practitioner from the policeman to the parole officer knows that the law in practice is not the same for rich and poor.

One of the results of this differential handling is probably an overrepresentation of the poor in official statistics relating to crime. Figures indicating arrests, convictions, and commitments show that poor people (lower-class people) commit crimes in numbers vastly disproportionate to their numbers in the population at large. Criminologists have long viewed these figures with some skepticism. Research, based on data gathered from anonymous questionnaires given to middle-class people, has indicated a surprising incidence of criminal conduct, including the commission of felonies, among groups the official statistics would lead us to believe are virtually crime-free. A study made by Herbert A. Bloch, a prominent sociologist, indicated that 91 percent of a group of college juniors and seniors admitted to having knowingly committed both misdemeanors and felonies. Women students were as delinquent as men. All those interviewed came from at least middle-class homes. An extension of the study, directed at professional men and women including physicians and lawyers, reported similar results.[5] An even more well-known study by Austin L. Porterfield found that middle-class college students, very few of whom had ever been charged or arrested, had committed virtually the full range of crimes with which juveniles in the Texas courts had been charged. These offenses averaged out at no less than eleven per student.[6]

Not only do middle-class people apparently commit the same kinds of crime as lower-class people, but in addition, they are prone to a considerable degree of what Edwin H. Sutherland, the late dean of American criminologists, has labelled "white-collar crime." These crimes, so called because they are perpetrated in the normal course of business by those in managerial or professional positions, include, in the business world, such practices as "misrepresentation in financial statements of corporations, manipulation in the stock exchange, commercial bribery, bribery of public officials . . . , misrepresentation in advertising and salesmanship, embezzlement, short weights . . . , and misapplication of funds in receiverships and bankruptcies."[7] Each profession has its own variety of illegal practices; for example, physicians have been known to sell narcotic drugs and prescriptions illegally, perform abortions, treat criminal fugitives and underworld characters, file fraudulent reports, perjure themselves in court, and split fees. A similar list could no doubt be drawn up for attorneys and other professionals. The money value of these crimes no doubt exceeds the total money value of traditional crimes, and their social effects may well be at least equally harmful. Yet perpetrators of white-collar crimes are seldom so much as charged, and are even more rarely committed to correctional institutions.

Police, as a group, have their own variety of white-collar crime. The charges, made by Lincoln Steffens in *The Shame of the Cities* (1904), of police connivance with and protection of racketeers, gamblers, prostitutes, and other criminals, have been repeated frequently since, and were not novel when made. Periodically, exposure is made of some particularly corrupt department which cooperates with underworld elements. These crimes fit Sutherland's definition of white-collar crime in that they arise out of the normal course of legitimate police business. They are regarded by the public at large and by most police practitioners as illegal, immoral, disfunctional activities. There is however, another

47

set of police activities which are in violation of the formal statutes, but which nevertheless are considered both moral and functional by almost all working policemen. These are the kinds of actions policemen take in acquiring and using informers. Many informed observers have described such police malpractice as harassment through illegal arrests and detentions, non-feasance of duty in refraining from arresting criminals, bribery, and illegal wiretapping. Some of these activities are related to the process of using petty criminals to inform on their bigger and more dangerous colleagues. Few policemen would deny the validity of this description of the informer system; fewer still would deny the necessity for the use of informers in police work. The evasions of the law necessitated by the informer system do, nevertheless, create a large body of lawbreakers within the police department.

The public at large is, for the most part, only dimly aware of the advantages that the well-to-do lawbreaker enjoys in contrast to his lower-class fellow criminal. In recent years, due in part to the publicity given to such cases as *Gideon v. Wainright* and *Miranda v. Arizona,*[8] there has been an increasing appreciation of the importance of adequate legal counsel in every criminal case. Access to such counsel is obviously easier for the rich man than for the poor. However, differential handling is a much more subtle and complex phenomenon than the relatively simple matter of providing counsel. The entire criminal justice system reacts differently to the rich man: he is less likely to be arrested; if arrested he can make bail; he will be treated considerately, if not deferentially, by the police; every avenue of legal appeal will be available to him; and should he be convicted, his punishment will be less severe, at least in terms of imprisonment.

Does society really wish it otherwise? While the average, strongly egalitarian-minded American would, in principle, vehemently reject the notion of one law for the rich and another for the poor, how many people really want to see rich and poor treated alike? In Philadelphia, Federal District Court Judge Ganby sentenced seven executives of leading electrical equipment manufacturers (including General Electric and Westinghouse vice-presidents) to jail for thirty days. He fined thirty-six men and twenty-one companies $931,500 for criminal violation of the anti-trust laws. The government had brought charges against forty-five individuals and twenty-nine companies for fixing prices and rigging bids for government contracts. Twenty received suspended jail terms.[9] Should these executives of the country's leading electrical manufacturers have received prison terms commensurate with the money value of the crimes they committed? In Case 2, cited above, involving an affluent peeping Tom, or in Case 4, concerning a middle-class sodomist, would any social purpose beyond simple vengeance have been served by committing the suspects to prison? If an offender is so situated that he can be rehabilitated and prevented from doing further social harm without being publicly disgraced and punished, is there a reason why he should be handled in a harsh and punitive manner?

Most people, except for those who think of justice in retributive terms, would probably agree that it is socially desirable to use only that degree of force and official action needed to accomplish the primary social goals of deterrence and reform. If this is so, then differential handling for the rich has considerable practical validity. What must not be overlooked, however, is that the poor are in many cases punished, disgraced, and publicly pilloried, not only because of the offenses they committed, but because their social position is such that other, less harsh alternatives are not available to the system of criminal justice. Lower-class, storefront clergymen simply don't have the strong families and resources that guarantee they will be kept out of trouble in the future. Poor people who commit violent crimes usually don't have relatives, business associates, and friends who will see to it that they are restrained in the future. The police and the jails must play the part that the psychiatrist and the good lawyer play in the lives of the rich. Thus the criminologist's skepticism as to the validity of official crime statistics is, in large part, justified.

DIFFERENTIAL HANDLING: BLACK AND WHITE

Black Americans bear a special relationship to our criminal justice system. They are more likely to become suspects or defendants in criminal cases than are white Americans, and once having become suspects, they suffer the double handicap of being both poor and black. All the disabilities suffered by a poor person in defending himself against a criminal charge are suffered by the poor black, and in addition, his color will add still another dimension of disadvantage to his case.

The incidence of crimes among Negroes is disproportionately high,[10] especially with regard to crimes of violence. The President's Crime Commission Report indicates that the arrest rate of Negroes for FBI Index Offenses* in 1965 was four times as great as that for whites; the Negro arrest rate for murder was almost ten times as high; and for burglary it was almost three and one-half times as high. We may not conclude from this, however, that a tendency toward crime is a genetic quality inherent in Negroes. One variable accounting for the disparity between white and Negro crime rates is a difference in level of income. There is a strong correlation between poverty (and especially slum living) and crime, and Negroes are disproportionately poor. Studies of ethnic groups in America have shown that crime rates decrease as the group moves from the core city to the suburbs. The difference in arrest rates between Negroes and whites living under similar conditions is far less disparate.

Secondly, the statistics which indicate these differential crime rates are incomplete, and therefore unreliable. The figures of the President's Crime Commission Report cited above are based on arrests. Other figures showing the disproportionate amount of Negro criminal activity are based on convictions. Neither of these figures bears any precise relationship to offenses committed. All that can be said with

*The FBI Index lists seven offenses: Willful Homicide, Forcible Rape, Robbery, Aggravated Assault, Burglary, Larceny (fifty dollars and over), and Motor Vehicle Theft.

certainty is that far more crimes are committed than are
known to the police, and infinitely more than result in arrests
or convictions. The differential in crime rates between Negroes and whites can thus mean one of two things: either
that Negroes commit disproportionately more crime, or that
they are arrested and convicted disproportionately more
frequently than whites. Probably both are true, but the discriminatory factor in the criminal justice system which leads
to disproportionate arrests and convictions has received far
less attention from the public than the hypothesis that
Negroes are more prone to crime than whites.

Poor people, as indicated in the previous section, do
not and cannot receive the same handling in the criminal
justice system as well-to-do people. They are more likely
to be suspected and arrested than the middle class. When
arrested, they are less likely to be admitted to bail or discharged on their own recognizance. If tried, they are less
likely to have the assistance of good quality counsel; if convicted, they are less likely to appeal; if sentenced, they are
more likely to receive prison sentences rather than fines or
probation; and, when sentenced to prison, their sentences
tend to be longer than those given well-to-do defendants.
All these disabilities apply to most black suspects enmeshed
in the toils of the law, because most blacks are poor. There
is however, an added dimension to the problem for the black:
his color alone, aside from his class, will make him more
likely to be suspected, arrested, convicted, and committed,
especially if his victim is white. On the other hand, the police
may under-enforce the law where black preys upon black,
thus reducing the protection of the law for black victims.[11]

The motion picture *In the Heat of the Night* depicts the
classic problem of the Negro vis-à-vis the police. When a
mysterious murder takes place in a small southern town, the
police, in searching for a suspect, automatically consider
first a strange Negro who was passing through the town. It
is quite clear that their decision to question him was based
almost entirely on his color, combined with the fact that he
was an outsider. Negroes have become increasingly bitter

51

in their complaints that police will arrest or at least stop to question blacks under circumstances under which whites would not be approached. In Louisville, Kentucky, one Thompson,[12] a Negro handyman waiting in a café for a bus, passed the time by "shuffling" to the music of the juke box. Despite the fact that neither the proprietor nor the other customers complained, city police officers on a routine check arrested Thompson for loitering, and when he protested verbally, added the charge of disorderly conduct. Thompson was convicted and fined in Louisville Police Court. Ultimately, the Supreme Court reversed the conviction on the ground that an arrest and conviction based on no evidence is a violation of due process rights under the Fourteenth Amendment.

Not many cases are as extreme as the *Thompson* case, fortunately, but many blacks feel that their color singles them out for especially harsh treatment by the police. One of the most troublesome problems in this area arises when the police decision to arrest or to question on the street is motivated largely by color. In *People v. Rivera*[13] two Puerto Rican boys were stopped, questioned, and searched by the police because their conduct seemed suspicious. The conduct in question consisted of looking intently for an extended period of time into the window of a bar and grill located in New York City's East Village. The police suspicions in this case were justified, in that Rivera was found to be carrying a revolver. The relevant question, however, is whether the very same conduct on the part of two students from nearby New York University would have produced the same reaction on the part of the police. There is some probability that it would not. From the police point of view, it is both logical and proper that poorly-dressed Puerto Ricans should be regarded with more suspicion than well-dressed college boys. The statistical likelihood that a boy of Rivera's type would stick up a bar and grill is greater than that a college student would do so. From the point of view of the black or Puerto Rican this attitude is simply a reflection of the bitter truth that he is suspect because of his color or ethnic background.

Merely being out of the ghetto is enough, on occasion, to single out the black man for attention. In 1969, in a case involving robbery and murder, two suspects were apprehended by the police, and subsequently convicted of homicide. In a second trial of one of the defendants on charges of felonious possession of a weapon arising out of the same incident, the conviction of the defendant was set aside by the appellate court because of inflammatory, allegedly racially biased remarks by the prosecutor. The basis for these remarks (which were in rebuttal to accusations of racial bias by the defense attorney) was that suspicion had fallen on the two suspects initially because they were black men in a white neighborhood.[14] Again, from the vantage of the police, black men running through a white neighborhood are unusual and suspect; to the law-abiding black, however, such law enforcement simply means that he is judged by standards more rigorous than those applied to his white counterparts.

Another area in which blacks feel they are at a disadvantage vis-à-vis the police is with respect to the question of identification. To the white man, all Negroes tend to look alike. Certainly, there is a far greater chance of error when a Negro suspect is identified by either a white victim or a white policeman, so much so that an authority on the problems of eye-witness identification suggests that far greater weight be given to identification of Negroes by other Negroes than to identification of Negroes by whites.[15] In practice however, it is doubtful that judges and juries are aware of the somewhat dubious validity of interracial identification.

The grievances of blacks against the criminal justice system are not, however, confined to complaints about overzealous or unduly harsh enforcement of the law. Curiously enough, precisely the opposite complaint may be made: that the police do not enforce the law vigorously enough when crimes are committed against Negroes by other

Negroes. It is notorious, for example, that assaults, especially those arising out of domestic quarrels, frequently do not end in arrest and prosecution when the parties involved are black unless the victim insists on filing a complaint and following through. LaFave states:

> This kind of unequal enforcement of the law frequently occurs when Negroes are involved, particularly in large metropolitan areas such as Detroit. Such offenses as bigamy and open and notorious cohabitation are overlooked by law enforcement officials, and arrests often are not made for carrying knives or for robbery of other Negroes. However, the practice is most strikingly illustrated by the repeated failure of the police to arrest Negroes for a felonious assault upon a spouse or acquaintance unless the victim actually insists upon prosecution.[16]

Similarly James Q. Wilson, in his study of police behavior in eight different American communities, says that:

> In Newburgh every Negro interviewed . . . agreed that the overriding characteristic of the Newburgh police was their tendency to under-enforce the law in Negro areas. One lawyer told an interviewer:
>
> "We can't get police protection in this [Negro] community. They [the police] ignore the crowds. There's a bar right next to where my parents live. . . . Every night there'll be a big crowd . . . that will gather in the streets in front of this place. Sometimes we'll have to call the police four and five times before they even come. When they do come, they often get out of their cars and just start joking with people standing there. The police are supposed to break up those crowds and move them along, but they don't do it."
>
> Another Negro . . . complained . . . :
>
> "Not long ago five men broke into my house. Five men! They came upstairs. . . . If I didn't have a .22 rifle with me, I don't know what would have happened. I called the police three times, and it took them a half hour to get there. . . . When you complain to the police about their not giving you any kind of protection, you get answers like the one X gave me. He said, 'I'll deny I ever said this if you repeat it, but you know how this police department is run. Our motto is, let the niggers kill each other off.' "[17]

The police rationale for such under-enforcement is generally that the mores of the Negro community are different, that Negroes don't regard these offenses as crimes, and that they want to be let alone by the police. They cite as evidence that Negro complainants are frequently uncooperative, refusing to file complaints or withdrawing complaints already filed. Some policemen see Negroes as preferring to take the law into their own hands and discipline the offender personally. Wilson quotes a Newburgh detective as saying that the police would permit this "discipline" only in "small cases . . . no more than fifteen to twenty stitches." The policemen will almost always deny that the under-enforcement of the law in Negro communities stems from contempt for the Negro community and a lack of concern for its well-being. He will justify his department's policy on the ground of suiting official conduct to the needs and desires of the client served. However, law-abiding Negroes, victimized by crime, see only that the law does not afford them the same protection it affords law-abiding whites. The policeman's case is somewhat weakened by the fact that an official laissez faire attitude towards crime by Negroes rarely exists when whites are the victims.

It is not only in the area of detention and arrests that color is a factor in official actions. Sentencing of Negro defendants also shows a differential pattern. In 1969, a study of the criminal justice system by Marvin E. Wolfgang of the University of Pennsylvania and Bernard Cohen of Queens College was published by the American Jewish Committee. It concluded that: "More blacks are arrested, jailed, convicted and given more severe penalties than whites." A specific example cited was that,

> between 1940 and 1964 in Florida 125 white men were convicted of raping white women and 68 black men were convicted of raping black women. In each category, approximately 4 percent of those convicted were sentenced to death. However, during that same period, 84 black men were convicted of raping white women and 54 percent of them were sentenced to death. Eight white men were convicted of raping black women and none were sentenced to death.[18]

To cite the most extreme example, in the South the death penalty for rape has been reserved almost exclusively for Negroes; white men convicted of the same offense have received varying terms of imprisonment.

Negro juvenile defendants are more often committed

to institutions, where white children are usually returned to their parents or are handled by unofficial agencies. Discriminatory attitudes on the part of those officials involved in handling such young offenders are only partially to blame for the situation; the lack of access by Negro children to the private agencies that service whites (especially Jewish youngsters) is also a highly significant factor. Nevertheless, studies show that Negro children are frequently committed at younger ages than whites, for less serious offenses, and with more promising case histories.[19] Thus, the criminal justice system for the black man, especially the poor black, is harsh and punitive to a degree experienced by relatively few whites. The black's consequent alienation from the system on which the white middle class pin their hopes of peace, order, and stability is easily understandable. As Professor Bloch has eloquently said:

> This is the inevitable price we pay for the social and cultural disenfranchisement of minority peoples, and the story can be duplicated in various parts of the country. The groups may change from time to time, but the effects of the cultural pattern of marginality remain largely the same.[20]

DIFFERENTIAL HANDLING: PARIAHS

In the discussion of deviance in Chapter 2, it was suggested that deviance was tentatively defined by some authorities as behavior that is pathologically different, pathological in the sense that it causes harm or disruption to society. Much of this antisocial behavior we label crime. There are, however, certain kinds of activities which are more distasteful than disruptive, and social attitudes towards the handling of such activities are frequently highly ambivalent. Most enlightened people today, for example, claim to look upon alcoholism as a disease. Alcoholics, thus, are not criminals but sick people. However, the sight of a drunk in the gutter arouses disgust rather than compassion in most onlookers, and their immediate reaction to the sight of the derelict inebriate is not so much "Help him" as "Get rid of him." Drug addicts, overt homosexuals, obvious prostitutes, mental defectives, hippies, skid row bums, and alcoholics all share a pariah status. Society wishes not so much to punish these people as to get them out of sight where they will cease to offend the sensibilities of "decent" people. We may agree that homosexual behavior in private between consenting adults is permissible, but we object to seeing a mincing, effeminate, rouged male on the streets. We may ultimately decide that smoking marijuana should not be punished, but we don't like to see groups of glassy-eyed adolescents wandering around in public. We may chuckle privately at extramarital sexual dalliance, but we object to the sight of groups of bizarrely dressed prostitutes soliciting clients in our downtown areas. In short, we object to the public display of conduct that good taste demands be kept private.

The police share the negativism of societal attitudes toward these types of deviants. The police, after all, are individuals drawn from the common ranks, and share the common ranks' prejudices. The public, furthermore, having no other agency to turn to in its effort to be spared the discomfort of seeing these deviates, turns to the police. The police reaction mirrors that of the community, but only more intensely.

Paul Chevigny of the American Civil Liberties Union discusses police reactions to undesirables:

> Bohemians, homosexuals, political activists (particularly of the left), derelicts, prostitutes, and narcotic users all evoke police action. A member of one of these outcast groups will not be harmed if he obeys the orders of the police, unless there is a drive on to round up homosexuals, derelicts or prostitutes. . . . On the other hand, the police do tend to take some action, short of arrest, against a member of such pariah groups, even without any verbal challenge or other threat. His mere presence seems to be enough challenge to make the police tell him to move on. Any sort of defiance of the police action in such cases is likely to be answered with violence.[21]

On the whole the aim of police conduct towards these outcastes is to get them out of sight: to get them to move on, beat it, get lost. Occasionally, in response to complaints from merchants, tourists, and others, there will be clean-ups of particular areas frequented by undesirables, in which case drunks, homosexuals, prostitutes, and others will be arrested and sentenced to short terms in jail. The police may also be rougher in their handling of these individuals than they are of other suspects, for very few of these pariahs complain. Most complaints, according to Chevigny at least, come from middle-class citizens who witness and are affronted by police conduct.

This type of police conduct, moreover, is typical of the handling of any minority group that has not yet achieved full acceptance. Negroes, Jews, Italians, Puerto Ricans, and even the Irish in the nineteenth century have experienced the underlying hostility of society towards them as filtered through the medium of police behavior. Conceivably, some of the groups mentioned by Chevigny will eventually lose their outcaste status and be accepted as unusual but not necessarily distasteful members of society (as some ethnic groups eventually have). In the interim, however, students of the criminal justice system must be aware that police handling of these individuals is by no means even-handed or comparable to the handling of commonplace suspects.

DIFFERENTIAL HANDLING: POLITICAL HERETICS

Another group that frequently receives unusually harsh and punitive handling by the criminal justice system is the politically unorthodox, especially radicals of the Left. There are two principal reasons why this type of differential treatment occurs: first, many law enforcement officials are unaware of the public policy implications of a commitment to the classical theory of democratic government on which the United States Constitution purports to be based; and second, radicals do not only speak—they act—and their actions sometimes pose real threats to the public order.

To many policemen and judges, the hortatory dogma of groups such as Communists, black militants, anti-war protestors, and students is a threat, not only to the stability, but to the very existence of the social order that law enforcement officials are sworn to protect. Such violent critics of the system are, moreover, not only dangerous but ungrateful. As many policemen see it, the freedom of speech that radicals enjoy is a gift bestowed upon them by a generous society, and when radicals use it to the detriment of that society, they are surely violating the rules of the game and behaving despicably.

This reasoning, though superficially plausible, is fallacious in terms of classical democratic theory. Freedom of speech is not a gift from society to the individual. On the contrary, freedom of thought, speech, and conscience are inalienable rights which inhere in every individual, and which no society may abridge. Moreover, such rights are socially justified only partially because of the fulfillment individuals may find in them. Their more important justification is that they are the salvation of a free society.

> The peculiar evil of silencing the expression of an opinion is, that it is robbing the human race; posterity as well as the existing generation; those who dissent from the opinion, still more than those who hold it. If the opinion is right, they are deprived of the opportunity of exchanging error for truth: if wrong, they lose, what is almost as great a benefit, the clearer perception and livelier impression of truth, produced by its collision with error. . . . We can never be sure that the opinion we are endeavoring to stifle is a false opinion; and if we were sure, stifling it would be an evil still.[22]

The practical implications of Mill's theory are that every idea must be heard—primarily for the benefit of society. However silly, destructive, hateful, or strange, no idea may be suppressed, because no one in society is capable of rendering an a priori judgment as to its worthlessness. History bears witness to the number of radical thinkers reviled in their own time whose thought is now revered and accepted. Moreover, the persecution of such thinkers has invariably resulted in a great loss to the society which suppressed them. The Athens which executed Socrates and the Hitler regime which drove Jewish scientists from Germany enfeebled their own civilizations. Thus, the radical is not an individual to be simply tolerated. He is a necessity to a society in a state of flux.

Most confrontations between police and radicals do not involve abstract questions of freedom of speech. They center on the policeman's duty—as he sees it—to maintain public order and the radical's right—as he sees it—to publicize his message wherever and however he can. Most such clashes involve public assemblies wherein a mixture of speech and action occurs. Action, unlike speech, is legitimately repressible by a democratic government. The dispute between radicals and the police normally concerns where the line should be drawn. The radical interprets his action as incident to his speech, hence beyond control; the police see the radical's speech as incident to his action, hence subject to restraint. No easy resolution of these disparate viewpoints exists. The best that can be done, perhaps, is to attempt to achieve some perspective on the dispute by reviewing some of the history and theory of our Constitution.

The absolute terms of the First Amendment to the United States Constitution reflect the healthy appreciation the founding fathers had for freedom of speech and conscience. "Congress shall make no law . . . abridging the freedom of speech, or of the press; or the right of the people to peaceably assemble . . . ." Despite this clear prohibition, however, certain kinds of speech—libel, obscenity, and sedition—have been legally suppressed in varying degrees by both the state and federal governments.

Although the first ten amendments to the Constitution, as originally passed, were restrictions on only the federal government, since 1925 the United States Supreme Court has increasingly applied these restrictions to the states, on the theory that the phrase *due process* in the Fourteenth Amendment means that which is unfair action for the federal government is equally unfair for the states. There is an ongoing controversy among members of the Supreme Court as to whether the phrase *due process* is the precise equivalent of the guarantees encompassed in the Bill of Rights, or whether the phrase can mean something either more or less than these guarantees. There is nevertheless agreement at this point that the First Amendment is applicable to the states. While libel and obscenity laws have caused relatively little political controversy, attempts to regulate sedition, that is, the bringing of the government into "hatred and contempt," have caused far greater problems.

The first federal attempt to regulate such speech was in the infamous and unpopular Alien and Sedition Laws, passed in 1798 and repealed two years later. From 1800 to 1917, the federal government had no peace-time regulation whatever of political speech. In 1917, however, coincidental with both our entry into World War I and the outbreak of the Russian Revolution, the federal government passed two statutes limiting speech that was disloyal and contemptuous of the United States government or that interfered with military operations. Since then the federal government has enacted several other similar laws, perhaps the most famous of which is the Smith Act of 1941. It is understandable that, in light of the absolute prohibition on regulation of speech in the First Amendment, challenges to these laws should have come to the United States Supreme Court in the form of cases involving individuals convicted under this restrictive legislation. The Supreme Court has had great difficulty in establishing a single yardstick for the test of the constitutionality of restrictive speech legislation. It has instead delivered opinions which range along a spectrum marked by two extreme positions. The more liberal of these positions is the famous so-called "clear and present danger test"; the more conservative position is the "bad tendency" or "gravity of the evil discounted by its improbability" test. In recent years the more customary position taken by the Supreme Court in cases involving "pure speech" has been the "clear and present danger" position, that is, all speech is permissible that does not create an imminent likelihood of antisocial action—riot or revolution. Although imminence is not readily definable, the Court appears to think of the time span involved in terms of days or hours rather than months or years. This standard refers to "pure speech," that is, speech unmixed with action. The best example of such speech might be publication of ideas in a book. Speeches before audiences, picketing, demonstrating on the streets, and distributing handbills are all examples of speech mixed with action, and are regulated in a somewhat different manner.

While the clear and present danger standard is the more usual position of the Court, at least since the late 1930s, there have been notable and significant exceptions. During the McCarthy era, from the end of World War II until well into the first Eisenhower administration, the Court refused to permit the advocacy of revolutionary ideas even though they were expressions of sentiment or desire rather than plans for overt action. Thus, Eugene Dennis and his co-defendant Communist party leaders were convicted for having preached the dogma embodied in such classical works of Communist literature as Marx's *Communist Manifesto* and Lenin's *State and Revolution*.[23] The reasoning of the Court seemed to be that a society had a right to protect itself from ideas which might in the future produce dangerous results—that there was no obligation on the part of the authorities to wait until the plans of the revolutionaries had been laid and action was about to take place. This standard is, of course, far more restrictive since it depends for its application on subjective judgment by administrators of the likelihood of events in the indefinite future. Timid or fearful officials, or those under political pressure, may easily see danger in every expression of dissent or dissatisfaction.

It is not surprising that, historically, the more restrictive standard of permissibility for speech has been invoked in times when the nation has, correctly or incorrectly, felt itself to be in danger, such as during and after World War I and during the McCarthy era following World War II. Thus far in the United States, the turmoil and criticism surrounding the Viet Nam War and the Civil Rights movement have not led to a retreat by the Supreme Court from the more liberal clear and present danger standard. If the historical parallel is correct, we may expect to experience such a retreat when and if our problems, internal or external, are perceived as a threat to our national integrity and stability.

The determination of a standard for the permissibility of pure speech is difficult conceptually, and controversial even theoretically. To the criminal justice system, however, difficult pragmatic problems are presented by situations where speech is mixed with action, and public-safety and crowd-control considerations present themselves. Even the most innocuous speech can, under the wrong circumstances, cause a riot; and flaming revolutionary rhetoric delivered over coffee cups to two sympathetic listeners is harmless in terms of danger to public order. Clearly, a speaker who waves an ideological red flag before the enraged bull of a hostile audience will provoke disorder. The problem presented to the criminal justice system under these circumstances is: who is to be restrained—the speaker or the audience?

As in the case of pure speech, the guidelines handed down by the Supreme Court have been ambiguous. In 1948, one Terminiello addressed eight hundred members of the Christian Veterans of America in a Chicago auditorium. In his address he referred to "Queen Eleanor Roosevelt, Queen of America's Communists," and referred to Jews and Negroes as "slimy scum," "snakes," and "bedbugs." Outside the hall two thousand opponents of Terminiello's Fascist adherents staged a riot, throwing bricks and bottles, and breaking into the hall. Terminiello was arrested and convicted of disorderly conduct.[24] During the 1948 presidential campaign, one Feiner, a student at Syracuse University, addressed a crowd of seventy-five to eighty people on a street corner in a Negro residential section of Syracuse, New York. He urged his audience to attend a meeting supporting the candidacy of Henry Wallace, and referred to President Truman as a "bum" and to the American Legion as a "Nazi Gestapo." He also made some remarks urging blacks and whites to join in and fight for their rights. His statements stirred up a little excitement and some muttering and pushing. A bystander with an infant in his arms

63

approached one of the two policemen in the audience and said that if the police did not get that "s.o.b." off the stand he would do so himself. The policemen thereupon arrested Feiner who was ultimately convicted of disorderly conduct.[25]

Both cases were appealed to the U.S. Supreme Court. The Court held that, in the *Terminiello* case, where an actual riot was in progress, the conviction should be reversed because it was the duty of the police to have restrained the crowd and protected the rights of the speaker. In the *Feiner* case, on the other hand, the court upheld the defendant's conviction on the ground that the police had the right to arrest a speaker who was threatening the peace, even though the imminence of the disorder was by no means clear.

.These two cases, although both involve speakers and hostile audiences, are not identical. Terminiello was speaking inside a closed auditorium, rented and paid for by his supporters; Feiner was speaking on the street, where problems of traffic obstruction, noise, and crowd movement presented themselves. Terminiello was speaking to an invited sympathetic audience. Feiner was speaking to an uninvited, somewhat unsympathetic, audience. Nevertheless, the two Supreme Court decisions taken together are somewhat contradictory and present grave problems. If the *Feiner* rationale is followed, there is freedom of speech only for those speakers who do not displease their audiences. This is, in effect, to limit street meetings to those who love mother, the home, and the flag. On the other hand, while the two thousand people who howled for Terminiello's blood might have been controlled by a police force the size of Chicago's, what if that size crowd had gathered in a small town with an inadequate police force, or for that matter, what if the Chicago crowd had numbered twenty thousand or two hundred thousand instead of two thousand?

The probabilities are that no court can draw a priori hard-and-fast rules for the guidance of police, prosecutors, and judges in such situations. Each case must be judged in terms of the realities of the situation: the actual ability of the existing law force to handle a realistically perceived threat to the public peace. On the other hand, the feeling on the part of many police officers, that a speaker who is inflammatory is ipso facto liable to arrest for disorderly conduct or disturbing the peace, does not square with the need of an open society for gadflies and critics. If the First Amendment is to be something more than a pious platitude, speakers who express the sentiments we most loathe must have protection comparable to that afforded speakers who preach the gospel of love, peace, and patriotism.

It is worth noting that even at the Supreme Court level there appears to be differential handling of political offenders of the Right and of the Left. There is no conviction of a right-wing speaker that has been upheld by the United States Supreme Court. On the other hand, left-wing speakers such as Schenck, Abrams, Gitlow, and Dennis have been convicted of abstract advocacy of ideas, and on review these convictions have been affirmed by the high court. Similarly, left-wing agitators are normally treated with more hostility than their right-wing counterparts by the police. Why this is true is not entirely clear, but two reasons suggest themselves. Many policemen conceive it their duty to maintain the status quo. The radical who threatens the status quo by advocacy of armed revolution is therefore more dangerous than the radical who threatens to protect the status quo from social change, albeit in an equally violent manner. A new Left student group advocating Maoism is more dangerous than a Minuteman group, even though the Minuteman group may advocate the arming of private citizens. That the forceable slowing down of the normal process of social change can be as subversive of stability as the forced acceleration of such change is perhaps not obvious to many police officials. At the Supreme Court level, the dearth of right-wing convictions may stem from the fact that liberals will oppose such convictions on civil libertarian grounds, and conservatives do not perceive right-wing ideology as sufficiently dangerous to warrant restraint.

Problems posed by public meetings aside, a technique which has gained increasing popularity during the past decade presents the criminal justice system with new problems, The use of civil disobedience, that is, the deliberate violation of a law to dramatize profound disapproval of the existing state of affairs, has been utilized increasingly by reformers of many political hues. Martin Luther King's leadership of the Montgomery bus boycott, the march to Selma, Alabama, the sit-ins at Selective Service headquarters, the demonstrations in Grant Park in Chicago at the Democratic National Convention in 1968 all involved conduct at least partially illegal in terms of existing local law. All were designed to bring to public attention conditions perceived as unjust and inexcusable by the demonstrators. The chief result of police attempts to break up such demonstrations was frequently the spread of social unrest. To justify their actions, demonstrators claim that there is a law higher than the statutes on the books, higher even than the Constitution. Such law is "natural law," "justice," "the principles of morality." The police, on the other hand, are paid by the public to enforce the very law the demonstrators claim is not binding on them. Inevitably, confrontation and conflict must result from these two opposing positions.

Civil disobedience takes two forms. In one, the demonstrators disobey a law which they hold to be basically unjust or even unconstitutional; for example, civil rights demonstrators' violation of southern segregation statutes. When the demonstrators are arrested for such violations they will appeal their cases to higher courts in the hope of obtaining a declaration of unconstitutionality. This technique has been very successful in eliminating legalized segregation throughout the United States in the last ten years.

The second type of civil disobedience is the deliberate breaking of a law to which one has no objection in order to demonstrate one's disapproval of some unrelated social policy. Students who seize college buildings are not protesting the criminal trespass laws. They seize buildings in order to make it impossible for the Establishment to ignore their objections to the Viet Nam War, research sponsored by the military, or racist admission policies.

Should such demonstrators be punished? And if so, to what extent? It must be appreciated at the outset that the

Judeo-Christian morality on which this country claims to be based clearly holds that there is a law higher than the stated law of the political sovereign, and that therefore, each individual has a moral right to resist injustice where he finds it. Demonstrators thus have a strong moral basis for their actions. The problem however, in terms of the criminal justice system, is whether they have a legal basis for their actions, that is, whether they can pursue their chosen course of conduct without the imposition of legal sanctions. As for those who, like Martin Luther King, challenge laws they feel are unconstitutional, if they win favorable verdicts in the appellate courts, they are clearly entitled to be free from legal punishment.

The situation with regard to the second type of demonstrator, the one who breaks a "legitimate" law, is far more complex. The great writers who developed theories of civil disobedience, Thoreau and Ghandi, held that such violators should offer themselves to the civil authorities for punishment in much the same way that Jesus offered to be crucified for the sins of mankind. Hopefully the sympathies of the uncommitted will thereupon be stirred to rectify the underlying social injustice and to prevent further punishment of the demonstrators. In the real world however, not too many people are capable of Christ-like conduct, and many demonstrators seek to avoid punishment. The uncommitted public, moreover, is seldom effectively stirred from its apathy. The problem thus usually takes forms such as: should students be punished for disrupting universities, though their cause is admittedly just, if the disruption is clearly illegal and produces great hardship to innocent people? Or, should anti-war protestors be permitted to disrupt the military operations of the government if they truly believe that we are engaged in an unjust war?

Once again, there are no clear guidelines for the police. Certainly, to exempt automatically all sincere protestors from punishment for their law-breaking is an invitation to anarchy. No society can realistically aid in the process of its own dissolution. Chaos would reign if each individual were free to exempt himself at will from the laws governing social conduct. On the other hand, to treat sincere moral protest in the same manner as the unprincipled violation of law for private gain is counterproductive in terms of achieving a just society. Probably some balance between the social costs of forgiving violations and the social benefit of the reform proposed is in order. The mothers who obstruct traffic in order to force the installation of a traffic light at a dangerous school crossing must be forgiven, because the social cost of their protest is small and the social gain proposed is great. The forceable kidnapping of school officials in order to change university policy with regard to military recruiting is probably indefensible because of the enormity of the social wrong involved in kidnapping and the marginal utility of the act in rectifying the alleged social wrong.

Thus, in civil disobedience situations the police become the men in the middle. They are the visible agents of a society which must decide on its proper course of action. It is those who make social policy who must determine the extent to which the civilly disobedient must be punished. The greater the extent of society's recognition and approbation of the protestors' cause, and the more defensible the techniques employed, the more lenient must be the instructions given the criminal justice system for the handling of demonstrators. If there is no public identification with the cause in question, harsh treatment may be meted out without risk of causing widespread social disorder. In any case, policy in regard to the treatment of the civilly disobedient cannot be made by the police, local prosecutors, or the courts. It must be made at far more politically responsive and responsible levels such as the presidency, Congress, and the state legislature. Police cannot function intelligently in this area unless they accept the fact that they are only agents of a policy that must be determined elsewhere.

Selected Readings

Abraham, Henry J. *Freedom and the Court.* New York: Oxford University Press, 1967.

Bloch, Herbert A. *Disorganization: Personal and Social.* New York: Knopf, 1952.

Bloch, Herbert A., and Flynn, Frank T. *Delinquency.* New York: Random House, 1956.

Chevigny, Paul. *Police Power: Police Abuses in New York City.* New York: Pantheon, 1969.

Harris, Richard. *The Fear of Crime.* New York: Praeger, 1969.

LaFave, Wayne R. *Arrest: The Decision to Take a Suspect into Custody.* Boston: Little, Brown, 1965.

Lindesmith, Alfred R. *The Addict and the Law.* New York: Vintage Books, 1967.

Mill, John Stuart. *On Liberty.* New York: Appleton-Century-Crofts, 1947.

Pettigrew, Thomas F. *A Profile of the Negro American.* Princeton: Van Nostrand, 1964.

Porterfield, Austin L. *Youth In Trouble.* Fort Worth: Leo Potishman Foundation, 1946.

President's Commission on Law Enforcement and Administration of Justice. *Challenge of Crime in a Free Society.* Washington, D. C.: U. S. Government Printing Office, 1967.

Reckless, Walter C. *The Crime Problem.* 4th ed. New York: Appleton-Century-Crofts, 1967.

Steffens, Lincoln. *Shame of the Cities.* New York: Sagamore Press, 1957.

Sutherland, Edwin H., and Cressey, Donald R. *Principles of Criminology.* 8th ed. Philadelphia: Lippincott, 1970.

Tenbrock, Jacobus, ed. *The Law of the Poor.* San Francisco: Chandler, 1966.

Wall, Patrick M. *Eye-Witness Identification in Criminal Cases.* Springfield, Ill.: Charles C. Thomas, 1965.

Wilson, James Q. *Varieties of Police Behavior.* Cambridge, Mass.: Harvard University Press, 1968.

Wolfgang, Marvin E., and Cohen, Bernard. *Crime and Race.* New York: Institute of Human Relations Press, 1970.

Notes

[1] *New York Times,* October 8, 1966, p. 27.

[2] James Q. Wilson, *Varieties of Police Behavior* (Cambridge, Mass.: Harvard University Press, 1968), p. 220.

[3] *New York Times,* October 31, 1955, p. 19; November 26, 1955, p. 1.

[4] *Newsday,* April 6, 1966, p. 1; December 22, 1966, p. 7.

69

[5] Herbert A. Bloch, *Disorganization: Personal and Social* (New York: Alfred A. Knopf, 1952), pp. 259–260.

[6] Austin L. Porterfield, *Youth In Trouble* (Fort Worth: Leo Potishman Foundation, 1946), p. 38ff.

[7] Edwin H. Sutherland, "White-Collar Criminality," *American Sociological Review* 5, no. 1 (February 1940): 1–12.

[8] *Gideon v. Wainright,* 372 U.S. 335 (1963); *Miranda v. Arizona,* 374 U.S. 436 (1966).

[9] *New York Times,* February 7, 1961, p. 1; February 26, 1961, p. 3.

[10] For fuller treatment of this subject, see President's Commission on Law Enforcement and Administration of Justice, *Challenge of Crime in a Free Society* (Washington, D.C.: U.S. Government Printing Office, 1967), p. 44ff; Thomas F. Pettigrew, *A Profile of the Negro American* (Princeton: D. Van Nostrand Company, 1964), Chap. 6; Walter C. Reckless, *The Crime Problem,* 4th ed. (New York: Appleton-Century-Crofts, 1967), pp. 103–107; Edwin H. Sutherland and Donald R. Cressey, *Principles of Criminology,* 8th ed. (Philadelphia: Lippincott, 1970), pp. 132–142.

[11] See Wayne R. LaFave, *Arrest: The Decision to Take a Suspect into Custody* (Boston: Little, Brown, 1965), pp. 110–114.

[12] *Thompson v. Louisville,* 362 U.S. 199 (1960).

[13] *People v. Rivera,* 14 N.Y. 2nd 441 (1964).

[14] *New York Times,* November 30, 1969, p. 53.

[15] Patrick M. Wall, *Eye-Witness Identification in Criminal Cases* (Springfield, Ill.: Charles C. Thomas, 1965), pp. 122–125.

[16] LaFave, p. 111.

[17] Wilson, pp. 161–162.

[18] Marvin E. Wolfgang and Bernard Cohen, *Crime and Race* (New York: Institute of Human Relations Press, The American Jewish Committee, 1970), pp. 80–81.

[19] Herbert A. Bloch and Frank T. Flynn, *Delinquency* (New York: Random House, 1956), pp. 45–46.

[20] Bloch and Flynn, p. 47.

[21] Paul Chevigny, *Police Power: Police Abuses in New York City* (New York: Pantheon Books, 1969), p. 114.

[22] John Stuart Mill, *On Liberty* (New York: Appleton-Century-Crofts, 1947), pp. 16–17.

[23] *Dennis v. United States,* 341 U.S. 494 (1951).

[24] *Terminiello v. Chicago,* 337 U.S. 1 (1949).

[25] *Feiner v. New York,* 340 U.S. 315 (1951).

Criminal Responsibility: Juveniles

4

"Under our Constitution the condition of being a boy does not justify a kangaroo court."

Abe Fortas, *In re Gault*

"Juvenile proceedings are not criminal trials. They are not civil trials. They are simply not adversary proceedings."

Potter Stewart dissenting, *In re Gault*

Horace Mann, the famed educator, was once invited to make a dedicatory address at an institution for the reclamation of juvenile offenders. At one point in the address he stated, with much enthusiasm, that all the money spent for that institution would be worthwhile, if only one boy was reclaimed. When the address was over, a rather cynical listener came to Mann and said: "Didn't your enthusiasm run away with you today, Sir? Do you really mean that it is worthwhile spending all the money for this institution if the end were to be the reclamation of one boy only? Didn't you exaggerate, Sir?" Horace Mann quietly but firmly replied: "Not if it were my boy."

Richmond News Leader, in *Federal Probation* 18, no. 2 (June 1954): 10

The classical school of criminology (which developed during the eighteenth century as one manifestation of the egalitarianism underlying the French Revolution) held that individuals were free actors who deliberately chose their paths of conduct, guided only by the relative amounts of pleasure and pain each chosen act produced. Therefore, to deter men from criminal acts it was necessary only for society to prescribe punishment of sufficient severity to make the pain of punishment far outweigh the pleasures of crime.

71

Punishment should be identical for identical crimes, and, since all individuals are basically equal, punishment for each should be the same, regardless of age, sex, physical condition, or class. Although this superficially plausible theory was intended to reform the criminal law by removing its class bias, it had grave weaknesses. It failed to cope with the problem of crimes committed by those who almost by definition were not equal to others: juveniles, idiots, and the insane.

THE JUVENILE JUSTICE SYSTEM

Historically, all societies have recognized that pre-adolescent youngsters are different from adults, and cannot be held accountable in the same way adults are. Rites of passage, such as puberty rites in primitive societies and confirmation ceremonies in modern Western religions, are indications that the child must be somehow transformed before he is deemed worthy of acceptance as a full member of society with full responsibility for his actions. In English Common Law, a child under the age of seven was considered incapable of *mens rea* (guilty intent), and since without intent there could be no crime, small children were thus immune from criminal prosecution for their acts. Below the age of fourteen (but over seven), the presumption of criminal responsibility was rebuttable; over that age, every person assumed full responsibility for criminal acts.

The recognition of the differential status of children came to the United States as part of the English Common Law.[1] Efforts to improve the handling of juvenile offenders were made as early as 1825 in New York and in 1826 in Boston with the establishment of houses of refuge for children. At first, reformers were more concerned with the post-conviction handling of children than with the processes that led to their detention and conviction in the first place. Gradually, however, attention began to shift from post-conviction handling to pre-conviction handling, and for example, in Massachusetts in 1869, statutes required that a state agent or his deputy be present in court, "whenever application for commitment is made for any child, to any reformatory maintained by the Commonwealth." An 1879 Suffolk County (Massachusetts) statute required that cases against children under sixteen should be heard in courts, "separate from the general and ordinary criminal business." In New York in 1892, "cases involving violations of the Penal Code that would ordinarily fall within the jurisdiction of a police court or the court of Special Sessions might be heard . . . separate and apart from the trial of other criminal cases." The first specialized court established specifically for the handling of juvenile cases (as distinguished from ordinary criminal courts with separate juvenile parts) was established in 1899 in Cook County, Illinois, to deal with neglected dependent as well as delinquent children. The approach of the court was the salvaging of children in trouble. As Judge Julian W. Mack, a pioneer in the juvenile court movement, said:

> The problem for determination by the judge is not, Has this boy or girl committed a specific wrong, but What is he, how has he become what he is, and what had best be done in his interest and in the interest of the State to save him from a downward career.[2]

The fruits of this humanitarian movement have been the establishment in the United States of a separate juvenile justice system. In every state of the Union children are handled separately from, and by standards different from those applied to adult criminals. The development of this system has, however, been highly idiosyncratic, and there are few uniformities in jurisdiction and procedures. In most states juveniles are handled in separate courts, but in some areas they are still handled in special parts of the adult courts. Some juvenile courts are state-wide, some county-wide, some purely local. The names of these courts vary: juvenile court, children's court, family court. While the lower age limit for the court's jurisdiction over children is usually seven years of age, the upper age limits vary. Eighteen is the customary upper age limit, but New York and several other states have established sixteen or seventeen as the appropriate cut-off point for the court's jurisdiction. A few states have extended the upper age limit to nineteen, and even to twenty-one in special cases.* Juvenile court jurisdiction in most areas extends not only to children accused of committing unlawful acts, but to children who behave in socially, rather than legally, unacceptable ways; for example, truants, runaways, and incorrigibles, as well as to neglected and dependent children (those whose welfare has not adequately been provided for by appropriate adults). In recent years there has been a tendency to label as delinquent only those acts which, if committed by adults, would be called crimes. Other behavioral offenses are given other labels, but the jurisdiction of the juvenile court remains broad and includes all problems relating to children, both criminal and non-criminal: those stemming from the child's behavior, and those stemming from the behavior of the adults responsible for him.

Unfortunately, the judges who serve in juvenile court are on the whole an unimpressive group. Though some progressive states have placed highly qualified men on the bench, there are wide variations in the stated qualifications for the position. A 1963 survey conducted by the National Council of Juvenile Court Judges indicated that only one-half the incumbent judges (mostly elected rather than appointed) had undergraduate college degrees and one-quarter lacked law degrees as well. Most reported that they spent less than 25 percent of their time on juvenile court matters. Their average salary (for full-time judges) was $12 thousand per year. Less than one-fifth of the courts reported regularly available services from psychologists and psychiatrists. Similarly, while the level of probation services for the juvenile courts was generally higher than for the adult courts, it was erratic and varied widely in quality and

*Some states provide for special handling of young adults, as for example New York State. The New York Criminal Procedure Law, Article 720 provides for special judicial processing of those between sixteen and nineteen so that they may avoid the stigma of an adult conviction. This is not part of the juvenile court system, but is a modification of the adult criminal court procedure.

quantity over the nation. Overall, with a few fortunate exceptions, the probation services available to the courts were inadequate, with high caseloads, low salaries, and insufficiently stringent qualifications for office.

As a result of the fine work of Judge Mack and other reformers, juvenile courts exist in one form or another all over the United States. Unfortunately, such courts generally suffer from a lack of adequately qualified personnel and services to their child clients. Serious as this problem is, however, it is more easily resolved than the most basic problem besetting the juvenile justice system: *that though the philosophy underlying the juvenile court has been rehabilitative, the court in practice has been punitive.* In practical terms, children don't need protection from government officials who are helping them, but they certainly do need protection from judges and probation officers who are hurting them. The juvenile court conceptually is like a kind but firm parent prescribing treatment for the child that, while possibly somewhat unpleasant, is rationally designed to help the child as quickly as possible. In practice, the court is usually far more like the adult court which, while it holds pious hopes for the ultimate rehabilitation of the offender, quite openly sentences for punitive and deterrent reasons rather than therapeutic ones.

The non-punitive handling of children perhaps comes closest to realization in advanced states such as New York. Intake is handled by trained probation officers who have both the ability and the legal power to arrange for informal handling of the child. Those cases which cannot be handled in this manner are passed on to a full-time qualified juvenile court judge who has at his command the auxiliary services of psychologists, psychiatrists, and social workers. He has a wide range of options available to him in the disposition of a case: the child can be released on probation to his parents, to a social work agency, or to an institutional or outpatient setting. As a last resort he may be committed to a training school, some of which, at any rate, have a high ratio of professional staff to patients and are highly reputed for their sensitive and humane treatment of their child inmates. At the opposite end of the spectrum is the Arizona juvenile court system, which gave rise in 1964 to the case of *In re Gault*.[3]

IN RE GAULT

Gerald Gault, age fifteen, was taken into custody by the sheriff of Gila County, Arizona, on June 8, 1964, as a result of a verbal complaint by one Mrs. Cook, a neighbor, who claimed to have received a lewd telephone call. At·the time the boy was arrested his mother and father were both at work. No official notice was left to advise them of their son's whereabouts. They learned of his detention from the neighbors. At a hearing before the juvenile judge the following day, neither Gerald's father, who was at work out of the city, nor Mrs. Cook, the complainant, was there. No witness was sworn, no transcript was made, and no memorandum of the substance of the proceedings was prepared. There are conflicting versions of what Gerald said at this hearing, but the weight of the evidence indicated that he had only dialed the number while his friend had made the lewd remarks. Following the hearing, Gerald was returned to the detention home in which he had been confined since his arrest. He was kept there two or three days longer and then, without explanation, released. At 5:00 P.M. on the day of his release the probation officer sent a one-sentence note on plain paper to Mrs. Gault, informing her that on June 15th there would be a further hearing on Gerald's delinquency. At the June 15th hearing, no new information was developed; at no time was the complainant called upon to testify, nor was she given the opportunity to hear Gerald's voice for identification purposes. At the conclusion of the hearing, the judge committed Gerald as a juvenile delinquent to the State Industrial School for the period of his minority, that is, six years. (Had Gerald been eighteen or over, the maximum penalty for his offense would have been a fifty-dollar fine or two months in jail.)

No appeal was permitted by Arizona law in juvenile

cases. A petition for a writ of *habeas corpus* was therefore filed with the Supreme Court of Arizona which referred it to the Superior Court for a hearing. In spite of the fact that the juvenile judge was shown to have had almost no basis in fact for his original findings, the Superior Court dismissed the writ. A further appeal was made to the Arizona Supreme Court, in which it was urged that the juvenile code of Arizona was unconstitutional because it did not require parents and children to be notified of specific charges, nor given proper notice of a hearing, nor did it have any provision for appeal. For all these reasons Gerald Gault had been denied his liberty without due process of law. The Arizona Supreme Court denied the appeal. The decision was then appealed to the United States Supreme Court which accepted the case for review.

Justice Fortas, speaking for five members of the Court, noted that while the United States Supreme Court would not, in this case, concern itself with the constitutionality of either pre-judicial or post-adjudicative procedures in juvenile courts, it would concern itself with the procedures questioned by the Gaults.

> A boy is charged with misconduct. The boy is committed to an institution where he may be restrained of liberty for years. It is of no constitutional consequence — and of limited practical meaning — that the institution to which he is committed is called an Industrial School. The fact of the matter is that, however euphemistic the title, a "receiving home" or an "industrial school" . . . is an institution of confinement. . . .
>
> In view of this, it would be extraordinary if our Constitution did not require the procedural regularity and the exercise of care implied in the phrase "due process." . . . Under traditional notions, one would assume that in a case like that of Gerald Gault, where the juvenile appears to have a home, a working mother and father, and an older brother, the Juvenile Judge would have made a careful inquiry and judgment as to the possibility that the boy could be disciplined and dealt with at home. . . . The essential difference between Gerald's case and a normal criminal case is that safeguards available to adults were discarded in Gerald's case. The summary procedure as well as the long commitment were possible because Gerald was fifteen years of age instead of over eighteen.[4]

While the Court refused to go so far as to require that all adult procedural safeguards be observed in juvenile cases, it specified certain rights which must be recognized for children as well as adults:

1. Notice of charges.
2. Right to counsel.
3. Right to confrontation and cross-examination.
4. Privilege against self-incrimination.[5]

In the instant case, no notice had been given to Gerald's parents when he was taken into custody, nor had formal notice been given of the dates of the hearings. The parents had not been notified at any time of the specific charges against Gerald. Mrs. Gault testified that she "knew" that she could have had a lawyer, but at no time had any official informed her of this right, nor requested that she make a knowing waiver of this right. The complaining witness was never asked to testify, and therefore could not be cross-examined. While there was conflict as to what admissions Gerald had actually made, at no time had he been informed of his right not to incriminate himself and to remain silent. There was no right of appeal from the findings of a juvenile court in Arizona so no transcript was made of what transpired at the hearings.

The response of the state to these obvious procedural irregularities was simply that since juvenile proceedings are designed to be confidential so as to avoid stigmatizing the child, formal procedures were neither necessary nor desirable. Furthermore, since juvenile procedures are not criminal in nature the constitutionally mandated procedures of the adult criminal trial were not applicable.

The United States Supreme Court rejected all these contentions. It saw no conflict between formal procedures and the goal of rehabilitative therapeutic treatment for the child. It quoted with approval a statement by the President's Crime Commission:

Fears also have been expressed that the formality lawyers would bring into juvenile court would defeat the therapeutic aims of the court. But informality has no necessary connection with therapy; it is a device that has been used to approach therapy, and it is not the only possible device. It is quite possible that in many instances lawyers, for all their commitment to formality, could do more to further therapy for their clients than can the small, overworked social staffs of the courts.[6]

Furthermore, to label juvenile proceedings non-criminal so as to avoid the need for procedural regularity is at best highly artificial and conceptually dishonest. Any procedure which results in the involuntary confinement of an individual for a lengthy period of time is coercive, no matter how euphemistic the appellation. As a matter of fact, as the Court itself pointed out, there is no assurance in many cases that a juvenile handled by the juvenile courts will remain outside the reach of the adult courts, since in over one-half of the states juvenile delinquents may be transferred to adult penal institutions after an adjudication for delinquency.

PROCEDURAL REFORM: STEP FORWARD OR BACKWARD?

While most criminal justice practitioners would agree that the Gault case presents a set of shocking and indefensible facts, the inadequacies of the juvenile justice system are not met by the remedies proposed by the majority opinion in this case. Although the procedural rules that the Court has imposed on the juvenile courts will undoubtedly protect children from the incompetence and neglect found in systems like that of Gila County, the decision does little to resolve the basic contradictions of the juvenile justice system. While it is true that juvenile courts act in a punitive and coercive manner, and therefore children are entitled to formal procedural protection, nevertheless, child wrongdoers are not adult criminals, and the assumptions and procedures of the adult criminal justice system are not always applicable to children.

The inflexible restrictions that the Constitution . . . made applicable to adversary criminal trials have no inevitable place in the proceedings of those public social agencies known as juvenile or family courts. And to impose the Court's long catalog of requirements upon juvenile proceedings in every area of the country is to invite a long step backwards into the Nineteenth Century. In that era there were no juvenile proceedings, and a child was tried in a conventional criminal court with all the trappings of a conventional criminal trial. So it was that a 12-year-old boy named James Guild was tried in New Jersey for killing Catherine Beakes. A jury found him guilty of murder, and he was sentenced to death by hanging. The sentence was executed. It was all very constitutional.[7]

While Gerald Gault needed and should have had a lawyer, the traditional role of the lawyer in an adversary proceeding is, if possible, to acquit his client. Not every case, however, is a Gault case, and not every child should be freed, even if a competent lawyer could secure his release. In the adult criminal proceeding, including the trial, the rules of the game are structured with two ends in view: the fate of the defendant, and the well-being of the community. It is assumed that the greatest good (from the defendant's viewpoint) which the court can confer is the restoration of his previous state of liberty. Neither the goal nor the result of such proceedings is the rehabilitation of an acquitted defendant. In juvenile proceedings however, the goal is quite different. Here the concern is far more with the future of the child than with the structuring of a style of social and political living. In a sense the juvenile court is like a hospital. To ensure the right of a sick child to avoid treatment would not be productive in terms of serving the child's welfare. In short, the traditional concern of the adult criminal justice system with the welfare of the accused has been whether or not the accused is to retain his liberty. Historically, the concern of juvenile justice has been to help the sick child get well. "The act simply provides how children who ought to be saved may reach the court to be saved."[8]

Thus, while some procedural safeguards are necessary simply because unchecked bureaucracies frequently function inefficiently and even corruptly, the scope and function of these safeguards cannot be quite the same for juveniles as for adults. Where the lines are to be drawn, and how the balance is to be struck, between the protection of the child from inappropriate official action and the need for administrative and judicial flexibility in the rehabilitative treatment of the child is not clear.

> It seems probable we cannot have the best of two worlds. If the emphasis is on constitutional rights something of the essential freedom of method and choice which the sound juvenile Judge ought to have is lost; if range be given to that freedom, rights which the law gives to criminal offenders will not be respected. But the danger is that we may lose the child and his potential for good while giving him his constitutional rights.[9]

The direction in which the U. S. Supreme Court may travel may have been indicated by the *Winship* decision in 1970.[10] This case involved a twelve-year-old boy who was adjudicated a delinquent by the New York Family Court when a "fair preponderance" of evidence indicated that he had taken $112 from a pocketbook. The boy was placed in a training school. An appeal was made to the New York State Court of Appeals on the ground that due process and equal protection of the law required that the same standards of proof for conviction apply in juvenile courts as in adult criminal courts, namely, that guilt must be established "beyond a reasonable doubt" for juveniles rather than merely by a "fair preponderance" of the evidence. The appeal was rejected by a divided Court of Appeals largely on the ground that juvenile courts require greater flexibility in carrying out their special mission, which is different from that of the adult courts. Justice Fuld dissented vigorously, suggesting that "where a twelve-year-old child is charged with an act . . . which renders him liable to confinement for as long as six years, then, as a matter of due process, as well as of equal protection, the case against him must be proved beyond a reasonable doubt."[11]

On appeal, the U. S. Supreme Court agreed with Fuld that the due process clause protects the accused against conviction except upon proof beyond a reasonable doubt of every fact necessary to constitute the crime with which he is charged. In the wake of the *Gault* decision, the Court held that the same considerations which protect innocent adults must apply to innocent children. At the same time Justice Brennan, for the majority, denied that such procedural protection would destroy the beneficial aspects of the juvenile process.

> Nor will there be any effect on the informality, flexibility, or speed of the hearing at which the factfinding takes place. And the opportunity during the post-adjudicatory or dispositional period for a wide-ranging review of the child's social history and for his individualized treatment will remain unimpaired.[12]

A major procedural issue which remained to be decided was settled by the U.S. Supreme Court on June 21, 1971, in a 6-3 decision in *McKeiver v. Pennsylvania,* wherein it was held that juveniles do not have a constitutional right to trial by jury. Justice Blackmun, writing for the majority, acknowledged that while "fond and idealistic hopes" with regard to juvenile courts had not been realized, if a jury trial were required the juvenile proceedings would be made into a full adversary process and would put an end to notions of an "intimate, informal protective proceeding."

Another issue, which may soon be adjudicated, is the police practice of compiling dossiers of unsubstantiated charges against juveniles which are then made available to the courts as well as other administrative agencies.[13]

However, even were the conceptual difficulty to be resolved, and even were we to know where in theory the balance between protection and administrative flexibility ought to be struck, formidable practical difficulties remain. The reality of our juvenile justice system is grim. There are in the United States thousands of Gerald Gaults adjudicated by courts that make a shabby pretense of rehabilitative handling of the child. Juvenile court judges are in many cases unqualified and uninterested: one-fifth have received no college education at all, and one-fifth are not even members of the bar. They command little professional respect from their colleagues, and the juvenile court is not looked upon as a promising or desirable forum for professional practice. The average juvenile hearing in many localities seems to be of no more than ten or fifteen minutes duration, and there is a general scarcity of psychologists, psychiatrists, and clinic facilities. Most jurisdictions do not have foster homes or group homes available for children who might do well in a different family setting, so that the range of dispositional alternatives open to most juvenile judges is very limited: outright release, probation, or institutionalization. Probation supervision, moreover, exists more in theory than in fact. Worst of all perhaps is that conditions in many of the institutions in which children are confined are not only more custodial than rehabilitative, but are also shockingly inhumane. A well-informed penologist states, "There are things going on, methods of discipline being used in the State training schools of this country that would cause a warden of Alcatraz to lose his job if he used them on his prisoners."[14]

In the face of the reality of a juvenile justice system that conforms very little to the ideals of its proponents, can the courts morally or legally refuse to extend to children the procedural safeguards that will prevent victimization by a system which is fully as punitive as the adult criminal justice system? It may well be that it is not in the best interests of the juvenile offender to be treated like an adult offender, but with mandated procedural safeguards he at least will not have gotten the worst of both possible worlds. Unless the juvenile justice system can be made to resemble the ideal more closely, it is hard to see how the courts can avoid further formalizing procedures.

> While there can be no doubt of the original laudable purpose of juvenile courts, studies and critiques in recent years raise serious questions as to whether actual performance measures well enough against theoretical purpose to make tolerable the immunity of the process from the reach of constitutional guarantees applicable to adults. There is much evidence that some juvenile courts . . . lack the personnel, facilities and techniques to perform adequately as representatives of the State in a *parens patriae* capacity, at least with respect to children charged with law violations. There is evidence, in fact, that there may be grounds for concern that the child receives the worst of both

worlds: that he gets neither the protections accorded to adults nor the solicitous care and regenerative treatment postulated for children.[15]

As matters stand now American society is faced with one of two choices: either to make the juvenile courts genuinely rehabilitative instruments, using modifications of adult legal safeguards, or in effect, to convert them to adult courts and extend to children the full range of safeguards available to adults. It would seem that the former is the preferable alternative, but unless the public apathy which permits the present shocking state of the juvenile system is replaced by an awareness of the problem and a willingness for public funds to be spent for the rehabilitation of the juvenile system, then the second alternative may be the more tolerable course.

Selected Readings

Cavan, Ruth A. *Juvenile Delinquency*. 2nd ed. Philadelphia: Lippincott, 1969.

Giallombardo, Rose, ed. *Juvenile Delinquency: A Book of Readings*. New York: Wiley, 1966.

Gilbert Criminal Law and Procedure of New York: Code of Criminal Procedure, Penal Law, Criminal Procedure Law. New York: Matthew Bender, 1970.

Glueck, Sheldon. *The Problem of Delinquency*. Boston: Houghton Mifflin, 1959.

Lerman, Paul, ed. *Delinquency and Social Policy*. New York: Praeger, 1970.

Matza, David. *Delinquency and Drift*. New York: Wiley, 1964.

Platt, Anthony. *The Child Savers*. Chicago: University of Chicago Press, 1970.

President's Commission on Law Enforcement and Administration of Justice. *Task Force Report: Juvenile Delinquency and Youth Crime*. Washington, D.C.: U.S. Government Printing Office, 1967.

Sellin, Thorsten, and Wolfgang, Marvin E. *The Measurement of Delinquency*. New York: Wiley, 1964.

Notes

[1] For a full treatment of the historical background of the juvenile courts as well as the problem of delinquency in America, see Sheldon

Glueck, *The Problem of Delinquency* (Boston: Houghton Mifflin, 1959); and Anthony Platt, *The Child Savers* (Chicago: University of Chicago Press, 1970). For a statement on problems of the juvenile justice system, see President's Commission on Law Enforcement and Administration of Justice, *Task Force Report: Juvenile Delinquency and Youth Crime* (Washington, D.C.: U.S. Government Printing Office, 1967).

[2] Julian W. Mack, "The Juvenile Court," 23 *Harvard Law Review,* 104 (1909), as quoted in Glueck, p. 324.

[3] *In re Gault,* 387 U.S. 1 (1967).

[4] *In re Gault,* at 27–29.

[5] *In re Gault,* at 10.

[6] *In re Gault,* at 38, fn. 65.

[7] Stewart, J. (dissenting), *In re Gault,* at 79–80.

[8] *Commonwealth v. Fisher,* 213 Pa. 48 (1905).

[9] *In the Matter of Samuel W.,* 24 N.Y. 2nd 196 (1969).

[10] *In the Matter of Winship,* 397 U.S. 358 (1970).

[11] *In the Matter of Samuel W.,* at 207.

[12] *In the Matter of Winship,* at 366.

[13] *New York Times,* August 9, 1970, p. 34.

[14] Quoted in President's Commission on Law Enforcement and Administration of Justice, *Task Force Report: Juvenile Delinquency and Youth Crime* (Washington, D.C.: U.S. Government Printing Office, 1967), p. 8.

[15] *Kent v. United States,* 383 U.S. 541 (1966), at 555–556.

5

Criminal Responsibility: Insanity

"A society that punishes the sick is not wholly civilized. A society that does not restrain the dangerous madman lacks common sense."

Jerome N. Frank, Introduction to *Murder, Madness and the Law*

A crime under our legal system is more than a physical act: it is an act accompanied by a state of mind. Evil intent, *mens rea*, must motivate the conduct, or no crime has been committed.* Where there is no *mens rea* there is no crime, and if the mind is too diseased to harbor guilty intent, no finding of criminal guilt can be made. Therefore, the insane person who violates criminal law must be handled differently from one who is of sound mind. Historically this distinction has been recognized and has posed few problems in regard to individuals who are obviously and totally out of contact with reality. A continuing problem, however, has been posed by those whose judgment is clouded in some areas but not in all, or who may function imperfectly at one time but not at others. In its less vindictive moods, at least, society has no wish to punish those who truly are not responsible for their acts. At the same time there is always a fear of providing the all too easy alibi of temporary insanity to a malefactor who is not deranged, but malevolent.

While there are variations among the state and federal governments in the method of handling allegedly insane suspects, the way in which such suspects are handled in New York City is probably fairly typical. If a policeman finds

---

*There are certain exceptions to this general rule. In some *mala prohibita* offenses, such as statutory rape, intent is inferred from the act itself, sometimes even where circumstances contradict the existence of criminal intent.

a suspect at the scene of a crime who is acting in a bizarre or irrational manner, he will report his observations of the defendant's conduct to the judge at the initial arraignment, which ordinarily will have been held as quickly as possible after the arrest. If the judge concurs with the policeman's observations, he will remand the prisoner to a city hospital psychiatric prison ward. There the prisoner will be interviewed by psychiatrists, and his mental condition evaluated. These recommendations will be forwarded to the judge who will then decide whether the defendant can stand trial and complete the normal course of legal processing, or whether he should be committed directly to a state hospital for the criminally insane. Should a seemingly rational suspect become irrational at any point between arrest and the completion of his sentence, a similar procedure involving psychiatric recommendation to a judge will be followed, with the exception that a defendant who has already been convicted of a crime and committed to a correctional institution will be sent to a maximum security hospital for insane criminals, rather than to an institution for the criminally insane. In any case, one committed to either type of institution will, in effect, serve an indefinite sentence; that is, he will remain in custody until "cured," even if the length of such custody is longer than the maximum sentence for the offense with which he was, or would have been, charged.

When the psychiatrist evaluates the accused, he does so for the purpose of determining the presence or absence of a mental disorder, a "pathology of the psyche," usually referred to by psychiatrists as a psychosis. The *Psychiatric Dictionary* defines psychosis as

> a [more] severe type of mental disorder in the sense that all the forms of adaptation (e.g., social, intellectual, . . . etc.) are disrupted. In other words, the disorganization of the personality is extensive.[1]

In layman's terms, the accused can be said to be out of contact with reality with respect to time, place, and identity. The identification of a psychosis within a given individual is an extremely difficult and complex task, complicated

87

even further by the disagreement among various schools of psychiatry as to which behavior syndromes indicate which, if any, psychosis. To confuse matters even more, the law does not recognize psychosis as a defense in a criminal prosecution. The law talks of insanity (a legal term), rather than of psychosis (a medical term). The relationship between insanity and psychosis is unclear, but essentially where the physician is looking for disease, the law is looking for a status designation indicative of the likely effect of the individual on society. The physician is concerned for the well-being of his patient; the judge is concerned with the well-being of the community.

> The test of insanity as laid down in the law centers about three matters; namely, the knowledge of right and wrong, the existence of delusion, and the presence of an irresistible impulse. . . . Insanity is purely a legal concept and means irresponsibility, or incapacity.[2]

The judge in a criminal court, then, is faced with the problem of translating medical concepts into legal ones, of using a psychiatrist's evaluation as the basis for a legal finding. This is an enormously difficult task made more difficult by the fact that differences of opinion among psychiatrists force the judge into an essentially subjective evaluation of the situation. The possibilities for error are great. Individuals whose conduct may seem highly irrational and disordered to middle-class observers such as judges may, in fact, be functioning quite rationally in terms of their own particular milieu. In New York State in 1962, one Victor Rosario was released from Matteawan State Hospital for the Criminally Insane, where he had been held for four years essentially because he told a story no middle-class official (including eleven psychiatrists) was willing to believe. Mr. Rosario, who was arrested and charged with assault for kicking and hitting his wife, told the police that his wife's love had been stolen from him by a boarder in their apartment, who had drawn blood from his (the boarder's) arms and drunk it in beer to prove his vigor. Mr. Rosario was sent to Bellevue Hospital for observation, and two psychiatrists who heard his story came to the conclusion that he was paranoid and unable to understand the charges against him. "The doctors told me that if I forgot that story, they might let me go, but the truth is the truth no matter what anyone says," said Mr. Rosario. After four years in a mental hospital, during which time he wrote letters to government officials and drew up six petitions for writs of *habeas corpus* (all of which were ignored by the courts), a lawyer to whom he had been referred believed his story sufficiently to check into it. She found that both Mrs. Rosario and the boarder verified Rosario's story. Rosario was released from the hospital and the assault charges against him dismissed.[3]

On the other hand, there are individuals whose conduct in many areas is rational, well-organized, and responsible, sufficiently so to hold a job or to make contracts. Such individuals may, nevertheless, be medically psychotic; their defenses are simply good enough to mask their loss of contact with reality in a particular sphere. For the judge to make an accurate determination or prognostication as to the defendant's future conduct is very difficult, and the consequences of error very serious. Either a sane person may be confined indefinitely with the mentally sick, there to become sick himself, or a sick person may be placed in a correctional institution where rehabilitation is impossible, and his conduct is a source of great difficulty for both prison officials and inmates.

In 1941, during an unsuccessful attempted payroll stickup, Anthony and William Esposito killed two policemen and wounded a third. A taxicab driver who assisted other police in apprehending the Esposito brothers was seriously wounded. The case attracted a great deal of news coverage and one enterprising newspaper reporter tagged the killers as the "Mad Dog" Esposito brothers. The two gunmen were quickly indicted and brought to trial, in spite of the attempts of their lawyers to have the Espositos declared insane and incompetent to stand trial. During the trial, the defense unsuccessfully attempted to convince the jury that the brothers were insane and hence not responsible for their actions. In

spite of the fact that the brothers engaged in violent out-
bursts, urinated, rolled on the floor, "simulated" uncontrolled
animal behavior, and made strange noises, the court was
convinced that the Espositos were malingering and attempting to escape the consequences of their killings by feigning
insane behavior. The jury found both brothers guilty, and
the judge, disregarding the pleas of the lawyers, sentenced
the Espositos to be executed. Even in the death house their
behavior continued to be bizarre, and on occasion they had
to be forcibly fed. The Court of Appeals of New York upheld
the conviction, the governor ignored pleas for clemency,
and both brothers were electrocuted. On autopsy, both
brothers were found to be paretic as a consequence of
syphilis. There was a good likelihood that the amount of
brain damage was sufficient to have caused both brothers
to have been in fact psychotic, and probably not responsible
for their actions.[4]

The Rosario and Esposito cases illustrate how subjective and culture-bound evaluations of insanity may be, even
when made by conscientious and honest judges and psychiatrists. It is to avoid such errors that the law attempts to
set objective standards in the form of definitions of insanity
and criminal responsibility. Unfortunately, these definitions
and the procedures associated with them have to some extent further complicated an already muddled situation.

PRE-TRIAL INSANITY HEARINGS

The adversary system of criminal justice presupposes a
contest between relative equals. At a very minimum the
defendant is supposed to be aware of his own self-interest
and capable of attempting to preserve it. However, when the
mentally incapacitated person is brought before the judge
in a pre-trial arraignment, he may be unaware of his illness,
and have no idea of how best to proceed in his own behalf.
It then becomes the obligation of the prosecutor, judge, defense attorney, or next of kin to point out the defendant's
condition and ask that the court take appropriate legal

action, usually a pre-trial sanity hearing. At this point the adversary system is nonexistent as far as the defendant is concerned. He is no longer dealing with opponents but with "friends"—friends who, while active in his behalf, may nevertheless send him away to what may amount to life imprisonment. He may indeed be mentally ill and require indefinite confinement in his own best interests. But what if he is not? Who can speak for him? Only he, himself—and he is presumed to be incompetent. His entire world is populated by enemies in the guise of friends. For such defendants there is no safeguard against the possibility of medical or judicial error. The justification for pre-trial sanity hearings relies on the infallibility of judges and psychiatrists. If the competence of the psychiatrist to diagnose the accused's mental state were beyond doubt, and the ability of the judge to translate a medical finding into legal action unquestionable, there would be no problem protecting the defendant's rights. Judges and psychiatrists, unfortunately, are far from infallible, and the pre-trial sanity hearing degenerates in some cases to a labelling process wherein the defendant is stigmatized.

Pre-trial sanity hearings are held before a judge, and without a jury. They can be held, moreover, over the objection of the defendant, his attorney, or his relatives, since the prosecutor is frequently considered to be a better judge of the defendant's interests than the defense lawyer. During the psychiatric examination, the defendant is often pressured to incriminate himself, either as to his guilt or as to his mental condition. The examining psychiatrist, employed by a state hospital or otherwise retained by the government, is perceived by the defendant (often correctly) as an adversary. He is not the patient's doctor in the normal understanding of that term. The defendant may therefore be understandably reluctant to confide to the psychiatrist any information relating to the offense with which he is charged, or to any of his past history, especially in relation to bizarre behavior or previous mental illness. Such uncooperativeness on the subject's part may be interpreted by the psychiatrist as evasiveness, escape from reality, or lack of contact. The defendant is thus in a position where he is damned if he does, and damned if he doesn't: if he speaks freely to the psychiatrist, his statements may be used against him; if he refuses to speak, his silence will be interpreted unfavorably.

Another hurdle encountered by defendants whose sanity is suspect is the prospect of multiple pre-trial sanity hearings. If a defendant has been considered incompetent to stand trial and remanded to a mental hospital, he is subject to another pre-trial sanity hearing before he can be tried at any later date. Thus, if he is not to serve what amounts to a life sentence, he must at some point be able to convince the state-appointed psychiatrists of his competence to stand trial. Even after he successfully passes the pre-trial examination however, he is not free from the prospect of further examination, because his sanity can again be questioned by the judge or prosecutor, and he can be ordered to submit to further examinations at the trial or sentencing stages. The accused must defend his sanity not once, but as often as the state seeks to question it.

The guidelines to be used by psychiatrists in evaluating the defendant's condition are by no means clear. The data on which the doctor's judgment is based may be scanty or inappropriate. Thomas Szasz, a psychiatrist known for his scathing indictment of the judicial handling of suspected mental incompetents cites the case of Major General Edwin Walker, who was ordered to submit to a pre-trial sanity hearing on the recommendation of psychiatrists who had never seen him and who based their judgments on newspaper stories which were later shown to be inaccurate.[5]

In light of the possible miscarriage of justice for an accused individual who cannot satisfy government authorities as to his mental health, Szasz and other critics have suggested substantial modification of the present system. They recommend that the issue of competence to stand trial be separated from consideration of the subject's overall mental condition. Since a judgment of mental illness is, in many cases, either an attempt to reconstruct events which happened in the past, or a prognostication as to the subject's future conduct, such judgments are highly problematical. The critics therefore hold that the state should confine this investigation initially only to the question of whether at the moment of trial the accused is able to understand the nature of the charges against him, and is able to cooperate with an attorney in his own defense. They also look askance at the paternalism underlying and implicit in the state's right to force a sanity hearing on an unwilling defendant "in his own best interest." The defendant himself or his attorney should be the sole determiner of his own best interest unless he is so disoriented and out of touch with reality as to make a trial obviously impossible.

The realities of the criminal justice system are such that in many cases even a mentally ill defendant will be better off pleading guilty to the offense charged and accepting punishment than permitting himself to be labelled insane either before or after trial. It is questionable whether the stigma of insanity is less than the stigma of conviction; certainly, the penalty for a minor offense will be far shorter than the time the accused may expect to spend in an institution for the criminally insane. Even if the accused is subsequently committed civilly to a mental hospital, his future prospects for release are less complicated than if his commitment were criminal. These criticisms suggest that when a sanity hearing is ordered over the objections of the defendant or his attorney, the burden of proof for the justification of such hearings must rest solidly on the state, and the standards for justifying such examinations must be clearly delineated and closely scrutinized. Provision should also be made for quick and inexpensive appellate review of such orders.

THE INSANITY DEFENSE

Defendants who were obviously deranged at the time of the crime present no problems with respect to criminal responsibility. Their mental condition is such that no true *mens rea* can be attributed to them and they must be acquitted by virtue of their insanity. Many defendants whose sanity is questionable, however, display no overtly bizarre behavior. To the casual onlooker, the individual in question may seem calm, well-oriented, and rational. Schizophrenics constitute the largest category of the criminally insane, and their behavior is often deceptive.

> Schizophrenics . . . can memorize lists of words, solve problems, and form concepts. . . . They are given complicated intelligence, personality, and concept formation tests, and are expected to understand instructions even though their performance on the tests themselves is likely to be abnormal. They, and psychotics generally, help maintain the hospital by doing work on the grounds, in the wards, and in the kitchens. They publish hospital newspapers and engage in athletics. Where there is a patient government, they take part in it.[6]

If institutionalized mental patients can behave in such an outwardly rational fashion, how can a judge and jury composed of non-psychiatrically trained laymen make an evaluation of a defendant's claim that he was insane at the time of the commission of the act charged? Somehow a formula must be developed which will permit a distinction to be made between the sane criminal seeking to avoid criminal responsibility for his act, and the seemingly rational but mentally incompetent defendant whose judgment was so impaired that he was not fully responsible for his conduct. It is in this context that the M'Naghten and Durham Rules have evolved.

In 1843, one Daniel M'Naghten, a Scotsman laboring under the delusion that the pope, the Jesuits, and Sir Robert Peel, prime minister of England, were conspiring against him, attempted to shoot Sir Robert, but because he did not know what Peel looked like, shot and killed Peel's secretary Edward Drummond instead. Eight doctors at the trial testified that M'Naghten really believed in the truth of his delusion. In addition, M'Naghten's conduct at the trial was bizarre and irrational. The presiding judge instructed the jury to bring in a verdict of "not guilty by reason of insanity," and M'Naghten was sent to an institution for the insane. The attack on Peel caused Queen Victoria much uneasiness, coming as it did during a period of economic distress and social unrest and following several abortive attempts at assassination of the queen herself. There was even suspicion that the killing was part of a plot instigated by the reformers of the Anti-Corn Law League. The verdict was a disappointment to many, including the queen herself who protested, "The law may be perfect, but how is it that whenever a case for its application arises, it proves to be of no avail?" As a result of public protest, the fifteen High Court judges were in effect asked to draw up rules applicable to such cases in the future. The judges decided that:

> to establish a defense on the ground of insanity, it must be clearly proved that, at the time of committing the act, the party accused was laboring under such a defect of reason, from disease of the mind, as not to know the nature and quality of the act he was doing; or, if he did know it, that he did not know he was doing what was wrong.[7]

Further, "he must be considered in the same situation as to responsibility as if the facts with respect to which the delusion exists were real."

In the years since its formulation, the M'Naghten Rule has been subjected to a barrage of criticism. For one thing, M'Naghten himself could not have been acquitted by reason of insanity, using the rule named for him. There was no reason to believe that he did not know that he was killing his victim, or that the act was wrong; nor would his delusion as to the conspiracy, even if true, have justified the killing. The most basic criticism however, is that the concept "disease of the mind" simply does not lend itself to modern psychiatric diagnosis, and without extensive stretching the language of the formulation hampers the presentation of useful psychiatric testimony to the court.

The word *know*, for example, interpreted narrowly and literally, refers to a kind of cognition absent only in the totally disoriented. A man may know what he is doing in a narrow sense, and yet not appreciate the total impact or consequences of his actions. Similarly, the word *wrong* is difficult to define. Does "wrong" mean moral or legal wrong? If moral wrong, by whose standards? What if the defendant honestly believes that he was commanded by God to kill? Did he think the act was wrong? If "wrong" means legally wrong, this surely is not proof of insanity. Many lawbreakers are ignorant of the law; many others know the law but willfully choose to disregard it. Neither category is necessarily insane.

Because of the ambiguities and limitations of the M'Naghten Rule, critics have charged that psychiatrists are impeded in giving meaningful testimony as to the mental condition of the accused. Obviously, a defendant could meet the standards of the M'Naghten test and still be mentally ill in a medical sense, certainly by present standards even if not necessarily by the standards prevalent in 1844. The case of *People v. Horton*[8] illustrates the difficulties the customary judicial interpretation of the M'Naghten Rule creates for the psychiatrist who wishes to testify meaningfully about the mental state of the accused. It also suggests that the rule does not help the jury to understand the components of mental illness, since it was clear that the intelligence and seeming rationality of the accused led the jury to conclude that he could not have been insane.

Norman L. Horton was an eighteen-year-old college student who left his dormitory at about 6:30 in the evening of May 23, 1953, and travelled sixty miles to his home in Chemung County, New York. He entered his father's garage and, taking a hammer and a pair of gloves, "because I knew they would be looking for fingerprints," waited several hours until the light was out in his parents' bedroom, and the whistle of a train due to pass nearby would muffle any noise he might make. When the train whistle sounded, he smashed the pane of glass in the French door, entered the house, and picked up a carving knife in the kitchen. Shoeless and shaking with fright, he crept upstairs to his parents' bedroom. "I kept telling myself," he said, "you have got to do it. It is the only way out. It isn't right but it is just circumstances that led me there and there is no way out." He then plunged the knife into his father's back, fatally wounding him. Leaving the bedroom, he restored the knife to the kitchen, retrieved his shoes, and fled, disposing of the gloves and hammer outdoors. He hitchhiked back to his dormitory, arriving between six and seven in the morning. Shortly afterwards, a message was given to him telling him simply that his father had died. His response was, "My father didn't have a heart condition." Horton was later arrested and indicted for murder in the first degree, to which he pleaded not guilty by reason of insanity.

At the trial, the testifying psychiatrist had great difficulty in answering meaningfully the classic question associated with the M'Naghten Rule: "Doctor, in your opinion, did the defendant know the nature and quality of his act, and did he know that it was wrong?" A categoric yes or no answer was required of him by the court.

Defense Attorney
Q. Doctor, did he know what he was doing when he committed those acts?
A. The answer is no. He was psychotic at the time and did not know the nature and quality of his acts. (This answer was stricken out.)

District Attorney
Q. You concede, then, Doctor, that this series of connected activities seemed to be rational?
A. Seemed to be rational just as the case of a paranoid praecox. They are a whole series of connected activities, yet they are a most serious and most malignant form of schizophrenia. Just the ability to rationalize doesn't make it rational. (This answer was stricken out, and the jury instructed to disregard it.)[9]

Horton's insanity defense was rejected by the jury, who obviously had not been able to deduce from the psychiatric testimony the nature of mental illness and how it might manifest itself in the defendant's conduct. The record suggests that the jury had difficulty believing that one intelligent and rational enough to have planned the crime in question could be insane.

Justice Van Voorhis, in his dissent, quoted feelingly from an article by Dr. G. H. Stevenson in the *Canadian Bar Review:*

> The psychiatrist's difficulties with the M'Naghten Rules begin
> with the administration of the oath. He is sworn to tell the whole
> truth, but the rules, because of their concern only with the
> intellective aspects of mental function, prevent him from telling
> the whole truth about the accused's mental condition. If he
> attempts to tell of the disorganized emotional aspects which
> may have caused the crime, he may be sharply interrupted by
> the trial judge and ordered to limit his comments to insanity as
> defined by the M'Naghten Rules. . . . He is in an impossible
> position — sworn to tell the whole truth and prevented by the
> court from telling it.[10]

In an attempt to remedy the inadequacies of the
M'Naghten Rule, Judge Bazelon of the United States Court
of Appeals in Washington, D.C., in 1954 enunciated the
famous "Durham Rule." This held that "an accused is not
criminally responsible if his unlawful act was the product of
mental disease or mental defect."[11] The court differentiated
between mental disease and mental defect in that the former
was considered capable of improvement or deterioration,
while the latter was considered incapable of change as the
result of congenital impairment, injury, or the residual effect
of disease.* Since 1954, only Maine and the Virgin Islands
have adopted the Durham Rule. Bazelon's decision however, has provoked an enormous amount of discussion and
controversy in legal circles.

Another attempt to remedy the deficiencies of the
M'Naghten test is the so-called "irresistible impulse" rule.
This rule instructs jurors to acquit the accused if they find
that he had a mental disease which made it impossible for
him to control his conduct. This new standard seems more
in keeping with the concepts of modern psychology because
it describes realistically the state in which a mentally dis-
turbed individual might find himself. Recently, however,
many lawyers and psychiatrists have become disenchanted
with irresistible impulse as a rationale for determining crim-

---

*The Durham Rule was not the first judicially suggested alternative to
M'Naghten. The Pike standard, handed down by the New Hampshire
Supreme Court in 1869, was almost identical to *Durham* but had been
largely ignored.

inal responsibility, because it either adds too little to *M'Naghten,* or too much. On the one hand, if narrowly construed, its meaning is very similar to the usual interpretation of *M'Naghten;* on the other hand, if broadly construed, it sets no viable limits for its application in a criminal case.

Generally whether *Durham* and irresistible impulse are used independently of, or together with *M'Naghten,* the same criticisms may be made of these tests as of earlier ones. The jury still receives no effective guidance as to whether the accused was in such mental condition as to be accorded diminished responsibility under the criminal law. It is extremely difficult for medical experts, especially when there are marked disagreements among them, to translate into usable legal terms a standard capable of being understood and applied by the laymen who sit on the jury. The reality of the situation is that regardless of what instructions are given to the jury, that is which test is used, the result is pretty much the same in terms of the verdict.[12]

Because of the difficulty of giving meaningful guidelines to the jury, and because of the possibilities of injustice inherent in an improperly adjudicated insanity defense, many critics of our judicial proceedings have suggested eliminating the insanity defense in toto. In its place they suggest a fact-finding hearing before a judge, with or without a jury, the purpose of which is to determine whether the act in question was committed, and whether the accused did in fact commit the act. Once the determination of fact is made, they suggest that a board composed of possibly a psychiatrist, a psychologist, a sociologist, and a judge dispose of the case in an appropriate manner. Within the confines of such an administrative tribunal, discussion as to the mental condition of the accused could proceed in a more informal and meaningful manner, and an intelligent decision could be reached on the best possible arrangements for the defendant's future.

In *The Crime of Punishment,* Karl Menninger imagines a colloquy between a judge and a psychiatrist in which the

99

psychiatrist points out the irrationalities of the present insanity defense. The judge then asks the psychiatrist for his suggestions for improvement. The psychiatrist replies:

Answer:
I have been waiting for this question, and now I would like to make my main point. Will your Honor indulge me?
Judge:
Proceed.
Answer:
In my opinion, what you should do, what all courts should do, what society should do, is to *exclude all psychiatrists from the courtroom!* Put us all out and make us stay out. After you have tried the case, let us doctors and our assistants examine him and confer together outside the courtroom and render a report to you, which will express our view of the offender—his potentialities, his liabilities, and the possible remedies.

If we doctors cannot agree, let us disagree in private and submit majority and minority reports. That probably will not be necessary; our differences are going to be on minor points. We are not going to raise legal issues like "sanity" and "responsibility" because we are not going to talk legal jargon. Nor should we talk *our* jargon. We should try to say in simple English why we think this man has acted in this way so different from the rest of us, and what we think can be done to change his pattern.[13]

Menninger's suggestion, which has been made by a number of other criminologists and sociologists, is very persuasive. It seems to make very good sense to leave the disposition of difficult cases involving diminished responsibility because of mental impairment to a panel of experts, rather than to a jury composed of uninformed laymen. Surely psychologists, psychiatrists, and sociologists have a better understanding of what makes this defendant "so different from the rest of us," and what to do with him. The problem is that if one accepts the rationale of expert handling at the administrative level of problem criminal defendants, one cannot stop logically with the mentally impaired. If mental disease makes it impossible for a man to control himself sufficiently to assume full responsibility for his acts, what of sociological disease — poverty, ignorance, alienation, or family disorganization? If schizophrenia entitles a defendant to administrative rather than judicial handling, why doesn't living in a ghetto? Surely, the life of a deprived child is as warping and detrimental to the development of internal controls as mental illness. If the mentally ill are to be judged outside the judicial process, why should not all other defendants who come before the bench damaged, destroyed, or impaired by the society into which they were unwittingly born?

There are indeed many critics of our society who hold that the concept of criminal responsibility is unfair and to some extent meaningless. The law is, of course, an expression of middle-class values, and the administration of criminal justice is weighted in favor of middle-class defendants. To this extent it is true that the ignorant, indigent defendant, like the insane defendant, is frequently given less than a fair shake by the system. But is the answer disposition by an administrative tribunal of experts? At least one noted legal scholar thinks not. Abraham S. Goldstein, dean of Yale Law School, objects to the Menninger type of reform precisely because, logically, it leads to administrative rather than judicial handling of many kinds of defendants. Experts, Goldstein argues, should not handle these cases because the issues being decided in the disposition of criminal defendants are ultimately moral questions, and not technical ones demanding professional expertise. The judge and the jury are, by definition, spokesmen for the community in the setting of moral standards: they are the keepers of the community's conscience.

Menninger himself recognizes this distinction.

> I oppose courtroom appearances [by psychiatrists] because I consider guilt, competence, and responsibility to be moral questions, not medical ones. The judge and jury are the community's representatives in this area. It is for them to make the judgment and apply the sanctions deemed appropriate, not us psychiatrists.*

---

*Menninger, p. 139. Menninger assumes apparently that the judge and jury will still make the final decisions as to the defendant's fate. So they will, but bureaucratic experience suggests that there will be a strong tendency for the judge to defer to the "experts" in these cases, so that the decision will in reality be theirs and not his.

To ask "What went wrong?" with regard to a defendant instead of "Is he guilty?" is to change completely the relationship of the individual to the law. It is to remove the notion that the individual has a responsibility to society to obey its laws, and to substitute therefor the notion that society has an obligation to the individual to see that he behaves, or at least that it is possible for him to behave, in the manner expected of him. While the latter goal is noble and praiseworthy, it is impossible of achievement both practically and conceptually. Even if we had the resources and political willingness to create a utopia in which no individuals were warped or harmed by their environment, we cannot even agree on what this utopia would look like. To substitute a standard of social responsibility for the individual for the present standard of individual responsibility to society is impractical, dangerous, and conceptually questionable. In the last analysis, the social and political theory underlying a free society presupposes individuals capable of acting with some degree of free will, and not automatons infinitely manipulable by the state. To remove the element of personal responsibility from the criminal law is to cut out the heart of democratic ideology.

> Most fundamentally, eliminating the insanity defense would remove from the criminal law and the public conscience the vitally important distinction between illness and evil, or would tuck it away in an administrative process. . . .
>
> This approach overlooks entirely the place of the concept of responsibility itself in keeping the mechanism in proper running order. That concept is more seriously threatened today than ever before. This is a time of anomie—of men separated from their faiths, their tribes, and their villages—and trying to achieve in a single generation what could not previously be achieved in several. Many achieve all they expect, but huge numbers do not; these vent their frustration in anger, in violence, and in theft. In an effort to patch and mend the tearing social fabric, the state is playing an increasingly paternal role. . . . As this effort gains momentum, there is a very real risk it will bring with it a culture which will not make the individuals within it feel it is important to learn the discipline of moderation and conformity to communal norms.

In such a time, the insanity defense can play a part in reinforcing the sense of obligation or responsibility. Its emphasis on whether an offender is sick or bad helps to keep alive the almost forgotten drama of individual responsibility. . . . It becomes part of a complex of cultural forces that keep alive the moral lessons, and the myths, which are essential to the continued order of society. In short, even if we have misgivings about blaming a particular individual, because he has been shaped long ago by forces he may no longer be able to resist, the concept of "blame" may be necessary.

. . . The concept of "blame" and insanity which is its other side, is one of the ways in which the culture marks out the extremes beyond which nonconformity may not go.[14]

The fact is that the principal importance of the insanity defense is in its conceptual impact on the system. The literature on the subject is voluminous, and it includes work by many of the first-rate scholars in law, sociology, and psychology. The actual incidence of claims of innocence by reason of insanity is statistically minute, however. Most criminal matters are disposed of by guilty pleas, and of the relatively small number that go to jury trial only about 2 percent involve the insanity defense. This means that probably far less than .5 percent of all indictments filed involve pleas of not guilty by virtue of insanity. Thus, the interest in the subject is occasioned far more by its implications for our political ideology than for the defendants involved. This is true for many aspects of the criminal justice system, but is especially marked in this area.

If then, the criticism leveled by Dean Goldstein at Menninger - type reforms in this area is to be taken seriously, what alternatives remain? Goldstein himself suggests several avenues of approach. He argues that the basic flaw in the M'Naghten Rule has not been in its substance but in its application. It has been unreasonably narrowly construed, and there is no basis for the continuation of such judicial interpretation. Judges can easily extend the definition of words like *know* and *wrong* so that they are more meaningful in terms of the determination to be made. The M'Naghten Rule can and should be modified further by statements such as those in the Durham and the irresistible impulse formulations. Steps along these lines have been taken in the Model Penal Code prepared by the American Law Institute (ALI) which suggests that:

1. A person is not responsible for criminal conduct if at the time of such conduct as a result of mental disease or defect he lacked substantial capacity to appreciate the criminality (wrongfulness) of his conduct or to conform to the requirements of the law.

2. As used in this article the terms mental disease or defect do not include an abnormality manifested only by repeated criminal or otherwise antisocial conduct.

Procedural impediments to raising the insanity defense should be reduced, possibly by guidelines such as the McDonald Rule, which places the burden of rebuttal on the state to show that the accused is in fact sane rather than vice versa, when evidence as to insanity has been offered by the defense. Above all, the rules of evidence must be sufficiently relaxed to permit psychiatrists to testify in a meaningful way about the mental condition of the accused, so that the kinds of answers demanded in the above-cited Horton case will be avoided. The inclusion of the word "substantial" in the ALI Model Penal Code is an attempt to accomplish this very purpose. The psychiatrist should be permitted to testify fully in terms of his own medical expertise. It is the burden of the judge to translate this testimony into useful legal guidelines for the benefit of the jury. Finally, the abuses attendant upon the practice of indefinite sentences (those with no maxima) must be remedied. Some system must evolve whereby the responsibility for the prognostication of the inmate's future conduct must be shared. Officials other than psychiatrists can review the record, and so avoid the horrifying spectacle of individuals indefinitely confined in a mental institution because no psychiatrist is willing to certify the inmate's future conduct.

The task of separating defendants who are sick from those who are bad is a challenge to a free society. There are no easy answers and no answers which can ignore the role of society itself in creating both sickness and badness. The success of our efforts in this area is, however, one indication of our success as an ongoing social system. As Judge Bazelon said:

> The law is neither a scientific instrument nor an adjunct to any absolute moral doctrine. . . . In the criminal law and the administration of the insanity defense the wisdom of the past, including the free-will postulate, meets modern scientific views, including the postulate of causal determinism. The legal process differs from religion in that . . . it cannot utter moral imperatives. It differs from science in that it cannot choose its experimental subject matter, it cannot plead ignorance and it cannot select its hypotheses freely. A court must resolve all conflicts presented to it, with or without adequate knowledge.[15]

Selected Readings

Biggs, John, Jr. *The Guilty Mind.* Baltimore: Johns Hopkins Press, 1955.

Goldstein, Abraham S. *The Insanity Defense.* New Haven: Yale University Press, 1967.

Halleck, Seymour L. *Psychiatry and the Dilemmas of Crime.* New York: Harper and Row, 1967.

Hinsie, Leland E., and Campbell, Robert J. *Psychiatric Dictionary.* 3rd ed. New York: Oxford University Press, 1960.

Menninger, Karl. *The Crime of Punishment.* New York: Viking, 1968.

Morris, Norval, and Hawkins, Gordon. *The Honest Politician's Guide to Crime Control.* Chicago: University of Chicago Press, 1970.

Szasz, Thomas S. *Law, Liberty, and Psychiatry.* New York: Macmillan, 1963.

Szasz, Thomas S. *The Manufacture of Madness.* New York: Harper and Row, 1970.

Szasz, Thomas S. *Psychiatric Justice.* New York: Macmillan, 1965.

Williams, Edward Bennett. *One Man's Freedom.* New York: Atheneum, 1962.

Notes

[1] Leland E. Hinsie and Robert J. Campbell, *Psychiatric Dictionary,* 3rd ed. (New York: Oxford University Press, 1960), p. 602.

[2] Hinsie and Campbell, p. 387.

[3] Thomas S. Szasz, *Law, Liberty, and Psychiatry* (New York: The Macmillan Company, 1963), pp. 166–168; *New York Times,* September 28, 1962, p. 18.

[4] *New York Times,* January 15, 1941, p. 1; March 13, 1942, p. 21.

[5] Thomas S. Szasz, *Psychiatric Justice* (New York: The Macmillan Company, 1965), Chapter 6.

[6] Abraham S. Goldstein, *The Insanity Defense* (New Haven: Yale University Press, 1967), p. 27.

[7] Edward Bennett Williams, *One Man's Freedom* (New York: Atheneum, 1962), p. 249.

[8] *People v. Horton,* 308 N.Y. 1 (1955).

[9] *People v. Horton,* at 20, 21.

[10] *People v. Horton,* at 21.

[11] *Durham v. United States,* 214 F. 2d 862 (1954), at 874–885.

[12] Norval Morris and Gordon Hawkins, *The Honest Politician's Guide to Crime Control* (Chicago: University of Chicago Press, 1970), p. 178.

[13] From *The Crime of Punishment* by Karl Menninger, M.D., p. 138. Copyright © 1966, 1968 by Karl Menninger, M.D. All rights reserved. Reprinted by permission of The Viking Press, Inc.

[14] Goldstein, pp. 223–224.

[15] David L. Bazelon, "The Awesome Decision," *Saturday Evening Post* (January 23, 1960): 56.

The Police

6

To the schoolboy, the policeman is the man who helps him across the street. To the middle-class white, he is the man who gives out traffic tickets, or the man who keeps an eye on his house or store after dark. To the drunk, the policeman is the person who says "Move on"; to the cardiac victim, he is the one who calls the ambulance and gets the patient to the hospital. To the bookie, the cop is the man to watch out for or to pay off; to the potential suicide, he is the man who will crawl out on a ledge to reach him. To the young black in the ghetto he is "The Man," the enemy; to the middle-aged, middle-class black, he is the man too often not there. To the rich man he is a public servant; to the poor he is the face of authority. He is the hero of the St. Patrick's Day parade; he is the scourge of the radical demonstration. To his Irish mother, he is "New York's Finest"; to the Black Panthers and white Weathermen he is "Pig."

Who is the policeman? What function does he perform? Is he hero or villain? Protector or oppressor? Corrupt or incorruptible? The last bastion of a decadent society or the thin blue line holding back the seas of anarchy?

The perspectives on the police are legion, as are the evaluations of their performance; nor is this a modern phenomenon. The police are obviously a socially necessary institution and have played a role in all modern societies.

107

Their utility, however, has not prevented their being a target of criticism. As Arthur Niederhoffer, a foremost student of police systems, has pointed out,

> Between the lines of [Magna Carta] can be deciphered the same problems and complaints about the police: abuse of power, false arrest, oppression, apathy, and their ignorance of, and contempt for the law. . . . And the remedies of that ancient time were no different from those proposed today: recruit better policemen, stiffen the penalties for malfeasance, create a civilian board as an external control upon the police.[1]

The traditional suspicion of the police remained endemic in England up to the time of the creation of the Metropolitan Police Force by Sir Robert Peel in the early nineteenth century, and it is to this distrust that scholars attribute the fact that English "Bobbies" have never been armed. In the United States today few domestic issues have excited as much controversy, or as furious partisanship, as the question of the police and their relationship to the poor, the black, the angry, and the criminal. Essential to any understanding of this problem is an awareness of who, in sociological terms, the police are. It is only after we know who they are that we can talk meaningfully of what they ought to be doing, and how well they are doing it.

WHO ARE THE POLICE?

Whatever their past sociological origins, today's policemen, especially in the large cities, are essentially lower-middle-class civil servants. Until recently, there was a widespread feeling among sociologists and others that policemen were a self-selected group, attracted to an authoritarian profession by deep-rooted personality needs. More recent research however, has suggested that policemen, far from representing the "Cossack" stratum in society, are more typically like lower-level bureaucrats. The attraction of the policeman's job is less likely to be the power inherent in the night stick than the security inherent in the pension that will be his at the end of twenty years. In New York City today, of all the job opportunities open to high school graduates, the policeman's job ranks as one of the highest in pay, fringe benefits, promotions, and job interest. Study after study of incoming recruits in the New York City Police Academy has shown that the recruits' own perceptions of their reasons for seeking a police job have far more to do with salary, pensions, and working conditions than with any sense of expected psychological fulfillment through the wielding of physical power.* Most authorities conclude that incoming rookie policemen represent a cross section of the American lower-middle and upper-working class,** rather than a self-selected group of potential authoritarians.

> Frustrated elsewhere, our job seeker turns to civil service where there is good pay, security, and decent working conditions. For which positions can he qualify? The obvious choices are jobs in the post office, sanitation, fire, and police departments. His high-school diploma is enough to satisfy entrance conditions. In each case there is a competitive test of roughly equivalent difficulty. But the post office position is federal, and does not pay as well, nor does it have the same early retirement policy as a city job. A sanitation worker does not enjoy as high a status as a fireman or a policeman. A fireman must live indoors with a small group of men and constantly be exposed to fire and smoke. On the other hand, the police position pays very well and offers

---

*This is especially true of black recruits. For an interesting study of the attitudes of black policemen, see Nicholas Alex, *Black in Blue: A Study of the Negro Policeman* (New York: Appleton-Century-Crofts, 1969), p. xviii: "Black policemen were motivated to enter police work more by the lack of alternative opportunities and by the relative absence of discrimination in civil-service employment than by any positive characteristics to be found in police work itself."

**Nelson A. Watson and James W. Sterling, in a survey made for the International Association of Chiefs of Police, claim that "the Police Opinion Poll data . . . casts doubt on the accuracy of the view that 'most policemen are products of lower-middle-class environment.' " The evidence that the authors introduce to support this statement however, is dubious, since they show that "today's police officers have come from the families of craftsmen and foremen, and service workers (including police) in larger proportions than is true for the general adult work force." These occupational groups are customarily subsumed under the heading of lower-middle class or upper-working class. It therefore seems appropriate to continue to describe policemen as belonging largely to these two classes. Nelson A. Watson and James W. Sterling, *Police and Their Opinions* (Washington, D.C.: International Association of Chiefs of Police, 1969), p. 119.

among its advantages a life outdoors with possibilities of romance and adventure. The police job is an obvious choice for a young man of lower-class background. *It matters little what type of personality he possesses.*[2]

If police recruits as a group do not over-represent authoritarian types, it does not follow, however, that fully trained policemen, socialized into the police system, are equally neutral in regard to authoritarian attitudes. Does the process of training and indoctrination take this rather average group of young men and transform them into the popular stereotype of tough, imperious, night stick–wielding brutes? Are policemen, as distinguished from police recruits, more authoritarian than the general population? As Niederhoffer describes it, they are not, *if one makes allowance for class background.* They may very well be more authoritarian than the population at large but are not more so than the social class, that is, upper-working or lower-middle, from which they are drawn. The concept of authoritarian personality grew out of post–World War II psychological research into the nature of the Fascist personality.[3] Some of the variables associated with this type of personality, as labelled by Robert Krug, are:

1. conventionalism.
2. cynicism.
3. aggression.
4. superstition and stereotype.
5. projectivity.
6. good versus bad people.[4]

That policemen are conventional is not surprising. If a potential recruit were an unconventional type to begin with, the chances are that the recruitment process, with its emphasis on the personal character investigation of the applicant, would be likely to weed him out. To police administrators, political extremists (of both Right and Left, but especially of the Left) and applicants with poor academic records, documented behavioral problems, or known unconventional sex lives are very much persona non grata, as are of course those with prior arrest or conviction records, even from juvenile court. The effect of these recruiting standards is to eliminate from consideration everyone but the individual who has so internalized middle-class values as never to have come into open conflict with school, parental, or legal authority. One of the difficulties in the use of such standards is that by definition, as it were, most candidates from the lower classes or from different ethnic cultures are, almost automatically in many instances, excluded from the pool of potential policemen. The police force of most large cities is thus largely white and at least second generation American. In recent years great efforts have been made to relax certain of these restrictions (especially those related to prior brushes with the law for minor offenses) for the purpose of recruiting more minority group policemen. These changes have generally met with great resistance and resentment from the men on the force.

Aside from the effects of recruiting standards in selecting a conventional type of recruit, the norms of police behavior reinforce the candidates' latent conventionalism. Policemen are expected to dress, wear their hair, and behave in a conservative, respectable manner. Recently a young, unmarried honor policeman was threatened with dismissal because he allegedly had sexual intercourse with an unmarried woman during his probation period. He was charged with conduct tending "to bring adverse criticism to the department."[5] The net result of these recruitment practices is to produce a cautious individual, firmly committed to the conventions of middle-class behavior and values.

Policemen also tend to be cynical, but this too is a by-product of the police training system; and they probably share their cynicism with others newly inducted into large bureaucratic systems: doctors, lawyers, college professors, and priests. The data suggest that rookies, on the day they enter the police academy, are quite idealistic about the department they are about to join and the police system in general. As they proceed with their training at the academy and are sent out onto the streets, their cynicism increases markedly, to the point where three-quarters of a representative cross section of the force believed that newspapers deliberately and malevolently give an unfavorable slant to news concerning police, and prominently play up police misdeeds; three-fifths of the group felt that the average departmental complaint was the result of pressure on superiors from higher authority to give out complaints; almost one-half of the men believed that when the policeman appears at the police department trial room, he will probably be found guilty even when he has a good defense; and almost two-fifths of the sample believed that the majority of special assignments in the police department depend on whom you know, not on merit.[6] This all-pervasive cynicism appears, however, to be a result of realities, or at least that part of reality visible to the recruit from his place in the police hierarchy, rather than the expression of internal psychological stress.

Moreover, police training of necessity teaches recruits to be both aggressive and suspicious. The policeman on his beat is faced with the need to make literally hundreds of decisions during a single tour of duty, and he must frequently take decisive action as a result of those decisions. Indeed, at least one police psychiatrist has testified that the personality factor causing the greatest number of washouts in the police department is the inability of the policeman to make a quick decision and live with it comfortably. A good policeman furthermore, must almost by definition be suspicious. In order to prevent crime or detect wrongdoing, he must watch others for signs of unusual, possibly undesirable, behavior. He must, in effect, sit in constant judgment on the behavior of those with whom he comes in contact, and, if he is to be effective, he must be more than usually suspicious.

It would appear then that policemen as a group exhibit many of the characteristics of the authoritarian personality, but so do many people, especially those with similar class backgrounds. It is questionable how much significance these findings have in terms of predicting police performance in a given situation. More relevant perhaps, in determining how police will react towards demonstrators, Negroes, rapists, or whatever, is their perception of the world in which they live, and the threat to the things they hold dear that they perceive in various types of conduct.

The policeman is frequently a marginal member of the middle class; that is, he or his family has struggled very hard to rise from a working-class background to the status and financial security of a police position. He has very little margin of safety: should he lose his job he would rapidly sink into the group he so painfully left only recently. Being insecure, he perceives any challenge to the social system, as he knows it, as a threat to his own personal well-being. Attempts to lower civil service standards for the purpose of recruiting minority-group policemen, Supreme Court decisions favorable to criminal defendants, left-wing political agitators, hippies, and homosexuals—all these he sees as dangerous, either to the police or to the social system that makes the police system possible. In this context it is understandable that the most furious anger of the police towards any type of demonstrator was reserved for those university militants who staged the first wave of campus riots in 1968 and 1969. These children of the upper-middle class, who held in their hands all that the policeman would sell his very soul for, were throwing it contemptuously away to be trampled under the feet of the mob. No wonder the students at Columbia inspired such feelings of outrage! No wonder the policeman sports his little American flag on his uniform and fights for the chance to display it on his patrol car. The policeman, in short, can rarely perceive social change as other than threatening. For this reason he tends to be personally and administratively conservative, and will exhibit his most extreme behavior in those situations where he feels most threatened.*

---

*All this is said, of course, in full recognition of the role elected officials play in determining and modifying basic police policy. This role will be discussed in greater detail at the conclusion of this chapter. It is interesting to speculate whether the 1969–1970 incidents involving the killing of Black Panthers by policemen in Chicago and elsewhere, were in fact examples of the police taking the law into their own hands

Police perception of change as a threat applies to change within the police world as well as to change in the outside world. Police attitudes toward the movement for increasing professionalization provide an insight into the nature of these fears. The official police line in regard to professionalization is one of hearty·approval. Every police organization, whether of superior officers or patrolmen, every police administrator, every policeman on the beat, will assure the outsider that his dearest wish is to see police work raised to the status of a profession. In some ways this is true. Professionalization will bring, it is expected, an increase in income and a rise in prestige in the eyes of the community, both goals understandably dear to police hearts.

If one probes beneath these surface manifestations of approval, however, one finds far more ambivalence towards professionalization than most policemen normally care to admit. Professionalization generally means raising the educational level of the police force, either through recruitment or through training of men already on the force. Generally, this training is conceived of in terms of college education, particularly in the social sciences and humanities, rather than as additional in-service training in traditional police-type subjects such as patrol, surveillance, or traffic. To the high school educated man on the force, this emphasis on further training may cause great uneasiness. On the one hand he may feel pressured to go to college himself, a prospect which may fill him with dismay. The mere fact that he did not attend college in the first place suggests that he was

---

because they felt especially threatened. In the Chicago incident there is considerable evidence that the police entered the premises illegally and killed and wounded occupants without proper legal cause. Most policemen consider groups like the Black Panthers to be extremely and imminently dangerous to the social order.

An even more shocking instance of police action taken directly and illegally against a group they perceived as threatening is the Brazilian "Death Squad," made up largely of off-duty policemen, who allegedly assassinate petty criminals. A Brazilian army captain justified this activity, saying "They're ridding society of bad elements—elements that would only be caught and sentenced anyway if our court system worked correctly." *New York Times,* July 21, 1970, p. 1.

less than academically outstanding in his youth, and many policemen enter the force with poor or mediocre high school records. At best, college will mean six to ten years of hard academic drudgery, to be undertaken at the end of a long day's work and in competition with the needs of family, friends, and community organizations. The reward for this education is moreover, in many communities, intangible, since many police departments offer no job credits or pay differential for additional academic training. On the other hand, should the police officer refuse to educate himself further, he must live in fear that one day he will be supplanted, in opportunities for promotion or desirable assignments, by some bright young college-educated rookie or by one of his more industrious colleagues.

Most policemen in the lower ranks are bitterly opposed to schemes for lateral entry, which they see as extremely threatening to their careers. Lateral entry would make it possible for better-educated candidates to be hired at levels above that of patrolman. In most traditional police systems, everyone enters at the bottom and achieves advancement through credits earned by competitive civil service examinations and seniority. The upper ranks, thus, are reserved for men who have served their time on the streets. This prospect, however, is uninviting to young college-trained, career-minded individuals. It is for this reason that suggestions have been made that such people be brought in above the patrolman level. It has also been suggested that police systems ought to be able to hire from other police systems experienced individuals in the higher ranks, much as universities hire each other's senior professors, or industry hires executives from competing firms. While these proposals have much merit from an objective administrative-management point of view, the patrolman on the beat perceives lateral entry proposals as taking away his all too few opportunities for promotion.

In addition to the unwelcome pressure exerted by the value placed on college education and the fears aroused by the threat of lateral entry, many policemen have a certain contempt for "book knowledge" as opposed to the lessons learned on the streets. This point of view is held by those whose intellect and performance are superior, as well as by those who might be considered mediocre or worse. It is a manifestation of the anti-intellectualism and scorn for the "egghead" that is endemic in American society. While this attitude cuts across class lines, it is probably most prevalent in the social classes from which most policemen are drawn, and it also fits into the construct of the authoritarian personality. Not surprisingly, policemen who have elected to go to college reflect this attitude less strongly than do policemen with equivalent service in the department who have not gone to college. (College-educated policemen also, incidentally, appear to be less authoritarian and less anti-intellectual than civilian college students of the same ethnic and class background.)[7] It is hard to assess precisely the contribution of academic knowledge to the police job. Certainly on-the-street practical experience is a sine qua non for successful performance. Education in the liberal arts, and especially in the social sciences, is, however, equally essential to achieve that sense of perspective which makes it possible for the policeman to relate to the public he serves, to the offenders with whom he must deal, and to the world of which he is a part.

It is in the area of these relationships to the non-police world that the policeman today expresses his greatest dissatisfaction.[8] His most heartfelt complaint is likely to be that the public does not appreciate his efforts on their behalf, does not value his willingness to sacrifice his very life for the public safety. The ungrateful citizenry is all too willing to criticize the police for rising crime rates or, perhaps contradictorily, for excessive zeal in the performance of their duties. The public is also eternally preoccupied with the subject of police corruption. Although in some ways his status may be rising, in an era of upward mobility the policeman feels somehow that he is being left behind.

The policeman today, far from being the authoritarian Cossack who for amusement growls at children in his spare time, is more likely to be a conservative, conforming, somewhat frightened, well-meaning but bewildered minor bureaucrat. He wants to believe in the system; he wants to do his job well; he wants to serve the public. For reasons about which he is not quite clear, the statistics seem to show that he is not doing his job well; that the public does not appreciate his efforts; and that he doesn't know how to go about solving his problems. He may become cynical and suffer from anomie. He is frequently somewhat bitter. He feels himself to be the man caught in the middle, between the criminal and the public, between the forces of stability and the forces of change. At the same time he feels isolated, a member of a persecuted, misunderstood minority. Truly, his lot is not a happy one.

TO ARREST OR NOT: AREAS OF POLICE DISCRETION

It is both impossible and undesirable for the police to enforce equally every law on the books. If they did, we would need a police force of mammoth proportions and scarcely a citizen would go through the day without official reprimand or arrest. The resources needed in terms of courts and correctional institutions would be of such magnitude as to be almost beyond imagination. Official discretion is obviously called for. In some cases the police will, of course, arrest offenders; in some cases they will warn; and in many more cases they will simply ignore illegal conduct. Wayne LaFave suggests that the decision not to arrest is particularly likely in four categories of offenses: trivial offenses; offenses where the conduct is thought to represent the subculture of a different ethnic or racial group; offenses where the victim refuses to prosecute; and offenses where the victim has also been involved in some kind of illegal conduct.[9]

Trivial offenses are the type of misconduct most frequently ignored by the police. Indeed, non-enforcement of laws relating to petty offenses may be the rule rather than the exception. Minor street arguments, panhandling, public drunkenness, peddling, spitting on the sidewalk, littering, and parking and minor traffic violations are often all handled by warnings, and more frequently are ignored completely by the patrolman on his beat. Normally, outside pressure, in the form of complaints by those who are being annoyed by such violators, will be necessary for the police to take action. Periodic drives against derelicts or drunks in the business areas of large cities are of this nature. Campaigns against certain kinds of parking violations are mounted when street congestion becomes unbearable; tickets rather than warnings are given to motorists when accidents become too frequent. Sometimes the complaint of a single individual is enough to affect the policeman's conduct. A New York City patrolman recounted an incident where an elderly lady approached him while he was on duty in a public park and demanded to know why he had failed to arrest a panhandler who was soliciting funds nearby. The policeman, who had already observed the panhandler and had decided on a live-and-let-live policy, rather uncomfortably approached the offender and started to speak to him. At that moment, a hippie couple approached and proceeded to berate the officer for harassing a poor man who, after all, was only trying to earn a living. The elderly lady joined in the conversation by scolding the hippie couple for interfering with an officer in pursuit of his duty. At that point, the officer said, "The bum walked one way; I went the other. I left the three of them arguing with each other."

Cultural patterns of subgroups affect police action most notably in the area of personal assaults. The complaint of a middle-class person that he has been the victim of an assault will almost always result in the arrest of the offender if that is physically possible. The lower-class complainant, however, does not evoke the same police response, especially if the assault is a result of a family quarrel or an altercation between friends. The police presumably operate on the theory that in the context of the particular group such conduct is far more acceptable and hence less deserving of legal sanction than it would be for society at large. This restraint on the part of the police is the basis for a large part of the complaints by Negroes of non-enforcement of the law in the ghettos.* Although this pattern of police action is perceived by blacks as racist, it is in reality more likely to be class-based. In the era when the Irish and Italians formed the bulk of the lower class who inhabited the urban slums, precisely the same police non-response was evoked when a drunken Irish hodcarrier beat up his wife or brother-in-law or when two Italian laborers cut each other in an affair of honor.

Frequently, when victims appeal to the police for relief against offenders, the relief they seek is not the arrest of the offender. They wish either to have the police make the offender stop doing whatever he is doing, or they wish the police to force the offender to make restitution. Small storekeepers, for example, may call on the police to evict troublesome customers or to chase away a crowd of boys obstructing the entrance to the establishment. They don't want the offenders arrested, because they don't want to take the time to appear in court as complaining witnesses. Nor are they really interested in seeing the offenders punished. They merely want the annoyance to stop. Similarly, in fraud cases the victims frequently want the threat of arrest to be used to force the swindler to give back that which he has stolen. Essentially, such victims are using the police and the district attorney as collectors for bad debts, dishonored checks, and the like. Sometimes victims call the police in a fit of anger and then almost immediately regret their action and refuse to press the complaint. This is most frequently true when the offender is a relative or one with whom the victim has a continuing relationship such as co-worker or neighbor.

Police frequently are reluctant to take action where the victim has been engaged in conduct that is illegal or embarrassing, either because they feel the victim got his just deserts or because they fear that the victim will be reluctant to cooperate in the prosecution. Men who are tricked out of

---

*See Chapter 3.

119

money which they gave to prostitutes or pimps; individuals who are swindled in get-rich-quick schemes that are patently illegal; victims of assaults which were provoked by actions on the part of the victim himself: all these are typical of cases where the police frequently decline to take action.

Another area in which police discretion is frequently invoked is the handling of juveniles. There is an unusually large number of options open to the police in the disposition of juveniles as compared with other kinds of cases; for example, the police may warn, reprimand, or pick up a child for questioning, may notify parents officially, investigate, and make official notation on the child's record, or refer a child to an appropriate social agency. All of these measures fall short of arrest, which is the ultimate sanction in the hands of the police. Arrest is usually avoided, if possible, because present-day progressive police practice recognizes the importance of labelling: that once the child is officially categorized as a suspected criminal it is hard for him to escape from this category. Some excellent sociological studies have, however, indicated that police discretion not to arrest juveniles is used in fairly predictable ways. Juveniles who act tough and unrepentant or who are dressed in a manner indicative of defiance tend to be dealt with far more severely than the meek, compliant youth, even when the facts confronting the police officer are the same. Black youths, especially those wearing leather jackets, sunglasses, and Afro hairdos, are particularly prone to more severe police reactions. Police tend to be more suspicious of such juveniles, keep them under closer surveillance, and arrest more frequently for conduct that would be handled informally if it occurred among youngsters they found less abrasive.

> One officer observing a youth walking along the street, commented that the youth "looks suspicious" and promptly stopped and questioned him. Asked later to explain what aroused his suspicions, the officer explained, "He was a Negro wearing dark glasses at midnight."[10]

The importance of the use of police discretion in juvenile cases is that frequently patterns of police enforcement become a kind of self-fulfilling prophecy in regard to certain

groups of youngsters. Because these youths perceive disproportionate suspicion and hostility on the part of the police,
they respond with the very kind of conduct—sullenness,
sassiness, and defiance—that the police perceive as cues
for punitive action. Once arrested, these juveniles are well
on their way towards attaining a criminal record and a
permanent status on the wrong side of the law. This in turn
leads the police to be even more suspicious of other youths
of the same type.

> Thus it is not unlikely that frequent encounters with police, par-
> ticularly those involving youths innocent of wrongdoing, will in-
> crease the hostility of these juveniles toward law-enforcement
> personnel. It is also not unlikely that the frequency of such
> encounters will in time reduce their significance in the eyes of
> apprehended juveniles, thereby leading these youths to regard
> them as "routine." Such responses to police encounters, how-
> ever, are those which law-enforcement personnel perceive as
> indicators of the serious delinquent. They thus serve to vindicate
> and reinforce officers' prejudices, leading to closer surveillance
> of Negro districts, more frequent encounters with Negro youths,
> and so on in a vicious circle. Moreover, the consequences of
> this chain of events are reflected in police statistics showing a
> disproportionately high percentage of Negroes among juvenile
> offenders, thereby providing "objective" justification for con-
> centrating police attention on Negro youths.[11]

LaFave and Piliavin discuss the police decision not to
arrest mainly in relation to offenses which are not very
serious: juvenile delinquency, swindling, traffic violations,
and simple assault. By their decision not to arrest, the police
are, in reality, informally structuring a system of priorities on
the use of their time so as to make the job of law enforcement more practicable given the limited resources usually
available to them.* By not arresting indiscriminately they are
conserving their efforts for the containment of more serious
offenders.

---

*Alexander B. Smith and Bernard Locke, in a survey of police attitudes
toward obscenity and pornography laws, indicate that while policemen
tend to be outraged by such "filth," enforcement of such laws has low
priority. Alexander B. Smith and Bernard Locke, *Response of Police and
Prosecutors to Problems in Arrests and Prosecutions for Obscenity and
Pornography.* Technical Report of the Commission on Obscenity and
Pornography, Vol. 2 (Washington, D.C.: U.S. Government Printing Office,
1970).

Another way in which the police utilize the decision not to arrest is in the operation of the informer system.[12] Studies of police departments have shown that it is very common for policemen to extend "protection" to pimps, prostitutes, petty thieves, addicts, small-time pushers, probationers, parolees, ex-convicts, bookies, numbers runners, and the like. This protection takes the form of freedom from arrest or, in some cases, freedom to continue to break the law, in return for which the suspect agrees to inform the police of the activity of more serious criminals of whom he may have knowledge. Prostitutes, for example, may be permitted to ply their trade free from police harassment if they cooperate by reporting to the police information regarding underworld activities that comes their way. Addict-pushers may be allowed to continue their activities in return for tips as to the identity of the wholesalers from whom they make their purchase. Addicts are also used as a source of information as to the disposition of stolen goods. Informants may be rewarded with money as well as freedom from arrest. The police may even undertake physically to protect a good informer from the colleagues he has betrayed. While the informer may not have absolute immunity from arrest when he is working for the police, he is usually assured that at least the police will attempt to get him the best possible plea bargain that can be arranged, as well as, if need be, an advantageous sentence from the court.

The informer system, which rests entirely on the ability of the police not to invoke the full process of the law, is not viewed by law enforcement officials as evidence of police corruption even though the police traffic with known criminals and may go so far as to give lawbreakers money which may be used for further illegal activities. In the police view, the system is essential for effective law enforcement, for without informers, police would lose their lines of communication to the underworld. The London police, for example, bitterly lamented legalization of prostitution because without the tips given to them by the girls their efficiency in solving important crimes in the metropolitan London area was seriously impaired. The symbiotic relationship between the police and the petty criminal-turned-informer may, in fact, be so essential to successful law enforcement in our present social system that it should not be eliminated, however unsavory and sordid the details of its operations may be. It is important to recognize however, that it is one manifestation of the very large amount of discretion residing in the hands of the police force as to *the degree to which the law should be invoked and against whom.* The police can never realistically meet criticism of their activities by saying they are only enforcing the law. The police constantly shape the law through a pattern of *selective enforcement.* They must recognize this reality and meet critics head on by indicating that the pattern of enforcement they have selected is justifiable in terms of agreed-upon societal goals.

POLICE DISCRETION AND POLICE CORRUPTION

It is obvious that police discretion not to invoke the law is greater for those offenses which are considered *malum prohibitum* rather than *malum in se.* Police generally enforce the law fully against murderers, rapists, arsonists; they enforce it much less fully against gamblers, prostitutes, and drug offenders. As the previous discussion indicated, non-enforcement may be the result of informal attempts to conserve police resources for more important crimes. Non-enforcement may also be the result of the need for informers. Sometimes, however, non-enforcement is the result of corruption of the police by criminals. Police corruption is the subject of enormous concern, to both practitioners within the criminal justice system and to the citizenry outside the system, and periodic exposés of such corruption are so regular as almost to be anticipated. There is scarcely a large city in this country which has not had a police scandal of major proportions. The most significant feature, however, of these exposés is that the pattern of corruption is virtually the same whatever the time and whatever the place. Almost always the police are bribed to overlook offenses that are *malum prohibitum* rather than *malum in se*, especially such morals offenses as gambling, drug use, and prostitution. It is unusual for the police to take bribes to overlook murders, rapes, robberies, or burglaries, or, in the case of the FBI, treason, espionage, or interstate kidnapping.*

The basic reason for the persistence of this pattern of corruption is that the criminal law does not reflect a true picture of community moral standards.[13] While many people pay lip service to the notion that gambling, prostitution, homosexuality, and marijuana smoking are evil, a very large minority either do not think these practices evil, or they hypocritically practice in secret what they publicly disavow. The result is that there is an enormous demand for the services which numbers runners, drug pushers, and prostitutes supply, a demand which potential consumers are willing to pay for in cash. Because these activities are illegal, some of this money is diverted to the police in the form of bribes. The police, for their part, are tempted by the availability of easy money, and many of them also share the modal belief of the public that gambling, prostitution, and marijuana smoking are not so very wrong. The police reaction to an exposé which indicates that police have been involved in the commission or protection of burglaries is very different from an exposé which shows police protection of gamblers. While both modes of conduct are illegal, the former will truly horrify most policemen; the latter will be greeted with shrugs of the shoulder.

Morals offenses, moreover, frequently have no victim, that is, the victim is an all too willing participant in the crime.[14] Gamblers do not force betters to play the horses, and prostitutes do not seduce their clients with guns. Thus, there are seldom any complaining witnesses to exert pressure on the police to enforce the law, nor is there as much risk of exposure of corruption.

---

*This is not to say that police have never covered up, or indeed been principals or accessories to serious crimes, especially those committed by organized mobsters. Nevertheless, the most serious, widespread, and common type of police graft is that received from pushers, prostitutes, and bookies.

This pattern of police corruption has several implications for public policy makers. It is probable that widespread corruption cannot be eliminated as long as the criminal law is used as a vehicle for foisting a morality on the public that the public does not really accept or has outgrown. It may seem incomprehensible why statutes that do not reflect community standards get into the statute books in the first place and are so difficult to remove once they are there. Students of the legislative process know, however, that laws are not so much the will of the majority as the will of whatever ad hoc coalition of interest groups is able to control the legislature at a given time. Well-organized interest groups, moreover, even though they represent a relatively small minority, can effectively veto the repeal of outmoded morals legislation, as witness the success of various religious groups in preventing divorce reform or the legalization of off-track betting. The problem of this type of police corruption must be handled at the level of making our legislatures more truly representative and responsive bodies.

The FBI has shown an interesting awareness of the likelihood of corruption in the enforcement of morals legislation by quietly but deliberately refusing to attempt enforcement in these areas. A very perceptive article in *The New York Times Magazine* points out that the FBI infinitely prefers to expend its resources catching bank robbers and kidnappers (of which there are relatively few in this country) than to become involved in investigating organized crime, the basis for which is the traffic in drugs, prostitutes, and illegal betting.[15] It is only in recent years that the pressure of public opinion has forced the FBI to concern itself with types of crime more relevant to the American social scene than the peccadillos of Bonnie-and-Clyde types. J. Edgar Hoover, who was appointed in 1924 as director of the FBI in the wake of the Harding administration Justice Department scandals, succeeded in cleaning up corruption within the FBI, and he has guarded the public chastity of his agents zealously ever since. One of his methods, however, has been to keep his men free from temptation by simply ignoring

those areas of law enforcement where corruption is pre-
dictably most likely to occur.[16]

POLITICAL DIRECTION OF POLICE ACTIVITIES

Discretion in law enforcement is exercised at three
levels.[17] A patrolman decides to warn rather than give a
ticket to a speeding motorist; to ignore rather than arrest a
prostitute; to calm rather than bring in an abusive, drunken
husband—all these are examples of discretion exercised at
the lowest level of bureaucratic hierarchy.

When a precinct commander orders his men to treat
hippies with courtesy and respect and to allow them unim-
peded use of the local park; when police administrators decide to saturate a difficult police precinct with foot police
in an attempt to reduce street crime; when the police commissioner decides that a fourth platoon is needed, the better
to deploy his forces during the high crime hours of the late
evening and early morning—these are exercises in police
discretion at the administrative or command level.

The mayor's office makes the most basic decisions of
all in regard to police policy. The ultimate decision at the
mayoral level is, of course, the portion of the city budget
that will go to the police. This determines how many men
will be available, what kinds of equipment will be purchased,
and by determining wage and pension levels, it even influences the kinds of men who will enter as recruits. Beyond
fiscal policy, however, the mayor's office is the conduit for
public opinion as to the kinds of law enforcement the public
wants. Does the public want prostitutes chased, arrested,
or tolerated? Is the traffic situation serious enough to warrant ten-dollar tickets or a tow-away program? Do the residents of the Upper West Side really need the additional
police protection for which they have been clamoring?

On some issues the policy-making process is clear and
easy to trace. The impulses of an aroused public opinion
are transmitted directly to the mayor, from the mayor to the
police commissioner, from the commissioner to his deputies,

and so on down the hierarchical ladder to the patrolman on the beat. When the number of deaths due to heroin over-doses among adolescents mounted sharply in New York City at the end of 1969, great public concern was expressed, especially because the use of heroin appeared to be spread-ing to middle-class youngsters. Newspapers, clergymen, civic groups, and educators all deplored the situation freely, and as with one voice turned to the mayor and said, in essence, "Do something!" The mayor's response was to turn to the police commissioner and repeat "Do something." The police commissioner turned to his deputies and to-gether they formulated certain departmental narcotics con-trol measures which included, among others, the formation of a special narcotics squad in every precinct in the city focused on the immediate problem of reducing heroin traffic.

The results of this policy were very plain, at least statis-tically: heroin arrests, for both felonies and misdemeanors, approximately doubled in the first two months of 1970, as compared to the same time period in 1969. At the same time, marijuana arrests (felonies and misdemeanors) declined. Superficially these statistics may appear simply to indicate increased heroin abuse and decreased marijuana use. The realities of the situation are, however, quite different, as any experienced observer can testify. By no stretch of the imagination could one suppose that marijuana use and sales had declined, and while heroin traffic may indeed have in-creased, there is no evidence to indicate an increase of such proportions as to justify the increase in arrests. It is a reasonable assumption that what the statistics actually reflect is the increased concern by the public about a social problem, which was transmitted through the mayor's office to the police department where it was transmuted into a dif-ferent deployment of police resources. Where formerly nar-cotics enforcement was mainly the responsibility of the city-wide narcotics bureau, under the new policy additional enforcement personnel was assigned at the precinct level. With the increased number of policemen available, arrests went up sharply. Thus the arrest figure is not necessarily a reflection of the amount of law-breaking occurring; rather it is a reflection of the discretionary enforcement of certain laws, in this case the policy decision to pay increased attention to heroin offenders and less attention to marijuana users. It should be noted that during the very same period that increasing public concern over heroin abuse was being expressed, a markedly more tolerant attitude towards the use of marijuana was manifest, partly because little scientific evidence of the harmfulness of marijuana use has been adduced, and partly because marijuana use was increasing among the "respectable" middle class.[18]

Not all policy making is so clear-cut however. Where an issue is controversial and public response is sharply divided, the cues coming to the mayor's office may be contradictory and ambiguous, and the mayor's response may be either unacceptable or unintelligible to the police department. The policy which then emerges may be quite different from what the mayor intended, and public response may be unpredictable. One of the touchiest issues confronting the Lindsay administration in New York City in the late 1960s was the police handling of street demonstrations. While the public was generally agreed on the need for public order, there was sharp polarization of opinion on the question of how much freedom of action dissenters should be permitted. Where should crowds be permitted to congregate? How much disruption of traffic should be permitted? How should the crowd be contained and controlled? How should disruptive incidents be handled? What level of violence, verbal and physical, should be tolerated? What proportion of the police department's resources should be diverted to the service of demonstrators? How best could crowd-control functions be handled administratively?

The response of the Lindsay administration to these questions reflected the mayor's sympathy for the poor, the black, students, and peace groups who were most aggrieved by Establishment policies during this period. His orders to his police commissioner were intended to provide a police contingent large enough to handle projected crowds with minimal use of direct physical force. Arrests were to be kept to a minimum, and only physically assaultive conduct was to be restrained. The general policy of the special events squad, designed to handle parades, demonstrations, and the like, was to break up disputes and altercations, making arrests only as a last resort or where there had been physical attack on a police officer. This sympathetic administration attitude toward demonstrators was difficult for many police officers to accept. Their personal political preferences often ran counter to those of the demonstrators; they were offended by the noisiness, untidiness, and unconventional appearance of many of the participants; and professionally, they were alarmed at the potential for riot and disorder in the milling and surging of large angry crowds. Because of the complexity of the problem and the disparity of views between the mayor's office and the patrolman on the street, the administrative officials of the police department were forced into an uneasy neutrality between their men and the mayor's office.

The record shows that the New York City police were remarkably successful in maintaining peace at a time when most of the major cities of the country were devastated by riots. The mayor's policies of non-provocative, relatively minimal law enforcement towards minority group demonstrators evoked some public and police criticism, but prevailed because they were effective in cooling an overheated situation. In at least two instances however, the results were not so fortuitous. In 1969, policemen in the City Hall area permitted largely black demonstrators for increased welfare rights to stomp and destroy several parked cars, including a Cadillac belonging to a conservative Republican New York City councilman. A year later in the same City Hall area, the police permitted several hundred helmeted construction workers to disrupt an anti-war demonstration and to physically and severely assault demonstrators, bystanders, and students at a nearby college.

In each case the stated reason for the inaction of the

police was the same: that the police force was inadequate to handle the crowd involved, and therefore could do nothing more than stand its ground and protect City Hall from invasion. While this statement may be accurate, it conceals as much as it reveals. A host of questions remain unanswered. Why was the police force inadequate? On what basis was the determination of the number of men available in the City Hall area made? Why was provision for reinforcements not made? Were the police as outnumbered as they claimed to be? Were their personal, political preferences in any way involved in their failure to take action? At the time of the incident involving the councilman's car, several police organizations commented bitterly that such violence was the inevitable result of the mayor's permissive policies toward demonstrators. Critics of the police responded by suggesting that the police had deliberately refused to stop the destruction of the car in order to discredit the mayor's policies. At the time of the second incident, even more vigorous charges were made that the police had refused to stop the beatings of students and peace demonstrators by the construction workers because their personal sympathies were entirely with the workmen. It is a fact that almost no arrests were made, although a substantial number of people were injured sufficiently to require hospital treatment. Once again the police line organizations remarked that such incidents were merely the results of the ambiguous and confusing directives on crowd-handling emanating from the mayor's office. They suggested, moreover, that the confrontation had been brought about by the intemperate remarks and misplaced sympathies of the Lindsay administration.[19]

Who, then, makes policy in New York City for the handling of street demonstrations? Certainly, the mayor's office did not intend for either the councilman's car to be stomped or the peace demonstrators to be beaten. Why then did these things happen? Was there simply an honest miscalculation on the part of police administrators as to how many men would be needed to contain the crowds, or was the miscalculation at least in part a result of the ambivalent feeling of police administrators toward official mayoral policy? Was the inaction of the police a response to the reality of the situation or an expression of hostility toward the official policies imposed on the department by "politicians"?

The answers to these questions are impossible to determine. It is evident, however, that while one may conceptually make distinctions in policy making at the various levels of the police system from patrolman to mayor, in practice the process is not nearly so clear-cut as one might wish. Where an issue is relatively non-controversial, such as the concern over heroin use, the response may well be straightforward and readily traceable from its inception in public concern to the mayor's office, to police administrators, and ultimately to the lowest levels of the police hierarchy. Where the issue is more controversial, the decision-making process becomes a blur of interactions and ad hoc adjustments between many levels of the hierarchy. What the mayor proposes is simply not what the policeman on the street disposes.

One must also note that a distinction should be made between political interference with the police department and political direction of police policies. It is legitimate for policemen to object if an elected official wishes to make his nephew a lieutenant or to award a contract for police cars to his brother-in-law. It is also legitimate for the police to object to instruction by non-professionals in the specifics of how to carry out a particular assignment, for example, where units are to be deployed or where reinforcements should be stationed. It is not legitimate, however, for policemen to object to the mayor's telling the police commissioner to make an effort to recruit more Negroes and Puerto Ricans, to increase the size of the force (possibly at the expense of wage increases for existing personnel), or to emphasize some areas of law enforcement even at the expense of lesser enforcement in other areas. Policemen, of course, have the right to criticize the mayor's decisions as ill-advised or misguided, but they cannot consider such suggestions as illegitimate. It is the mayor's obligation to control over-all policies of the police department in conformity with the wishes of the electorate in much the same way as the president and the civilian secretary of defense control policies of the armed forces. Police organizations frequently express such hostility to this type of political control as leads to the inference that they feel police policy should be made by policemen for society at large. This point of view is wholly unacceptable in a democratic society. Police officials and patrolmen have the right and duty to offer technical advice to elected officials; beyond that they have an obligation to accept and implement policies formulated by those responsible to the voters.

A suggested approach to the problem of political control of police policy is to eliminate as many areas of police discretion as possible through mandating full enforcement of the criminal law as opposed to the de facto discretionary enforcement which now exists in almost all jurisdictions. Since it is largely through these selective enforcement decisions that police policy is made, law professors such as Joseph Goldstein of Yale have suggested that, by insisting that all laws be fully enforced, the police will be removed from policy making that is not responsive to the community.

> The ultimate answer is that the police should not be delegated discretion not to invoke criminal law. It is recognized, of course, that the exercise of discretion cannot be completely eliminated where human beings are involved. . . . But nonetheless, outside this margin of ambiguity, the police should operate in an atmosphere which exhorts and commands them to invoke impartially all criminal laws within the bounds of *full enforcement*. If a criminal law is ill-advised, poorly defined, or too costly to enforce, efforts by the police to achieve *full enforcement* should generate pressures for legislative action. Responsibility for the enactment, amendment, and repeal of the criminal laws will not, then, be abandoned to the whim of each police officer or department, but retained where it belongs in a democracy — with elected representatives.[20]

While superficially plausible, this is a naive suggestion. In the first place, it is predicated on the assumption that legislatures will be willing to remove from the statute books obsolete, unenforceable, popularly disregarded morals legislation (such as Sunday blue laws), an assumption which is highly unrealistic politically.

In the second place, even if the deadwood of the criminal code were cut away, the total enforcement of what remains would fantastically overstrain the resources of the criminal justice system.

> If each patrolman made an arrest [in the ghetto] in every case where he observed a crime, or had probable cause to believe that a crime had been committed, there would be literally no policemen at all patrolling the precinct. They would all be at the station house or at court on legitimate police duty in connection with the arrest. The station houses, the courts, and the prisons, would be swamped by the sheer magnitude of the numbers of prisoners. Under these conditions is it wise, or possible, to enforce the law to its fullest extent?[21]

In the third place, as the discussion of policy in regard to street demonstrations illustrated, total enforcement of law is, in many cases, a meaningless term. What, for example, would total enforcement of the law in regard to parades mean? Should the same measures be taken in relation to the annual parade of the Sunday school union as to a parade of anti-war protesters? If not, what guidelines should be established, and by whom? How would this guideline-establishing process differ from police department policy making as now instituted in our "non-total enforcement" police departments?

It would appear that willy-nilly, for better or worse, police policy making is a fact of life that must be accepted by analysts of the criminal justice system. While such policy making cannot be eliminated, it can and should be controlled by the elected officials to whom the police, both on the beat and in administrative capacities, must be subservient. One of the most urgent tasks facing many localities is that of educating the police into an understanding and acceptance of this subservience.[22]

Selected Readings

Adorno, T.W.; Frenkel-Brunswik, Else; Levinson, Daniel J.; and Sanford, R. Nevitt. *The Authoritarian Personality*. New York: Harper and Row, 1950.

Alex, Nicholas. *Black in Blue: A Study of the Negro Policeman*. New York: Appleton-Century-Crofts, 1969.

Banton, Michael. *The Policeman in the Community.* New York: Basic Books, 1964.

Bayley, David H., and Mendelsohn, Harold. *Minorities and the Police.* New York: Free Press, 1969.

Black, Algernon D. *The People and the Police.* New York: McGraw-Hill, 1968.

Bordua, David J. *The Police: Six Sociological Essays.* New York: Wiley, 1967.

Chevigny, Paul. *Police Power: Police Abuses in New York City.* New York: Pantheon, 1969.

Cook, Fred J. *The FBI Nobody Knows.* New York: Macmillan, 1964.

Cray, Ed. *The Big Blue Line.* New York: Coward-McCann, 1967.

LaFave, Wayne R. *Arrest: The Decision to Take a Suspect into Custody.* Boston: Little, Brown, 1965.

Niederhoffer, Arthur. *Behind the Shield.* Garden City, N.Y.: Doubleday, 1967.

Niederhoffer, Arthur, and Blumberg, Abraham S. *The Ambivalent Force: Perspectives on the Police.* Waltham, Mass.: Ginn and Company, 1970.

Packer, Herbert L. *The Limits of the Criminal Sanction.* Stanford: Stanford University Press, 1968.

The Report of the Commission on Obscenity and Pornography. Washington, D.C.: U.S. Government Printing Office, 1970.

Richardson, James. *The New York Police: Colonial Times to 1901.* New York: Oxford University Press, 1970.

Schur, Edwin M. *Crimes Without Victims.* Englewood Cliffs, N.J.: Prentice-Hall, 1965.

Skolnick, Jerome H. *Justice Without Trial: Law Enforcement in Democratic Society.* New York: Wiley, 1966.

Turner, William. *The Police Establishment.* New York: Putnam, 1968.

Watson, Nelson A., and Sterling, James W. *Police and Their Opinions.* Washington, D.C.: International Association of Chiefs of Police, 1969.

Westley, William A. *Violence and the Police.* Cambridge, Mass.: The M.I.T. Press, 1970.

Notes

1. Arthur Niederhoffer, "Restraint of the Force: A Recurrent Problem," *Connecticut Law Review* 1, no. 2 (December 1968): 288.

2. Arthur Niederhoffer, *Behind the Shield* (Garden City, N.Y.: Doubleday, 1967), p. 156. Italics added.

[3] T. W. Adorno, Else Frenkel-Brunswik, Daniel J. Levinson, and R. Nevitt Sanford, *The Authoritarian Personality* (New York: Harper and Row, 1950).

[4] Robert E. Krug, "An Analysis of the F Scale: 1. Item Factor Analysis," *Journal of Social Psychology* 53 (1961): 288, 291.

[5] Niederhoffer, *Behind the Shield,* p. 115.

[6] Niederhoffer, *Behind the Shield,* pp. 199–248.

[7] Alexander B. Smith, Bernard Locke, and William Walker, "Authoritarianism in College and Non-College Oriented Police," *Journal of Criminal Law, Criminology and Police Science* 58, no. 1 (1967): 128–132; and by the same authors, "Authoritarianism in Police College and Non-Police College Students," *Journal of Criminal Law, Criminology and Police Science* 59, no. 3 (1968): 440–443.

[8] For comment by police on the negative aspects of their jobs, see Watson and Sterling, Chapter 1.

[9] Wayne R. LaFave, *Arrest: The Decision to Take a Suspect into Custody* (Boston: Little, Brown, 1965), pp. 102–124.

[10] Irving Piliavin and Scott Briar, "Police Encounters with Juveniles," *American Journal of Sociology* 70 (September 1964): 212. This is an excellent study of the interaction between police and juveniles based on observations in the San Francisco–Oakland area.

[11] Piliavin and Briar, p. 213.

[12] Jerome H. Skolnick, *Justice Without Trial: Law Enforcement in Democratic Society* (New York: John Wiley and Sons, 1966), Chapters 6 and 7.

[13] See Herbert L. Packer, *The Limits of the Criminal Sanction* (Stanford: Stanford University Press, 1968).

[14] Edwin M. Schur, *Crimes Without Victims* (Englewood Cliffs, N.J.: Prentice-Hall, 1965).

[15] Tom Wicker, "What Have They Done Since They Shot Dillinger?" *New York Times Magazine,* December 28, 1969, p. 5.

[16] For further discussion of the FBI, see Fred J. Cook, *The FBI Nobody Knows* (New York: The Macmillan Company, 1964).

[17] Police use of the discretion available to them is covered from several points of view by many social scientists, among them: David J. Bordua, *The Police: Six Sociological Essays* (New York: John Wiley and Sons, 1967); Arthur L. Stinchcombe, "Institutions of Privacy in the Determination of Police Administrative Practice," *American Journal of Sociology* (September 1963): 150–160; and Skolnick, in the work cited above.

[18] See discussion, Chapter 2.

[19] *New York Times,* May 11, 1970, p. 1; May 12, 1970, p. 18.

[20] Joseph Goldstein, "Police Discretion not to Invoke the Criminal Process: Low-Visibility Decisions in the Administration of Justice," *Yale Law Journal* 69 (March 1960): 586–587.

[21] Arthur Niederhoffer, "The Quantity and Quality of Justice," *The Administration of Justice in America: The 1968–69 E. Paul duPont Lectures on Crime, Delinquency and Corrections* (University of Delaware, 1970), p. 42.

[22] Paul Chevigny, *Police Power: Police Abuses in New York City* (New York: Pantheon Books, 1969), Chapter 15.

Lawyers, Prosecutors, and Judges: The Bureaucratization of Justice

7

"I should like to have every court begin, I beseech ye in the bowels of Christ, think that we may be mistaken."
Learned Hand, *Morals in Public Life*, 1951 (quoting Oliver Cromwell)

"There is no such thing as justice—in or out of court."
Clarence Darrow, Interview (Chicago, 1936)

For the man in the street, the criminal justice system means the courtroom and its related procedures. It is in the courtroom that the sheep are separated from the goats, the bad from the good, and the label of guilt is finally affixed to one who previously had passed unmarked among his fellows.

The courtroom scene is unquestionably the most dramatic portion of the sequence of events by which justice is administered. In the public mind, truth is discovered through courtroom trial by combat between two equally armed lawyer-gladiators, with the struggle presided over by the judge (as repository of the wisdom of the community). The adversary model of courtroom procedure is England's contribution to world culture; and, in the United States, not only do the descendants of the original British settlers look upon this model as holy, but the most recent arrival from abroad, not yet English-speaking, still acculturated in the ways of an alien society, seizes upon this model and proclaims it the very symbol of the freedom for which he came to this country.

The picture is an attractive one. For most defendants in most courtrooms in the United States, *it is not true. It is not true, and probably never has been.* In pre-industrial America, the adversary–due process model of criminal justice may have existed in small towns and rural areas which were essentially classless; it may also have existed for some members of the urban upper and middle classes. For all others, and especially the poor, justice frequently was dispensed by vigilantes, lynch mobs, or tyrannical magistrates, if indeed the victim or other members of the community had not already handled the matter informally. Urbanization and industrialization have been accompanied by a vast increase in the number of criminal acts requiring adjudication. At the same time, especially in the last twenty-five years, there has developed an increasing sensitivity to the need for protecting individuals from the vast public and private bureaucracies which structure our complex society. Our response in the criminal justice system has been to provide increasing numbers of courts, judges, prosecutors, and defense attorneys who theoretically function according to the role models of the adversary system, but who in fact have transformed the adversary system into a bureaucratic machine for the handling of presumed malefactors. This transformation has occurred because of the necessity of dealing with vast numbers of defendants in a society that has not allocated (possibly because it cannot) sufficient resources to the criminal justice system to make the dream of Anglo-American justice come true.

PROSECUTORS

The crusading D.A. is an American folk hero. In movies, radio, television, and newspapers, he is the twentieth-century urban equivalent of St. George, Sir Lancelot, and all the other heroic gentlemen who defended goodness and virtue against the dragon of corruption. Not only was a series entitled "Mr. District Attorney" an enormous popular success on radio and television for a good many years, but Thomas E. Dewey, Earl Warren, and Hugo Black, to mention a few out of hundreds, are men whose public reputations were first established as public prosecutors. The position of district attorney, or state's attorney, or attorney general is one of the most frequent jumping-off places for a career in politics and public office.

While the popular image of the prosecutor is that of an avenging angel, strangely enough his role, according to the standards of Anglo-American justice, is not that of inquisitor but of one who sees that justice is done. The prosecutor is supposed to defend the public interest in its largest sense, and as defender he is required to secure the release of any defendant whom he feels is unjustly held. Thus, in the words of the Canon of Ethics of the New York State Bar Association,

> The primary duty of a lawyer engaged in public prosecution is not to convict, but to see that justice is done. The suppression of facts and the secreting of witnesses capable of establishing the innocence of the accused is highly reprehensible.[1]

These noble precepts are honored probably more in the breach than in the observance. With some notable exceptions, such as Homer S. Cummings (upon whose exploits the movie *Boomerang* was based),* most prosecutors are interested in a "batting average" of convictions. The boast that he has never lost a case is considered to be worth many votes at election time. While some prosecutors are interested in the position as an end in itself, most look upon the job as a way station on the road to higher office. Frank Hogan, district attorney for New York County, is an exception remarkable for his dedication and devotion to the office he has held for almost thirty years. Unlike most other prosecutors he has made the district attorneyship the culmination of his career. His office is unusual not only because of his continued incumbency but because of his de-politicization of the process whereby the assistant district attorneys are chosen. In most jurisdictions the assistants to

---

*The plot of the movie concerned an unpopular drifter who had been charged with the murder of a clergyman, and who was saved from almost certain conviction by the efforts of a public prosecutor who was convinced that the wrong suspect had been arrested.

the prosecutor (who is usually himself an elected official) are patronage appointments. These subsidiary positions are rewards to the politically faithful for previous political services rendered. Since salaries are frequently low, and the selection process is dictated by political considerations, many prosecutors' offices suffer from poor quality, part-time, largely uninterested assistants. Hogan's office, on the contrary, has become a model for the country because of his continuing battle to upgrade salaries and appoint young lawyers on merit rather than for political reasons, and his insistence on full-time service. This is not to say, of course, that patronage appointments cannot result in dedicated, highly competent assistant prosecutors, only that the patronage problem, compounded by an inadequate salary scale, frequently mitigates against quality appointments.

Prosecutors, like the police, exercise discretion in their enforcement of the law. Whereas the policeman may decide whether or not to arrest, the prosecutor may decide whether or not to prosecute.* For example, in New York County since 1962, assistant district attorneys have been assigned to the complaint room to supervise the drawing up of complaints against recently arrested suspects. If the assistant district attorney feels there will be no conviction in the case (either misdemeanor or felony), he will file a form which advises the judge that there is insufficient evidence in the case and asks for a dismissal, a request the judge almost invariably grants. While 10 to 15 percent of the cases brought into the

---

*In Kings County (Brooklyn, New York), a progressive police practice in most felony arrests is to set up a conference at the station house between the arresting officer, his superior, and an assistant D.A. If the assistant district attorney feels there are insufficient grounds for holding the suspect, the case will be dropped and he will not be charged with the crime. (If however, a suspect has been brought into the station house against his will, the motion to dismiss the case will not be made by the district attorney until the initial arraignment. This is to guard against suits for false arrests.) How widespread this kind of station house conference between police and the prosecutor's office in felony cases is, is impossible to say. It would appear to be a useful device, however, for sparing the accused unnecessary time in detention and the courts unnecessary time in considering an improper charge.

complaint room are dismissed as a result of this preliminary screening, the remaining cases which go to court are very rarely dismissed (except when witnesses fail to appear). Even where there is evidence sufficient to sustain the *prima facie* case necessary for the initial arraignment in felony court, if there is a lack of additional corroborative evidence the prosecutor may still recommend dismissal.

The decision not to prosecute can also be made after the initial arraignment. Indictments in felony cases in New York (and other states which use the grand jury) come, of course, from the grand jury rather than from the prosecutor's office. Theoretically, the district attorney presents all cases to the grand jury and leaves the decision as to the filing of the bill to the jurors. In practice, however, the district attorney usually has sufficient influence over the grand jury to get the decision he wants, that is, the jurors return a "true bill" when the district attorney wants to prosecute, and dismiss when the district attorney wants to dismiss.* There are times however, most especially in politically hot cases, when the prosecutor may prefer to be relieved of the responsibility of decision. In those cases he will present his witnesses and evidence in such a neutral manner as to throw the burden

---

*Ideally, the grand jury is supposed to be a panel of responsible citizens who independently determine whether there is sufficient evidence to warrant proceeding with the prosecution of the accused. In reality, the grand jury is frequently under the control of and completely responsive to the district attorney. This has come about because it is the district attorney who determines the manner of presentation of the case to the grand jury; that is, he decides on the witnesses to be summoned and the evidence to be adduced. Since no defense is presented, and the defendant rarely risks self-incrimination by appearing, it is difficult for the grand jury to do other than that which the district attorney requests. On occasion, grand juries have been known to rebel against prosecutors and judges and proceed independently. The rarity of such occurrences is indicated by the headlines which "runaway grand juries" invariably inspire. On the whole, it is fair to say that district attorneys influence the preliminary pre-trial stages of a prosecution through their initial decision whether or not to prosecute and through their control of the indictment process.

Although the grand jury was abolished in England in 1933, it is still used for felonies in all the federal district courts of the United States as well as in many state courts.

of continuing the prosecution on the grand jury. Cases involving political disturbances, well-publicized homicides, and accusations of police brutality are examples of the kinds of cases for which prosecutors prefer to share responsibility with the grand jury.

After the indictment, information, or complaint has been filed against the accused, some district attorneys will feel obliged to prosecute every case. Others however, have a somewhat different view.[2] Some are reluctant to press forward in a case where they feel the evidence is weak and an innocent man might be convicted. Some feel that it is morally wrong to prosecute where they have strong doubts as to the guilt of the accused; and some district attorneys, for example, have even been known to go so far as to use polygraph (lie-detector) examinations in robbery cases where time has elapsed between the crime and the arrest and there is no corroborating witness. It is true that, by singlehandedly making the decision to terminate a prosecution (judges rarely deny the prosecutor's motion to dismiss), the prosecutor is in effect trying the case by himself, without benefit of judge or jury, and thus short-circuiting the judicial process. On the other hand, such a concerned prosecutor is perhaps doing no more than the standards of his office and the canons of ethics require: defending the public interest by seeing that the guilty are prosecuted but the innocent released.*

BAIL

The bail system is the process whereby, for a financial consideration, an accused individual is released from cus-

---

*LaFave and others have pointed out the racial and class discriminatory patterns underlying the exercise of police discretion in the matter of arrests. If there are similar patterns in the exercise of prosecutors' decisions in the matter of prosecutions, they are more subtle and complex. Probably an important factor underlying the exercise of such discretion is the state of public opinion and the likely repercussions of the decision on the district attorney's political career. Whether there is any marked favoritism toward wealthy and upper-class people, for example, is hard to document. In the Woodward case, cited in Chapter 3, the wealthy defendant was released without indictment; in the Sam Sheppard case, the wealth and prominence of the accused seemed only to whet the determination of the prosecutor to prosecute.

tody pending his later appearance in court. The purposes underlying the bail system are first, to permit the defendant (who is legally *innocent* until proved guilty) his freedom so that he may continue his normal pursuits, support his family, arrange his affairs, and aid his attorney in the preparation of his defense; and second, to protect the community by insuring his subsequent court appearance through damaging financial penalty if he does not appear.

The bail system originated in England at a time when real property was frequently the security for the bail bond, the loss of which was extremely serious for the accused. In the United States today the system has lost much of its rationality. Judges frequently set bail for defendants according to the severity of the alleged offense; that is, the bail for armed robbery will normally be higher than the bail for shoplifting. If, however, the defendant is well-to-do he will be able to meet any reasonable bail; if he is poor he may not be able to raise even the most nominal sum. Thus, in terms of protecting the community, money bail determined by the severity of the crime is entirely irrational. It serves only to keep the poor, no matter what their characters, their roots in the community, or their alleged offenses, in jail, while more well-to-do defendants are set free virtually without regard for the consequences in terms of public safety.

Bail, furthermore, has become a commercial enterprise of dubious propriety. In many big city jurisdictions it is customary for defendants to raise bail through the services of a commercial bail-bondsman. The bondsman will provide the bail needed upon receipt of a fee, the amount of which is a percentage of the required bail. This fee is actually the premium on an insurance policy furnished by a commercial insurance company that undertakes to indemnify the court should the defendant fail to appear at the appointed time. In addition, the bail-bondsman may request (particularly if the defendant is not known to him personally) collateral, in the form of bank accounts, insurance policies, and real estate, for the reimbursement of the insurance company if

143

the defendant forfeits his bail through non-appearance. Defendants who are too poor to pay the premium, or who cannot post acceptable collateral, may be refused by the bail-bondsman. The net result of the bail system thus, in the words of former Supreme Court Justice Arthur Goldberg, is that, "at best, it is a system of checkbook justice; at worst, a highly commercialized racket."[3]

The only legitimate use of the bail system is to insure the presence of the defendant at a future court proceeding. Bail itself is not a punishment or a form of restitution for an offense.

> A recognizance of bail, in a criminal case, is taken to secure the due attendance of the party accused, to answer the indictment, and to submit to a trial, and the judgment of the court thereon. It is not designed as a satisfaction for the offense . . . but as a means of compelling the party to submit to the trial and punishment which the law ordains for his offense.[4]

It is, however, a common occurrence for judges to use bail to detain in custody defendants whose release is felt to be either dangerous or unpopular. Those accused of capital offenses, for example, are frequently denied bail, or bail is set so high as to be virtually unattainable. The same can be said for those accused of other particularly heinous, violent crimes, such as forcible rape or felonious assault. Similarly, political protesters are frequently held in custody prior to trial because they are unable to meet the bail requirements set by unsympathetic judges. Communist defenders such as Eugene Dennis and Elizabeth Gurley Flynn, who were tried during the 1950s for their preaching of Communist doctrine, could not realistically have been held to be a physical danger to the community; nor were they likely to fail to appear for trial; yet high bail was set for each. Similarly, nonviolent civil rights demonstrators, such as Martin Luther King, Jr., and the thousands of white and black youngsters who joined with him in the many marches he led protesting segregation in the South during the 1960s, could not be considered a physical danger to the communities in which they were arrested; yet they too were forced to post thousands of dollars of bail money before they could be released. It is obvious in these cases that bail was used by the courts to harass and make more difficult the work of political organizations sponsoring protests that were unpopular, either with the courts or with the communities in which the trials were to occur.

It is clear that the use of the bail system as a weapon against political protesters is indefensible in a free society and is simply a manifestation of the weakness of local courts in protecting the constitutional rights of this type of defendant against public pressure. The relationship of the bail system to defendants who are felt to be *dangerous* rather than unpopular (or even subversive) is more ambivalent however. While the community, under our Constitution, has no right to be protected from opinions it deems loathesome, it has a right to protection from those who would murder, rape, or rob. Although it is true that the accused is presumed innocent until his guilt is legally established by a court trial, there are many circumstances in which freeing of the accused may reasonably be thought a danger to the community. The release of a suspect caught committing a violent crime, for example, is properly viewed with trepidation. The bail system, however, provides a very poor mechanism for the handling of such a suspect. To set bail so high as to be unattainable is simply to deny bail and therefore operate outside the context of the system. To set it high enough for an affluent suspect to reach, but too high for the poor man, is to give unjustifiable preferential treatment on the basis of financial means. To set bail low enough for any suspect to reach is, if the suspect is truly dangerous, to deny protection to the community.

In 1835, a man named Lawrence fired two loaded pistols at President Jackson. He missed, and when he was brought up for preliminary examination, Chief Judge Krantz of the District of Columbia Circuit questioned the prisoner and supposed that in view of his very limited economic circumstances, $1,000 bail would be enough, because, "To require larger bail than the prisoner could give would be to require excessive bail."

When the government objected because of the danger to the President's life, Judge Krantz in effect threw up his hands,

increased the amount to $1,500 and remarked that if the *ability
of the prisoner alone were to be considered, $1,500 was too
much, but if the atrocity of the offense alone were to be considered, it was too small.*

That there is not, then, a single intellectually respectable
judicial decision on this problem in the ensuing 129 years is
probably a testimonial to the fact that *the riddle is insoluble in
the context of the bond system.*[5]

The rising crime rate in the District of Columbia led the
Nixon administration, in 1970, to urge passage of legislation
permitting "preventive detention" of dangerous suspects.
The impetus for a law of this type came from the feeling
that recent reforms of District of Columbia bail procedures,
whereby the amount of bail was determined by the financial
circumstances of the accused rather than the nature of the
offense, had led to a sharp rise in violent crimes by suspects
who were out on bail. The legislation, enacted in July 1970,
provides that prosecutors can, in prescribed cases, request
the court to permit pre-trial imprisonment of accused persons considered to be dangerous. Such detention would be
authorized for suspects meeting stated criteria only after a
hearing, to be held shortly after arrest, wherein a high
standard of proof of the dangerousness of the accused is
required of the prosecution, and right to counsel and the
right of appeal are insured for the defendant. If the court
grants the prosecutor's request for the detention of the
accused, the date for the trial must be set within sixty days.[6]

Proponents of this legislation felt that it would provide
a method of holding dangerous suspects without relying on
the misuse of the bail system, or the hypocrisy of two standards of justice: one for the poor and one for the rich. Those
defendants who were not dangerous would be released on
minimal bail; the others would be held for a relatively speedy
trial. More defendants would be freed, the jails would be
unencumbered, and the community would be protected.
Opponents of this system, however, are fearful that the
device will be used to harass and detain in custody political
opponents of the administration, Negroes, and poor people.

They suggest that the solution to the problem of the dangerous suspect is a speedy trial. A speedy trial as a practical matter, however, is not always possible, and in at least some cases may even work to the disadvantage of the defendant by not giving him sufficient time to prepare his defense. While many of those detained undoubtedly will be Negroes (most suspects, like most residents of the District of Columbia, are black), it is also true that the victims of crime in the District of Columbia are predominantly Negro, and there is evidence that community sentiment in the District is heavily in favor of preventive detentioń. Ronald Goldfarb, a civil libertarian and probably the outstanding authority in the United States today on the subject of bail, has taken the position that with proper procedural safeguards preventive detention is probably on the whole less unjust to criminal suspects of all kinds, rich and poor, black and white, than the present money bail system.[7] In reality the law has been drafted with sufficient ambiguity that either the hopes of those who drafted it or the fears of those who oppose it can come to pass (and therein, perhaps, lies its real threat). Whether the District of Columbia Act will be a device for denying bail to the poor and unpopular, or a highly sophisticated tool used with fairness and objectivity in the war against crime, depends almost entirely on how the law is administered.

In respect to defendants whose release does *not* pose a threat to the public safety, the bail system is likewise of dubious value. Again, if the bail is set high enough to be a real deterrent to flight, it may well be beyond the reach of many criminal defendants except the very well-to-do. Thousands upon thousands of those brought into court are literally unable to make *any* bail. For them, unless the system is revised, there is no such thing as pre-trial release; for them, the bail system in effect does not exist. For many people, moreover, bail is superfluous because they simply cannot leave and become fugitives from justice. They don't know where to go, how to support themselves when they get there, or who will care for their families while they are gone. Frequently they haven't even the money with which to flee.

Aside from the hardship to individual defendants, the social cost of an unreformed bail system is great. The defendant who is in prison cannot support his family, which then frequently requires public support. When he is released, moreover, even if he is acquitted, his job may be gone and his family may have lost their home through eviction. He, himself, may have become embittered, and he certainly will have had undesirable exposure to experienced criminals in the institution in which he was confined. There is a good probability that he may have been subjected to unwanted homosexual advances, or, if he is physically slight, he may even have been raped by fellow inmates. The cost of maintaining him in jail, moreover, is considerable. A large percentage of the inmates in city and county jails are those awaiting trial. Were they to be removed from these facilities, either the cost to the public would be less or, with the same budget, far better services could be provided for those who should not be released or who are serving short term sentences.

In recent years several experiments in bail reform have been successfully mounted. Probably the most publicized has been the Vera Foundation's Manhattan Bail Project. The Vera Foundation was founded in March 1961 by Louis Schweitzer, a businessman-philanthropist, as a non-profit charitable institution to further equal protection of the laws for the indigent through research into neglected aspects of criminal law and procedure. The Manhattan Bail Project was begun in October 1961 in cooperation with the New York University Law School, and was designed to determine whether selected indigent offenders, released without bail, could be relied upon to appear in court when scheduled. Defendants brought into Manhattan's Criminal Court were interviewed by N.Y.U. law students, asked a series of questions, and scored on the basis of their answers. The questions related to the defendant's community ties, residence, family, job, background, prior criminal record, and associations. The information provided was then checked for accuracy by one of the Vera staff, and normally, within an hour, a summary of the findings and a recommendation for disposition of the accused was ready for consideration by the court. Those charged with homicide, most narcotics offenses, and certain sex crimes were not eligible for consideration. The project appears to have been very successful. As of August 31, 1965, more than thirty-five hundred accused persons had been released on their own recognizance, and of these 98.4 percent returned to court when required. The rate of non-appearance was lower than the 3 percent forfeiture rate of bail bonds. Vera officials believe, moreover, that some cases of non-appearance were due to mishap or misunderstanding rather than willful failure to attend. The Manhattan Bail Project has since been taken over by the New York City Office of Probation. An interesting sidelight on the effect of pre-trial release is that defendants released on bail are subsequently convicted far less often than those not released, even when the backgrounds and offenses of the two groups are similar. Vera kept records on a control group of accused persons whose release was not recommended although they were eligible by Vera standards. Sixty percent of those recommended by Vera for pre-trial release were not convicted, while only 23 percent of the control group were not convicted. Of those in the first group who were found guilty only one in six went to jail; in the control group 90 percent were given jail sentences.

Success of the bail project led Vera to undertake a summons project whereby desk officers in precinct station houses screen those arrested in a manner similar to the screening of defendants in the bail project, for the purpose of issuing summonses to appear in court rather than subjecting the accused to the usual arrest and arraignment procedures. The summons procedure is not only a more dignified way of handling the accused; it avoids the disruption caused by an overnight jail stay and the delays attendant on the arraignment process. It also frees the arresting officer from the necessity of spending hours in the station house and in court processing the accused prior to the initial arraignment, and permits the police officer to go back to his post for his normal duties. The Manhattan Summons Project, during the two years of its operation under Vera auspices, showed a "jump" rate of 2.6 percent, which compares favorably with the rate for bail jumping. In July 1967, the Summons Project was taken over by New York City and instituted on a city-wide basis. During its first year of operation the jump rate rose to 4.5 percent, a low rate still but one sufficient to cause concern to the municipal authorities. There is reason to believe, however, that refinement of the screening process will improve the situation.

It seems clear that the bail system as presently constituted is inefficient, hypocritical, and archaic. Basically, the problem of handling arrested persons before trial should be considered on two levels: for suspects whose release may pose a danger to the community, and for all others. In regard to the latter group, the pattern for reform seems fairly clearly indicated by the successful pilot projects which have been mounted recently. It may even be that bail is meaningless for this latter group of defendants, and the system as we know it may be close to dissolution. For the small group of dangerous defendants, money bail is not the answer either. New methods of handling such persons must be devised, keeping in mind the constitutional rights of the accused as well as the safety of the community.

DEFENSE LAWYERS

Of all the rights claimed for accused persons, the one most accepted by and acceptable to all segments of our society is the right to counsel. Even the most non-civil-libertarian types, who normally view with despair or alarm attempts to "coddle" criminals, will concede that, for the person enmeshed in the toils of the law, the lawyer is a necessity if the outcome of the trial is not to be a mere travesty of justice. While state and local officials may have gotten administrative and budgetary jitters over the prospect of providing thousands of defendants with counsel, few criminal procedure decisions have been as uncontroversial in principle as *Gideon v. Wainright,* wherein the Court declared,

> Reason and reflection require us to recognize that in our adversary system of criminal justice, any person hailed into court, who is too poor to hire a lawyer, cannot be assured a fair trial unless counsel is provided for him.[8]

The most obvious problem in regard to providing counsel for the accused arises when the accused is indigent. Who will pay for the cost of his lawyer? The response in most jurisdictions has been either a public defender's office (the counterpart of the public prosecutor's office), or services provided by a legal aid society. For the past several years, poor defendants in many localities have also had available to them the services of lawyers employed by the Office of Economic Opportunity's Legal Services Program. Dozens of neighborhood law offices have been opened throughout the country, where help is available in both civil and criminal cases. There are, however, still many areas of the country where unfortunately there are neither legal aid societies nor legal services programs.

Public defenders are paid, of course, from public funds, just as judges and prosecutors are. Legal aid attorneys, however, are usually employees of a legal aid society whose funds traditionally came from private sources (including bar associations). In recent years, however, these funds have been supplemented by grants: on the federal level from poverty program funds, and on state and local levels from general tax funds. Most indigent defendants are thus represented either by public defenders or by legal aid or legal services lawyers. A relatively small percentage may also have private attorneys who are appointed by the court, and who generally do not receive compensation except in capital cases. Some defendants, of course, can afford to hire attorneys of their own, and are represented by private counsel. Whereas conceptually the defense attorney is the champion of the accused, whose only concern is the safeguarding of his client's interests, in reality, the relationship is somewhat more ambivalent. In addition to his concern for

151

his client, the defense attorney must also consider his own relationship to the prosecutor, the judge, and even to other court officials. To understand why this is so, one must examine the principal method of disposing of criminal cases in most metropolitan courts today: plea bargaining.

PLEA BARGAINING

In a study of the handling of criminal cases in a major American city, Abraham S. Blumberg, a sociologist-attorney, found that well over 90 percent of felony cases that were processed past the indictment stage were disposed of by guilty pleas on the part of the accused. To put it another way, fewer than 10 percent of those accused of a major crime elected to go to trial. More than nine-tenths pleaded guilty and, in effect, threw themselves at the mercy of the court. In this survey which covered fifteen years (from 1950 to 1964 inclusive), the percentages of those who pleaded guilty ranged from 91.05 percent in 1956, to 94.58 percent in 1961. While this may be a rather high figure (especially for felony indictments), almost every other study of guilty plea practices in the United States confirms the general picture, and it can probably be safely said that fewer than one-third of all those accused of crime will ever go to trial.*

The picture revealed by these statistics is very different from the conceptual model of the adversary system that is normally thought to be the reality of courtroom practice. Instead of each accused standing trial before an impartial judge and jury, with skilled legal counsel who examine the case from different points of view, we find rather that most defendants arrive in the courtroom only to stand before the judge and plead guilty. The differences between the adversary system that is supposed to be and the plea bargaining system that exists in most jurisdictions are great, and are

---

*Abraham S. Blumberg, *Criminal Justice* (Chicago: Quadrangle Books, 1967), p. 29. In a nationally televised speech on August 10, 1970, Chief Justice Warren E. Burger stated that 90 percent of all criminal suspects plead guilty and do not stand trial. *New York Times,* August 11, 1970, p. 1.

differences in quality, not simply in degree. Why has this change occurred? Why do so many defendants agree to waive their right to trial and content themselves with appearing before the judge for sentencing?

The reasons for the growth of the plea bargaining system are complex, but probably the single most important factor has been the necessity of handling a vast and increasing number of criminal defendants. While statistics purporting to show a rapidly rising crime rate are in many cases of dubious validity, there is no question that the absolute number of crimes is rising and the absolute number of defendants to be processed is also rising. At the same time, the amount of money the public is willing to invest in courts, prosecutors, and jails is not keeping pace with this increase. The result is a court system that is overburdened to the point of near breakdown in some communities.* Under these circumstances there is enormous pressure on the prosecutor, the judge, the defense attorney, and the defendant to handle the case in whatever manner will dispose of it most quickly.

The prosecutor faced with more cases than his staff can handle knows that if he holds out for trial, the trial will be inordinately delayed. If the defendant is in jail awaiting trial, a possibly innocent man may be incarcerated for months, and his family may become destitute and have to be supported at public expense. The defendant, moreover, is taking up jail space of which there is a desperate shortage (which the newspapers frequently comment upon). If the defendant is out on bail pending trial, he may be committing further crimes — a phenomenon on which the mass media also frequently comment. The longer the trial is delayed, furthermore, the harder it is to round up the witnesses and present an effective case. The prosecutor is thus very much disposed towards any acceptable method that will cut down

---

*In January 1968, all civil trials were suspended in Supreme Court in Bronx County, New York, so that all the judges, courtrooms, and facilities could be used to help clear up the backlog of criminal cases awaiting trial in that county. Administrative Board of the Judicial Conference of the State of New York, "Report for the Judicial Year July 1, 1967–June 30, 1968," *Legislative Document* no. 90 (1969): 40–41.

the number of cases awaiting trial. The obvious way out, in most cases, is to accept the offer of a defense attorney to plead his client guilty to an offense less than that charged on the indictment or information; for example, a defendant accused of felonious assault will be willing to plead guilty to simple assault, or one charged with armed robbery will admit attempted robbery. So great are the pressures on a district attorney to bargain pleas rather than bring cases to trial that defense lawyers can at times actually use the threat of going to trial as a weapon against a hard-nosed prosecutor.

The defense attorney may thus find the prosecutor receptive to an offer to bargain a plea. The former is restrained, however, by the necessity of acting responsibly in terms of what the prosecutor requires. The defense attorney cannot risk forcing a plea on a prosecutor which will result in adverse publicity for either the prosecutor or the judge. A client who is dangerous to himself or the community must be put away, and a plea bargained accordingly. While superficially this may seem a convenient and efficient way to handle accused persons, it is obvious that it is a short-circuiting of the entire judicial process, because the determination of guilt has been made, not by judge or jury in open court, but by two lawyers in private conference. The defense attorney, moreover, needs to maintain good relationships with the prosecutor and the judges, since long after his client of the moment has passed from the scene, the defense attorney will be practicing in the same court, and will need the good will of other actors in the system to perform his own roles as efficaciously as possible. It is this almost symbiotic relationship with the prosecutor, the judge, and sometimes even court personnel that makes the relationship of the defense lawyer to his client ambivalent. He cannot devote himself exclusively to the interest of his client if he must also show some concern for the interests of the prosecutor, and even the judge.

The judge too, is co-opted into the system by the pressure resulting from the overload. Although judges routinely question defendants as to whether they have received any consideration in return for their guilty pleas, no matter how vigorous the denial on the part of the accused, the judge knows the truth: that these pleas are the results of deals between the lawyers on both sides. The judge closes his eyes to the obvious and permits the process to go on because he, too, knows that he must clear up the backlog of cases awaiting trial. The trial system itself is moreover so cumbersome in many jurisdictions that, even were the calendars not overloaded, inordinate delays would occur. Cases may be called for trial many times, and each time a continuance may be requested by one side or another. Sometimes witnesses are not present, sometimes counsel is occupied at another trial, and sometimes even the defense counsel wishes to give his client more time to raise the fee before proceeding with the trial. Innumerable motions are made and appeals taken from the rulings on those motions. It is sometimes difficult to impanel an acceptable jury. Judges therefore welcome an opportunity to dispose of a case without trial. For the judge who is insecure, incompetent, or inexperienced, moreover, accepting the recommendation of the prosecutor is an easy way to solve many problems and maintain good working relationships with the members of the legal fraternity with whom he is likely to have day-to-day contact.

> It is clear that the "grand tradition" judge, the aloof, brooding, charismatic figure in the Old Testament tradition, is hardly a real figure. The reality is the working judge who must be politician, administrator, bureaucrat, and lawyer in order to cope with a crushing calendar of cases. A Metropolitan Court judge might well ask, "Did John Marshall or Oliver Wendell Holmes ever have to clear a calendar like mine?" The Metropolitan Court judge who sits in a court of original jurisdiction, in his role as trial judge, arbiter, sentencer and awarder, cannot avoid the legal, interpersonal, and emotional dynamics of the small group of court regulars and those hangers-on who are inevitably present in a criminal court.[9]

So socialized into the system are many judges that they become angry with a defendant who refuses to avail himself of the opportunity to bargain a plea, and who insists instead on going to trial. It is a rare judge, if indeed there is any, who can avoid a feeling of institutional rejection when confronted with a recalcitrant defendant. Almost all judges become angry at this rejection, either openly or secretly, and express their anger in the form of sentences more severe than would have been dispensed had the defendant pleaded guilty to the same charge.

The willingness of judges to accept prosecutors' recommendations is reenforced by the tendency of judges to associate covertly, and perhaps unconsciously, with the prosecution in criminal cases. This is probably because they see themselves as defenders of the state, and as such tend to be more solicitous of the rights of the community than of the rights of the accused. It is noticeable that judges are far more impartial in their handling of opposing counsel in a civil, rather than a criminal case.

> When the charge is a serious crime the judge often drops the facade of objectivity and patience. He frequently excoriates the defense, and the jury as well when they bring in a verdict of "not guilty." So jealous is the judge in pressing for a conviction that his wrath burns the prosecutor who seems to lag in the pursuit. In the Spock conspiracy case Judge Francis J. W. Ford "was heard whispering urgently to his clerk 'Tell that son of a bitch (the prosecutor) to cut it out! He'll blow the case if he keeps this up and get us all in trouble.' "[10]

Once the judge sees himself as the ally of the prosecutor, it is easy for him to reject the adversary model of criminal justice and accept the bureaucratic model. He loses his mediator role and becomes an opponent of the defendant.*

---

*In fairness it must be said that, at least up to the present, one area in which the judge performs in conformity with the stated role model of a judge is in his relationship to the probation officer assigned to the case. Probation is essentially an institutionalized method for personalizing justice, that is, a formal way of taking into account the individual circumstances and history of each defendant, and tailoring the disposition of the case to fit those circumstances. In spite of heavy caseloads, in the more progressive court systems probation officers have not yet been entirely co-opted by bureaucratic considerations, and perform their jobs vis-à-vis defendants with considerable integrity. Judges also, at least in those cases where there are no outside pressures, use probation recommendations properly: to individualize sentences in order to achieve whatever beneficial results may be possible.

DUE PROCESS: THE ADVERSARY MODEL V. THE BUREAUCRATIC MODEL

It is obvious that the reality of our judicial process conforms far more closely to the bureaucratic model than to the adversary ideal. Criminal defendants are adjudicated, not by a trial involving two equally matched lawyer-champions arguing before a neutral judge and jury, but by private negotiations between actors who have at least as much claim on each other as the defendant has on any one of them. The judicial process, in short, is one of bargaining and compromise; it is informal, and indeed exists only through its ability to short-circuit and bypass the prescribed, formal procedures.

The development of the plea bargaining system was not planned. There are no heroes or villains (depending on one's point of view) in this story. The bureaucratic mode of handling most criminal defendants rose from necessity: the necessity of handling with limited public resources vast numbers of accused persons. To make the adversary model a reality would require an almost unimaginable increase in the outlay of tax funds: enough money to re-create for each criminal defendant in our vast megalopoli the unhurried, personal attention that can only exist in small, well-integrated communities. To say that such an increased outlay is unlikely is an understatement. If such funds are to be obtained, an intense struggle by reformers will be necessary, and to succeed in such a struggle they will have to be prepared to answer the obvious question of the economy-minded: What's wrong with the bureaucratic model anyway?

What, if anything, *is* wrong with the bureaucratic model? Isn't it in reality just as good as the adversary ideal that is so hard to effectuate? The plea bargaining system, it must be conceded, works better than many purists would care to admit. Given honest, reasonably conscientious officials and attorneys, it is quite unlikely that a totally innocent person, with no past record, will be wrongfully convicted. The chances of such a miscarriage of justice are probably less under the plea bargaining system than if the accused were forced to appear before a jury of his peers. Further, the informality and flexibility of the system makes it possible for errors to be corrected with a minimum of difficulty at various stages of the process, even occasionally beyond conviction (though before sentence). The defense attorney, prosecutor, or judge who feels that something is wrong in the way that the case is developing, that some bit of evidence does not ring true, that some witness is not what he appears to be, can easily and quickly call an informal conference of the participants in the case to convey his disquiet. This would be far more difficult if formal adversary procedures were adhered to. The plea bargaining system is also economical in terms of both time and money. This economy is, of course, its supreme virtue, and its virtual raison d'être. While this may not provide conceptual justification, it is of enormous practical importance because it is quite possible that our society cannot afford the outlay of man-hours and money needed to create an adversary system for the overwhelming number of accused persons our present laws and criminal justice system produce.

However, the plea bargaining system cannot be looked upon with complacency. Despite its very considerable virtues, it has inherent within itself some very dangerous defects. For one thing, it is more vulnerable to corruption at the hands of dishonest, incompetent, or lazy participants than is the adversary system. The very informality and secrecy of the procedures and the negotiations out of court lend themselves to questionable arrangements which may be adverse to the interests of both defendant and society at large.

Even, however, assuming the honesty and competence of the actors, the plea bargaining system has serious drawbacks. While it is true that a totally innocent man with no previous record may benefit from the system, an accused with a previous criminal record is almost certain to be harmed. There are few persons in prison who are totally innocent; there are many who are innocent of the specific crime for which they were convicted, but who are or were guilty of something else. The defense attorney considers that a client's past criminal record impairs his (the attorney's) bargaining power vis-à-vis the district attorney. This is particularly true if the client has a record, not only of past convictions, but of arrests which did not lead to conviction due to considerations such as lack of evidence. In such a case, the defense attorney will in all likelihood feel (probably correctly) that the district attorney will not settle for anything less than a plea of guilty to some charge somewhat less than that in the indictment, complaint, or information. The result is that any defendant with a questionable past record is going to be pleaded guilty by his attorney, even if he is innocent of the specific charge against him. In a true adversary system, in which evidence of the specific charge would be needed for conviction, he might be found not guilty; in the plea bargaining system he will surely plead guilty to something. A member of the Fortune Society* with a long criminal record recently recounted an occasion when he wished to face trial for the crime with which he was charged, but his attorney (who was privately retained by the defendant's family) threatened to withdraw from the case unless the accused agreed to bargain a guilty plea. When the defendant protested, the lawyer explained that, should the client go to trial and be convicted, he could be sentenced to sixty years in prison. Such a sentence would not only be hard on the defendant, the lawyer explained, but would be bad for his own reputation as a defense attorney.[11]

The plea bargaining system, while it may under-protect certain kinds of criminal defendants, may also over-protect others, thus denying society the protection it ought to have against some dangerous criminals. In a large city, the pressure of moving the cases of thousands of defendants is so great that frequently district attorneys are virtually forced to accept pleas of guilty to charges far less than the offense in question warrants. Murder is reduced to homicide, rape is reduced to simple assault, and burglary is reduced to unlawful entry. Minimal punishment is sometimes dispensed

---

*A group of ex-convicts organized for self-help.

by the judge in accordance with a previously struck bargain. The bitter comments by policemen about revolving-door justice, where arrested persons plead guilty, are sentenced, and are out on the street again repeating their nefarious crimes, stem partly from the practice of accepting very much reduced guilty pleas and imposing perfunctory sentences. In New York City, for example, a threat by the Legal Aid Society, which handles 70 percent of the criminal cases in the New York City criminal courts, to take these cases to trial is enough to bring the toughest district attorney to the bargaining table in a chastened mood. With the court calendars crammed to the point of chaos, the thought of any substantial proportion of the Legal Aid cases going to trial is so horrifying that other considerations pale by comparison. This does not mean to say, of course, that any hardened criminal can get a minimal sentence by simply demanding a trial. Many defense attorneys will cooperate with the prosecutor in seeing that "bad men" are sent away for a long time. While in one sense this may be reassuring to the public, it is at the same time a clear indication of how, under the plea bargaining system, the determination of guilt is removed from the hands of the judge and the jury to the hands of the "defense" attorney and prosecutor.[12]

Serious as these criticisms of the plea bargaining system are, they are perhaps not as great as a drawback which is apparent to very few defendants, attorneys, or public officials. The bureaucratic model of criminal justice has an adverse social effect on society not only because it may harm individuals caught up in the system, but because it has a stultifying effect on the law itself. The very essence of the bureaucratic system is that each member performs the task assigned to him and works harmoniously with other members of the system. Each actor, as they say, goes along to get along. Every one plays ball with everyone else, and so the ball game goes on. But therein lies the difficulty: there is no one on either team to stand back and say, "Is this what we should be doing? Is this the game we ought to be playing?" In short, everyone is concerned with procedure, no one with the nature of the law itself. Everyone concentrates on what to do with a particular defendant under the system as it currently operates. No one has time or motivation to wonder whether the system itself may not need change.

Oliver Wendell Holmes said that the law grows in response to "the felt necessities" of the time. A meaningful system of law is a dynamic system, one which changes as society changes. The plea bargaining system tends to make static what should be dynamic, to blunt those felt necessities. The criminal law cannot change or respond as long as those who participate in the adjudicatory process are concerned primarily with not rocking the boat, that is, disposing of the accused in such a way as to cause the least possible disruption to the system.

The naive observer may, at this point, protest, "But the criminal law has changed! It is changing so rapidly that the courts are in a state of chaos and confusion. Never have criminals had so many rights. Why, look at Miranda and Escobedo!" Our naive friend is quite correct. The criminal law *is* changing rapidly, and at the very same time the adjudicatory process has become increasingly bureaucratized. The point is, however, that these changes in the criminal law *have not been brought about by the normal actors in the plea bargaining system. They have been brought about by outsiders.* These outsiders have acted as mavericks, goads, sometimes even thorns in the flesh. They have forced the system, often painfully, to reexamine the rules by which it operates.

Who are these outsiders? Most frequently they are attorneys for civil liberties or legal defender groups whose interest in a particular case is centered on the law itself rather than on the needs of a particular client. A great proportion of recent defendants whose cases have established significant precedents relating to a change in the criminal law have been represented by attorneys affiliated with the Legal Aid Society, the NAACP Legal Defense Fund, or the ACLU. Many others have been represented by a court-appointed attorney who has volunteered his services to the court primarily because of his ideological interest in the law itself. These attorneys tend to see justice not only in procedural terms but in substantive terms as well. In the case, cited in Chapter 1, of Edward Johnson confined as a narcotics addict in a punitive rather than rehabilitative program, it is very doubtful that one of the courtroom regulars who normally defend indigent criminals would have done for the defendant what Counsellor Meltzner did for Johnson: freed Johnson through mounting an attack on the unfairness of the law itself. Similarly, Miranda's attorney claimed not that his client was handled badly by the police but that the "good" handling of prisoners was basically unfair. Attorneys who make claims such as these must be outsiders. No working system can tolerate the disruption caused by their iconoclasm.

Not many attorneys have the temerity (or even the inclination) to play the role of gadfly. The system is not kind to those who do play such a role, and in fact many criminal lawyers have been punished for defending a client by attacking the system. In a recent study of courtroom behavior, Niederhoffer and Smith point out that small-time criminal lawyers, "the courtroom regulars," can commit minor transgressions against the propriety of the courtroom and established courtroom procedures with impunity.[13] At worst they will be subjected to a reprimand by the judge. Outstanding criminal lawyers such as Clarence Darrow, Samuel Leibowitz, F. Lee Bailey, Melvin Belli, Jake Ehrlich, and William Fallon, on the other hand, have all been in serious trouble stemming from their courtroom defense of a client. Clarence Darrow and William Fallon, for example, were tried for subornation of perjury; others were threatened with disbarment. Though these attorneys were probably less ideologically oriented than legal defender organization attorneys, their relationship to the system was the same: they were outsiders. By refusing to take a plea and forcing the case to trial, they were fighting the system. They bargained with neither the court nor the district attorney, and once their independence of the system had been established, their transgressions could not be forgiven as they might have been for those who played in the regular ball game. While legal defender lawyers probably suffer less direct punishment, those who are outstandingly aggressive in support of particular clients, for example, William Kunstler defending the Chicago Seven or northern attorneys defending civil rights clients in southern courtrooms, find themselves punished in such ways as citations for contempt of court.

The plea bargaining system is the reality of criminal adjudication in the big cities of the United States, and despite its obvious imperfections, it works reasonably well to process the multitude of criminal defendants brought before the courts each year. It is fortunate that it works as well as it does, because the likelihood of creating or re-creating a true adversary system consonant with the ideals of Anglo-American jurisprudence is slim indeed, given the present political complexion of our government and the prevailing ordering of priorities on the use of public funds. In a sense, however, the plea bargaining system is a temporary expedient, a device whose usefulness may decrease with the passing of time. Its effect on the growth and change of the law itself is slow and imperceptible, but it is real and, with the passage of time, will become ever more apparent. Only to the extent that outsiders, in the form of non-co-opted attorneys and interest groups, enter the system, will this stultifying effect be counteracted.

It is very difficult even to suggest reforms that would lead toward the realization of the adversary system, which unquestionably is a superior system for the handling of accused persons in a democracy. The likelihood of sufficient men, money, and time to handle each defendant as he should be handled in the name of justice and liberty seems almost hopelessly remote. Perhaps this is simply another way of saying that a free, open society that creates so many criminal defendants cannot perform as a free, open society should, at least insofar as these most unfortunate of its citizens are concerned.

Perhaps the answer is that a successful democratic

society must find ways to reduce the number of those accused of crime. Perhaps we make too many modes of conduct criminal; perhaps we warp too many personalities so that they become enemies of society instead of builders of the social order. Perhaps we must think, not in terms of tinkering with the criminal justice system, but in terms of basic, needed reforms, both in the law as a device for social control and in the larger institutions of society itself, so that fewer individuals will come to be regarded as criminally deviant. It is totally unrealistic to think of providing adversary system treatment for all offenders, ranging from those who go through stop lights, to alcoholics, to marijuana-smoking students, to pugnacious husbands, to burglars, muggers, rapists, and murderers. It may conceivably be feasible to provide such handling for those who commit serious *malum in se* crimes of violence or potential violence. Other ways need to be found for handling other types of defendants. Are their offenses really so antisocial that they need be labelled criminal? Can their conduct be corrected without sanctions of such seriousness that they must be dispensed by a court rather than an administrative agency? Certainly no simple, short range solutions will resolve the dilemma in which our courts find themselves: desiring to do justice to each individual, and at the same time to protect society with resources that are not only inadequate but which can in no foreseeable way be made adequate for the job that needs to be done.[14]

Selected Readings

Blumberg, Abraham S. *Criminal Justice*. Chicago: Quadrangle Books, 1967.

Blumberg, Abraham S. *Law and Order: The Scales of Justice*. Chicago: Aldine, 1970.

Carlin, Jerome E. *Lawyers' Ethics*. New York: Russell Sage, 1966.

Frank, Jerome. *Courts on Trial*. Princeton: Princeton University Press, 1949.

Friedman, Laurence, and Macauley, Stewart. *Law and the Behavioral Sciences*. Indianapolis: Bobbs-Merrill, 1969.

Goldfarb, Ronald. *Ransom.* New York: Harper and Row, 1965.

Schur, Edwin M. *Crimes Without Victims.* Englewood Cliffs, N.J.: Prentice-Hall, 1965.

Schwartz, Richard D., and Skolnick, Jerome H. *Society and the Legal Order.* New York: Basic Books, 1970.

Simon, Rita James, ed. *The Sociology of Law: Interdisciplinary Readings.* San Francisco: Chandler, 1968.

Notes

[1] New York State Bar Association, *Canons of Professional Ethics; Canons of Judicial Ethics,* adopted January 1909, amended January 1963 (Brooklyn: Edward Thompson Company), p. 13.

[2] The information concerning the activities of district attorneys in the New York area was gathered from informal conversations with present and former assistant district attorneys. See also David S. Worgen and Monrad G. Paulsen, "The Position of the Prosecutor in a Criminal Case," *The Practical Lawyer* 7, no. 7 (November 1961): 44–58.

[3] Arthur J. Goldberg, "Foreword" to Ronald Goldfarb, *Ransom* (New York: Harper and Row, 1965), p. ix.

[4] *Ex parte Milburn,* 34 U.S. 704 (1835), as quoted in Goldfarb, p. 10.

[5] Caleb Foote, as quoted in Goldfarb, pp. 13–14. Italics added.

[6] P.L. 91-358 District of Columbia Court Reform Act, July 29, 1970.

[7] For a full discussion of bail and preventive detention problems, see Goldfarb, *Ransom,* and Goldfarb, "A Brief for Preventive Detention," *The New York Times Magazine,* March 1, 1970, p. 28.

[8] *Gideon v. Wainright,* 372 U.S. 335 (1963).

[9] Blumberg, pp. 122–123.

[10] Arthur Niederhoffer and Alexander B. Smith, "Power and Personality in the Courtroom: The Trial of the Chicago 7," *Connecticut Law Review* 3, no. 2 (Winter 1970–1971): 240.

[11] Statement made by Chuck Briganski, a member of the Fortune Society, Brooklyn College, July 21, 1970.

[12] Blumberg, pp. 92–94.

[13] Niederhoffer and Smith, p. 240.

[14] For a somewhat different approach to the problem of reform of the criminal justice system, see Herbert L. Packer, "Two Models of the Criminal Process," *University of Pennsylvania Law Review* 153, no. 1 (November 1964): 1–68. For a discussion of the labelling of modes of conduct as criminal, see Edwin M. Schur, *Crimes Without Victims* (Englewood Cliffs, N.J.: Prentice-Hall, 1965).

8

The Rights of the Accused: The Supreme Court, Due Process, and Police Procedure

"We must never forget that it is a *constitution* we are expounding."
John Marshall, *McCulloch v. Maryland* (1819)

"We are under a Constitution, but the Constitution is what the judges say it is."
Charles Evans Hughes, Speech at Elmira, New York (1907)

"The history of liberty has largely been the history of the observance of procedural safeguards."
Felix Frankfurter. *McNabb v. United States* (1943)

"A policeman's affidavit should not be judged as an entry in an essay contest."
Abe Fortas dissenting, *Spinelli v. United States* (1969)

The Supreme Court and the American System

If the adversary system is England's contribution to jurisprudence, the United States Supreme Court is strictly an American contribution. The Constitution, which was adopted in 1789, established a high court with power to sit in judgment on and reverse the actions of both national and state legislatures—or at least so John Marshall said. Article III provides for a court called a Supreme Court in which "the judicial power of the United States shall be vested," and whose jurisdiction will "extend to all cases, in Law and Equity arising under this Constitution, the Laws of the United States, and Treaties made . . . under their Authority." In this brief, ambiguous section the founding

fathers set up an institution which has had enormous influence on the shape of American law and society.

Whether those who drew up the Constitution meant for
the Court to have the power of judicial review, that is, the
power to sit in judgment on legislative (especially congressional) acts, is a question about which historians have
argued heatedly since 1803. Nor is it clear whether, if the
Supreme Court were intended to have such power, the
electorate who voted to ratify the Constitution understood
this to be the case. In any event, in 1803, in deciding the
politically explosive case of *Marbury v. Madison,* John
Marshall announced that the Supreme Court did indeed
have not only the power, but the duty of reviewing such
acts of Congress as were relevant to the cases under litigation and determining whether those acts were in conformity with the Constitution. Having thus confidently
asserted its power, the Supreme Court then very prudently
refrained from exercising that power vis-à-vis Congress for
the next half-century, until the disaster of *Dred Scott* on
the eve of the Civil War.

Whatever the merits of the historical arguments, judicial
review is today a fait accompli and an accepted part of
American government. The Supreme Court can hear cases
brought to it from the highest state courts, as well as from
the intermediate federal appellate courts. It hears a very
limited (largely insignificant) number of cases on original
jurisdiction, and a similarly small number of cases from
lower state courts.[1] While the rules of jurisdiction and procedure which have evolved since the *Marbury* decision are
fairly complex, two features are significant. In the first place,
the Court can speak *only in the process of deciding a case.
It does not render advisory opinions.* This means that if the
Court has something to say, it must wait until a suitable
vehicle in case form happens to present itself. It also means
that if any individual or group in the United States wishes to
elicit from the Court an authoritative statement or definition
of constitutional rights, it may approach the Court only by
litigating a suitable case. In short, no matter how brilliant,

167

how wise, how urgent the opinions of the justices may be, they will remain forever unheard and unsaid unless a case presents itself wherein these thoughts may be appropriately included. No law, no matter how outrageous or how patently contrary to the Constitution, is unconstitutional until the justices declare it to be unconstitutional; and they cannot so declare it until it is challenged by a case or controversy which the procedural rules of the Court permit it to hear.

Secondly, the caseload of the Court is almost entirely discretionary; that is, the Court has the power, in over 90 percent of cases requesting review, to decide which ones it wishes to hear. Furthermore, the number of cases that the Court hears is miniscule compared to the number of cases it *could* theoretically hear, and is a small fraction of even those cases requesting a hearing. For most litigants, thus, the Supreme Court as a court of last resort does not, in reality, exist. The Court itself recognizes that its function is far more subtle and complex than that of the ordinary appellate court. As Justice Frankfurter once said, "After all, this is the Nation's ultimate judicial tribunal, not a super-legal-aid bureau."[2] The Court, in deciding which cases to hear, is not primarily motivated by the justice or injustice of the lower court's verdict, or by the fate of the defendant should the review not be granted.* Its chief motivation is presumably that the question to be decided is of national significance. The Court's formal rules of procedure provide some guidance: for example, cases must arise under the laws or Constitution of the United States and present a federal question for decision; litigants must have suffered a personal injury or damage in order to have standing to sue and must have exhausted all previous remedies. In the last analysis, however, the rules of procedure are only

---

*There is evidence, however, that the justices heartily dislike, and hesitate to reject cases involving capital punishment where the defendant will be executed in the absence of Supreme Court action. See for example, Barrett Prettyman, Jr., "The Electric-Chair Case," in C. Herman Pritchett and Alan F. Westin, eds., *The Third Branch of Government* (New York: Harcourt, Brace, and World Inc., 1963), pp. 83–117.

guidelines to be more or less flexibly applied; the Court hears what it thinks is important for the Court to hear, and the definition of "importance," like the definition "national significance," is determined by the justices themselves.

While the members of the Court make the final determination as to which cases will be heard in a given term, it is worth noting that almost all the important cases decided by the Court (especially in recent years) have been shaped to some extent by judicial pressure groups. In *Griswold v. Connecticut* (the Connecticut birth control case) for example, the appellant Griswold was the director of the Planned Parenthood League of Connecticut, and the allegedly illegal acts charged were committed at her direction while acting in her official capacity; PPLC retained the attorneys who defended her and paid for the entire course of litigation; Planned Parenthood of America, of which PPLC was an affiliate, also entered a brief *amicus curiae* at the Supreme Court level. The *Griswold* case, in short, would not have reached the Court for adjudication except for the activities of a group which (at least at that point in its history) existed in large part specifically for the purpose of challenging restrictive legislation in the courts.

Griswold and Planned Parenthood is perhaps an extreme example, but dozens of others come to mind. The American Jewish Congress has been involved in almost all cases where church-state relations have been challenged; the NAACP has been active in segregation cases; and the ACLU has argued in scores of civil liberties cases. Pressure group involvement can take many forms, but probably the most frequent is the presentation of an *amicus curiae* brief at the U.S. Supreme Court level, or the providing of counsel or money to defray expenses at any level of the case. Sometimes a group may provide the litigants (as in *Griswold*) or even witnesses. Although the ACLU and the NAACP are currently the most active and well-known judicial pressure groups, not all such judicial pressure groups represent liberal points of view. Many conservative groups on occasion provide either counsel, financing, or *amicus curiae* briefs for cases in which they are interested. Administrative officials, moreover, frequently band together and act in a manner very similar to the ACLU; for example, in the *Miranda* case, the attorneys general of many states filed briefs *amicus curiae* in opposition to the position taken by the ACLU briefs *amicus curiae.*

Thus, the contribution of judicial pressure groups (whether permanent or ad hoc) is to shape the caseload of the Court by making it possible for certain cases to reach the highest appellate levels, and to influence the thinking of the justices themselves by the arguments made before the Court. Even private attorneys sometimes play a role similar to that of a judicial pressure group, as did, for example, Abe Fortas in his appearance for Clarence Gideon, in *Gideon v. Wainright.*[3]

In 1963, one Clarence Gideon, a drifter with a long criminal record, was convicted in Panama City, Florida, of breaking and entering a poolroom, a felony offense. Gideon, an indigent, had requested court-appointed counsel to represent him at the trial. The request was denied, since Florida law provided court-appointed counsel for indigents in capital cases only. After his conviction, and while confined in the state penitentiary, Gideon appealed, first to the Florida courts (which denied him relief), and then *in forma pauperis** to the U.S. Supreme Court, on the ground that the failure of the state to provide him with counsel was a denial of his due process right.

The Supreme Court not only agreed to hear the case on its merits, but appointed Abe Fortas (later Justice Fortas), of the prestigious Washington firm of Arnold, Fortas and Porter, as counsel for Gideon.

In appointing Fortas, the Court was no doubt looking for a competent attorney to represent Gideon; Fortas, in accepting the appointment, was, to be sure, motivated by his desire to help an unfortunate prisoner. It is impossible how-

---

*The procedural rules of the United States Supreme Court permit prisoners who are poor and without access to a lawyer to file an appeal in whatever way they can. Appeals have been received and heard from men who have written in pencil on grocery bags and lined note paper— misspelled and ungrammatical, but decipherable.

ever, to read Anthony Lewis's splendid study of this case without becoming aware of the fact that at least as important as the concern for Gideon as a man *was the concern, on the part of both the Court and Mr. Fortas, with the state of the criminal law.*[4] The Court was essentially looking for a lawyer good enough to reevaluate the old precedents relating to the right to counsel; Fortas, for his part, was interested in reshaping an area of constitutional law in a manner he thought desirable. Gideon's case was in effect heard by the Supreme Court, not so much because of the personality or problems of Gideon as because of the national significance of the issue presented by that case, and Abe Fortas's involvement related directly to that issue. Fortas, in this case, though he acted as an individual, did precisely what attorneys affiliated with organized judicial pressure groups do: he discussed the state of the law from a previously determined ideological vantage point.

The function of the judicial pressure group or the ideologically motivated attorney is, thus, to introduce arguments relating to value systems—the preference for one set of norms over another. To phrase the matter somewhat differently, they argue the case in its political and philosophical context. Those unacquainted with the true role of the U.S. Supreme Court are frequently horrified that such considerations should be introduced. They conceive of the judicial decision-making role in technical terms—as the finding of justice in the law books in a manner analagous to the finding of a good recipe for chocolate cake in a cookbook. But not only is it not nefarious for ideology to enter into Supreme Court arguments, it is vital that such considerations appear. Supreme Court decisions are essays in law, but law conceived in its broadest sense—as the basis on which society rests. In this context, law is almost synonymous with political philosophy. It is healthy and essential that adversaries representing different ideological points of view appear before the Court, because it is from such interchanges that the shape of the law is slowly changed to meet the changing needs of society.

In the last thirty-five years, a large proportion of the

major decisions of the United States Supreme Court have been concerned with individual rights. This is probably a reflection of increasing social concern over bureaucratization, centralization, and other institutional changes in our mass society that threaten the uniqueness and integrity of the individual. These decisions have been made in many fields: the rights of Negroes to equal treatment in education, transportation, and voting; the rights to freedom of speech and press, and equality before the law for the politically and sexually unorthodox; and the rights of suspects and defendants in criminal cases. It is important to note that concern for criminal defendants is simply part of the larger picture of concern for the rights for all individuals of whatever status and capacity. Concern for criminals is not evidence of weakness in society or of over-permissive attitudes toward evil and violence. It is, instead, merely another manifestation of the struggle to preserve the sanctity of the individual and his personality from the dehumanizing effects of over-mechanization and subordination to senseless technology.

The interest of the United States Supreme Court in the rights of the criminal defendant has gained momentum in the last ten years. While criminal procedure decisions have been handed down from time to time throughout the entire history of the Court, since World War II their number has been increasing, and in the last decade they have formed a significant part of the Court's caseload. The earliest decisions in this area attracted little public attention; more recent ones, particularly in the area of confessions and the right to counsel, have been quite controversial and have attracted attention from the public at large, as well as from those directly involved in the law enforcement field. A large number of these decisions have been concerned with the legality of various kinds of police procedures, such as how and under what circumstances the police may arrest a suspect, or search him or his home; whether wiretapping or electronic eavesdropping is permissible; how rigorously the police may question a suspect for the purposes of obtaining incriminating information; how voluntary a "voluntary" confession must be; and when a suspect is entitled to confer with counsel. While police procedure probably constitutes the largest single category of criminal procedure decisions made by the Supreme Court, several other important issues have also been of concern: the conglomeration of rights that ensure a fair trial, such as the right to a jury selected without social or racial prejudice; the right to be free from excessive prejudicial publicity; the right to reasonable bail; the right not to be placed in double jeopardy; and the right not to be subjected to cruel and unusual punishment. All of the cases in the above areas considered by the United States Supreme Court have raised new questions even while they have settled others. Basically, these cases, while seemingly concerned with the technicalities of criminal procedure, are really concerned with the kind of world we wish to live in. The questions that are left unanswered relate not only to the way this world will look, but whether such a world is even possible to achieve.

Search and Seizure

The restriction on the right of the police to arrest is the hallmark of a free society. The basic condition for freedom, as far as any individual is concerned, is that he cannot legally be seized in an arbitrary or capricious manner at the discretion or whim of any government official. It is customary to refer to the writ of *habeas corpus,* the "Great Writ," as the guarantor of personal freedom in a democracy. The reference is correct; but it should be noted that *habeas corpus* is merely a method of remedying wrongful administrative action. The writ of *habeas corpus* is a challenge to an arrest or other detention which has already occurred and which may have been illegal. The statutory and constitutional standards for the making of an arrest are of crucial importance because they prevent police action which may be very harmful to the individual. Furthermore, by establishing a standard for legal police action, they make it possible to obtain *habeas corpus* relief from other kinds of action.

No other constitutionally guaranteed personal rights are

meaningful in the absence of strict controls on the right of the police to arrest. To say that the individual enjoys freedom of speech or freedom of religion when he may be arbitrarily arrested for exercising either freedom is a contradiction in terms. In the United States, historically, purely political arrests have been relatively infrequent, at least as compared to the vast numbers of arrests that have been made for criminal activity. It is very important, nevertheless, that stringent controls be maintained over the right to arrest, for at least three reasons: (1) the Constitution exists for criminal suspects just as much as for any other individuals, and it is important that their rights be protected; (2) erosion of rights in one area leads to erosion of rights in other areas, and the protection of the criminal suspect's rights is essential for the protection of other people's rights; and (3) many activities which are political in nature, such as street assemblies, picketing, and mass demonstrations of all kinds, also fall afoul of the criminal law, and it is essential for political freedom that standards for the enforcement of the criminal law be strict and evenhanded.

The Fourth Amendment of the United States Constitution is the source of constitutional protection from arbitrary arrest.

> The rights of the people to be secure in their persons, houses, papers, and effects, against unreasonable searches and seizures, shall not be violated, and no warrants shall issue, but upon probable cause, supported by oath or affirmation, and particularly describing the place to be searched, and the persons or things to be seized.

As interpreted by the courts, the standard for a legal arrest is "probable cause." Probable cause has no precise definition but has been described as something more than mere suspicion and something less than "beyond a reasonable doubt." The policeman, therefore, can arrest only if he has sufficient reliable information to establish a fair degree of certainty in his mind that a particular individual has committed an offense warranting an arrest. Similarly, he may search either a suspect or the premises to which a suspect has had access only on the basis of probable cause, rather than on mere suspicion or a hunch; and when he does search he may normally do so only for certain categories of evidence: the instrumentalities of a crime, the fruits of a crime, or contraband (that which it is illegal to possess, such as heroin or policy slips).

Searches and seizures may be made either with or without a warrant. A warrant is an order issued by a magistrate who in effect certifies as to the soundness of the policeman's judgment that probable cause exists. If time and circumstances permit, warrants must be obtained prior to arrests or searches. Frequently, however, the fleeing of a criminal caught in the act or the threat that important evidence will be destroyed will necessitate on-the-spot police action. Such proceedings without benefit of warrant are legal, providing the police officer had probable cause for his actions.

The Constitution forbids unreasonable searches and seizures, but it does not define the term "unreasonable." The courts have held, however, that at a very minimum, an *illegal* search is unreasonable, hence unconstitutional. Theoretically, the police are thus deterred from making any but legal searches and seizures. Practice, unfortunately, does not conform with theory. The police have made in the past, and continue to make at present, thousands of illegal arrests and searches each year. The justification offered for this illegal activity varies with individual cases, but the chief reason is probably that, in the opinion of the officer, the act was necessary in order for him to fulfill his function of maintaining law and order. In the practice of his profession the policeman acquires an expertise which leads him to look upon certain kinds of people in certain circumstances as suspects and to take action against them. The fact that his standards for action vary from the legal standards established by the courts does not deter him, because in his eyes, his standards are both more relevant and more binding than the court's standards which, after all, were established by a judge who likely had never walked a beat. Where there has been a particularly nasty rape, for example, and the victim describes her attacker in general terms, it makes sense to many policemen to round up everyone in the immediate area who looks anything like the assailant. This may or may not result in the arrest of the real culprit; it positively *will* result in the arrest and detention of many entirely innocent people. The courts, presumably, weigh the claims of the community for security from rapists against the need of individuals for freedom from arbitrary arrest. The policeman, however, is not a social scientist, nor does he ordinarily wax philosophical. His job is to find criminals, and he frequently goes about it in the most direct way he knows.

Another reason for the frequency of illegal arrests and procedures in this country is that police forces often see themselves as the agents of the most politically powerful groups in the community—the Establishment. And while they treat members of these groups with respect and even deference, they may treat politically impotent individuals, such as Negroes, hippies, petty criminals, homosexuals, and drug users, with contempt or brutality. Occasionally, the illegality of police methods can be attributed to corruption within the police force. This is less frequent, however, than illegality resulting from the distortions of the police role due to faulty perception of their function and place in society.

Whatever the reasons, however, it is unfortunate but true that American law enforcement, especially at the local level, has in the past been notorious for the frequency with which police officials utilized illegal methods. It was in an attempt to remedy this condition that the "exclusionary rule" was developed and adopted by the courts. In 1914, for the first time, the United States Supreme Court ruled that evidence seized in an illegal search could not be used in federal courts.* The purpose of this ruling was obvious: to

---

Weeks v. United States, 232 U.S. 383 (1914). *Weeks* excluded illegal evidence only if seized by *federal* agents. Illegal evidence seized by state law enforcement could be turned over to federal agents and was admissible in federal courts. This so-called "silver platter" doctrine was declared unconstitutional by the United States Supreme Court in *Elkins v. United States,* 364 U.S. 206 (1960), which held that no matter who seized the evidence, if the seizure was illegal, its use in federal court was not permitted.

deter federal agents from making illegal searches by removing the incentive, that is, by forbidding the use of the seized evidence in obtaining a conviction. Thus, since 1914, no convictions have been obtained in federal courts on the basis of illegally seized evidence. Federal agents have continued, however, to make some illegal searches and seizures. The evidence thus obtained has either been used for the purpose of obtaining leads or informers, or, when appropriate, has been turned over to state law enforcement officials for use in the state courts.

Contrary to federal practice, up until 1950 relatively few states employed an exclusionary rule to deter police lawlessness. In 1949, police in Colorado illegally broke into the office of one Wolf, a physician who was suspected of being an abortionist. They seized his appointment book, which was subsequently used to obtain Wolf's conviction in state court. Wolf appealed on the ground that the use of illegal evidence by the state to obtain a conviction denied him due process of law and thus contravened the Fourteenth Amendment. Essentially, Wolf's claim was that for the state to break the law in order to convict him was basically unfair. A majority of the Supreme Court, in a decision written by Felix Frankfurter, agreed that an illegal search was contrary to the concept of "ordered liberty" and fell within the protection offered by the Fourteenth Amendment, but that the exclusionary rule was not per se required of the states. If the states chose to use the exclusionary rule as a method of disciplining their police forces they were free to do so, but there was no constitutional requirement for them to follow the federal practice adopted in the *Weeks* case. Frankfurter pointed out that, as of 1949, only seventeen states were in agreement with the *Weeks* doctrine.[5]

The force of Frankfurter's reasoning was considerably weakened when, three years later, he wrote a somewhat contradictory opinion in *Rochin v. California.*[6] Rochin was a suspected narcotics dealer whose house the police entered illegally. When they entered, they found Rochin in his bedroom, partially dressed, sitting on his bed where his wife

177

was lying. On the night table were two capsules which Rochin seized and swallowed upon seeing the officers. Assuming that the capsules contained illegal narcotics, the police grabbed the suspect, rushed him off to the hospital, and had his stomach pumped. The recovered evidence was used to obtain a conviction. Rochin appealed on the same grounds as Wolf: that the state's use of illegally seized evidence was a violation of the Fourteenth Amendment. This time Frankfurter agreed, not only that the search was a violation of the Fourteenth Amendment, but that the fruits of the search could not be used in court. The police-directed stomach pumping, Frankfurter said, was conduct that shocked the conscience.

Wolf and *Rochin,* taken together, present a confusing picture. The use of illegally seized evidence was clearly a violation of the Fourteenth Amendment and the evidence could—or could not—be used in state courts to obtain a conviction. The confusion was further compounded when the court held, in *Irvine v. California,*[7] that evidence obtained by *repeated* illegal entries by the police into the premises of the accused was admissible for purposes of obtaining a conviction. There seemed to be very little rhyme or reason behind these declarations of admissibility or non-admissibility, except perhaps the use of physical force on the defendant. Even this rationale was not clear, since the Court upheld a conviction based on the blood samples, drawn without consent from the accused, to prove his intoxication.*

There was, moreover, considerable protest both within and outside the United States Supreme Court against the notion that the states were free to do what was forbidden to the federal government. Many commentators felt that standards of due process must be comparable for state and federal

---

Breithaupt v. Abram, 352 U.S. 432 (1957). In all fairness it should be noted that the blood sample was drawn by appropriate medical personnel from an unconscious (and therefore unprotesting) patient. It is conceivable that had the defendant kicked, screamed, or otherwise struggled, or had the sample been taken by police rather than physicians, the decision of the Court might have been otherwise.

authorities; that is, what is sauce for the goose must be sauce for the gander. The dissenters in the *Wolf* case, moreover, protested that to hold a search illegal but not apply the exclusionary rule was ridiculous, because the exclusionary rule was what made the Fourth and Fourteenth Amendment guarantees against illegal seizures a reality. After several years of confusion and heated controversy, the Court finally resolved the issue in the *Mapp* case,[8] by declaring unconstitutional the use of illegally seized evidence in state courts.

Dolree Mapp was a Cleveland woman whose home was entered by the police acting on the basis of a tip that Miss Mapp was hiding a fugitive and/or a large amount of policy paraphernalia in her two-story home. When the officers initially demanded entry, Miss Mapp, after telephoning her lawyer, refused to admit them without a search warrant. Three hours later the police reappeared and forcibly entered the premises. When Miss Mapp demanded to see their warrant, a paper was held up by one of the officers. She snatched the paper and placed it in her bosom, whence it was immediately forcibly retrieved by a police officer who then handcuffed her. In the course of the ensuing search, neither the policy slips nor the fugitive was found. Some obscene literature was discovered in a basement trunk, and on the basis of this evidence Miss Mapp was subsequently tried and convicted of the crime of possession of obscene literature. On appeal, the Supreme Court held that her conviction must be set aside because the requirements of the Fourth Amendment, as incorporated in the Fourteenth, make unconstitutional the use of illegally seized evidence. The Court specifically required the states to apply the exclusionary rule to illegally seized evidence. In *Mapp*, the majority apparently bought the argument of the dissenters in *Wolf:* that the exclusionary rule was the only effective method of deterring police lawlessness and effectuating constitutional guarantees. The Court also noted that, by 1961, more than one-half of the states had adopted the exclusionary rule.

While the *Mapp* decision put an end to confusion over

the admissibility of illegally seized evidence, it did not, unfortunately, end the problem of illegal law enforcement. Critics claimed that only some of the worst excesses and the more blatant disregard of the procedural niceties were curbed, but other procedures of dubious legality continued unchecked, such as the time-hallowed police custom of indiscriminately stopping and searching "suspicious" people on the street. The police argued that to perform their function of maintaining the peace through preventing crime, they must be permitted to stop and question individuals who look or act "wrong," and they held that the professional expertise gained from years of on-the-street observation gave them a rational basis for such judgment. Others charged that to give the police such wide discretion in the matter of on-the-street stops might expose everyone who was either unconventional or disliked by the police to harassment.

In 1968, three cases came to the U.S. Supreme Court questioning the constitutionality of such on-the-spot searches and questioning. *Terry v. Ohio*[9] involved a suspect who was stopped and searched by an experienced police officer who had observed the suspect apparently "casing" a store for robbery. *Sibron v. New York*[10] concerned a patrolman who questioned, and then reached into the pocket of a man whom he had observed over a period of eight hours to be in conversation with known drug addicts. In *Peters v. New York*[11] the suspect was collared and searched by an off-duty veteran policeman who saw Peters prowling around his (the policeman's) apartment house hallway. In each of these cases incriminating evidence was found: Terry had a gun, Sibron had heroin, and Peters had burglar's tools. Each defendant moved to suppress the incriminating evidence on the grounds that the police in each case had not had probable cause to make either the stop or the search.

In deciding these cases the Court was faced with a number of difficulties, some conceptual and some practical. If the Court were to declare that under certain circumstances policemen need not have probable cause in order to conduct a stop and search, then how much meaning would be left in *Mapp v. Ohio?* If probable cause was not to be the clear-cut constitutional standard for legality in searches and seizures, what standard would take its place? On the other hand, if the Court were to insist on a far higher standard for action than the police had traditionally observed regarding on-the-street stops and searches, would, or even could, the police obey such a decision? Were the police, in fact, correct in maintaining that a more flexible standard for street questioning was essential for proper law enforcement?

The Court decided that an on-the-street stop for brief questioning accompanied by a superficial search or patting down of external clothing was something less than a full-scale arrest and search in the constitutional meaning of those terms, and therefore could be conducted on grounds somewhat less than the traditional probable cause. In *Terry,* the Court felt that the policeman's expertise, acquired through thirty-four years on the job, invested his decision to stop and search Terry with sufficient reasonableness to pass constitutional muster. In *Peters,* the Court split on the question of whether the patrolman had probable cause, or only reasonable suspicion as a justification for his search and seizure of the suspect.* All the justices agreed, however, that the search under the circumstances was not unreasonable. In *Sibron,* however, the Court agreed with the defendant's contention that the policeman had insufficient grounds for his search of Sibron's pocket. The state had justified the patrolman's search on the ground that an experienced officer could logically have deduced from Sibron's lengthy conversation with known addicts that Sibron was selling drugs, since only selling and the negotiations connected with such sales would have required such protracted interaction. The Court rejected this argument and held that the officer had no reasonable grounds for the search.

---

*"It is difficult to conceive of stronger grounds for an arrest short of actual eyewitness observation of criminal activity." C. J. Warren, *Peters v. New York,* at 66. "I do not think that Officer Lasky had anything close to probable cause to arrest Peters." J. Harlan (concurring), at 74. Truth is in the eye of the beholder.

Very few working policemen would agree with the Court's finding in *Sibron,* and many policemen will see the police action in this case to be fully as reasonable as the police action in *Terry* or *Peters.* This suggests that something more than reasonableness or unreasonableness underlies the divergent result in *Sibron. Terry* and *Peters* were concerned with crimes of violence or potential violence; *Sibron,* however, involved infraction of a morals law. It may be that in balancing the equities, that is, the need of the community for protection against the right of the individual to be free from police harassment, the Court was willing to tip the balance in favor of community protection only where violent crime was concerned, especially in cases where the policeman had reason to fear for his own safety. In *Sibron,* however, the alleged offense was not a violent one, and traditionally it has been in the area of the enforcement of morals legislation that the greatest amount of police harassment of suspects has occurred. In the eyes of the Court, thus, *Sibron* may have appeared to be a case where neither the community nor the policeman was endangered by a *violent* criminal suspect, and the alleged offense was of such nature that an unchecked police force might resort to considerable illegal harassment of suspects. The Court therefore tipped the balance in favor of the defendant, apparently concluding that Sibron was more likely to need protection from the police than the community from Sibron.

To the criticism that in *Terry* and *Peters* the Court was backing away from the *Mapp* decision, Justice Warren responded,

> Street encounters between citizens and police officers are incredibly rich in diversity. . . . Encounters are initiated by the police for a wide variety of purposes, some of which are wholly unrelated to a desire to prosecute for crime. Doubtless some "field interrogation" conduct violates the Fourth Amendment. But a stern refusal by this Court to condone such activity does not render it responsive to the exclusionary rule . . . it is powerless to deter invasions of constitutionally guaranteed rights where the police either have no interest in prosecuting or are willing to forego successful prosecution in the interest of serving some other goal.[12]

The Court said, in short, that no purpose would be served by too slavish an adherence to the exclusionary rule since the exclusionary rule only deterred the police *to the extent that the police wished to carry a case to the courts for prosecution.*

There are many reasons why a policeman may arrest or search other than a desire to prosecute the offender for a crime. The most important of these, perhaps, is that often when a policeman detains a minor offender, he is not so much interested in arresting him as in obtaining him as an informant. Once incriminating evidence is found, it matters little to the suspect that the search was illegal: the path of least resistance is to purchase freedom by supplying the police with information on more important criminals. Even in important cases, moreover, where prosecution rather than information is the controlling consideration, the finding of contraband, for example, inevitably shifts the balance of forces against the suspect. Courts tend to rationalize the legality of police behavior when the results in terms of evidence prove the police to have been correct in their original suspicions. The norms of police organization also put pressure on the police to confiscate harmful objects such as narcotics or weapons, so that even if prosecution fails, the policeman feels that at least he has protected the community to the extent of removing dangerous commodities from circulation. For all these reasons, the exclusionary rule is only a partially effective deterrent to illegal police action, and the *Terry, Peters,* and *Sibron* decisions are not so much a backing away from *Mapp* as a recognition of the realities and necessities of police procedure.[13]

There is some evidence that the U.S. Supreme Court is willing to give the police considerable leeway in obtaining reliable, objective evidence against a suspect, especially where the crime is one of violence or potential violence. In recent cases, the Court has indicated that even a dragnet fingerprinting campaign might be permissible if the police had prior permission from a judge.[14] The Court has also permitted the use as evidence of a robber's clothing—"mere evidence"—as opposed to the usual fruits of the crime, instrumentalities of a crime, or contraband.[15] The Court has also lowered the standards for the use of wiretap evidence and non-testimonial evidence, such as blood and urine samples drawn from the body of the accused. (The use of body fluids as evidence presents Fifth Amendment as well as Fourth Amendment problems. As least one justice— Black—has consistently held that if a man's conversation cannot be used to convict him, then neither can his blood, urine, or exhaled breath. Black's concept of *self*-incrimination extends to the flesh as well as the spirit.)

Thus, in the area of searches and seizures, the U.S. Supreme Court has shown itself quite sensitive to the implications for a free society of a lawless police force and, through the extension of the exclusionary rule, has attempted to apply the most effective judicial deterrent available. At the same time it has shown a sophisticated awareness of the realities of police procedures in our big cities and is willing to be permissive of police action that results in the prosecution of the obvious culprit, but has relatively little potential for harassment of innocent, though perhaps unpopular, citizens.[16]

Wiretapping and Electronic Eavesdropping

In considering the constitutionality of government wiretapping and electronic eavesdropping, the basic problem is that the authors of the Constitution were not acquainted with telephone taps or electronic microphones. The Constitution talks of invasions of privacy in terms of unreasonable searches and seizures, referring obviously to physical entries by police officials into private premises. With the advent of modern electronic devices, snooping without physical penetration of the premises became a reality, and the question immediately arose whether a search for evidence via a tapped wire, or by means of an electronic listening device, was a search within the meaning of the Fourth Amendment. In *Olmstead v. United States,*[17] a case involving wiretapped evidence against a bootlegger, Chief Justice Taft, writing for a majority of the United States Supreme Court, held that a wiretap was not a search within the meaning of the Fourth Amendment, since there was no seizure of a tangible object, and since the evidence in question was obtained through the sense of hearing rather than by the usual physical act of searching. Four justices dissented vigorously, including Brandeis who protested that the intent of the founding fathers was obviously to protect the right of privacy—the right to be let alone—and that the Fourth Amendment must, therefore, be interpreted broadly enough to handle problems stemming from technological advances. Holmes was repelled by the "dirtiness" inherent in wiretapping and the unattractive role that governmental officials were forced to play.

> We have to choose, and for my part I think it is a less evil that some criminals should escape than that the government should play an ignoble part.[18]

Six years later, the question of whether a wiretap was a search within the meaning of the Fourth Amendment was mooted when Congress passed the Federal Communications Act, Section 605 of which provides:

> No person not being authorized by the sender shall intercept any communication and divulge or publish the existence, contents, substance, purport, effect, or meaning of any such communication to any person.

The courts subsequently interpreted this passage as applicable to both state and federal agents as well as private persons, and to messages both within the state or between two states.[19] While the average English-speaking layman might thus conclude that wiretapping was made illegal for everyone all over the United States, the United States Department of Justice and the Federal Bureau of Investigation read Section 605 and came to the conclusion that unauthorized interception of telephone messages was permitted *if no divulgence takes place.* Moreover, divulgence in the Department's lexicon was interpreted as to forbid publication or use in evidence but to permit use by agents in the preparation of cases for prosecution (that is, as leads). As a result of this somewhat unusual interpretation of Section

605, federal agents continued to employ wiretapping as a method of gathering evidence in federal cases. In 1939, the United States Supreme Court held that neither interception nor divulgence was permissible, and that even leads developed from wiretaps could not be used in federal courts.[20] State agents however, continued to wiretap despite Section 605, and in 1952, in *Schwartz v. Texas,*[21] the United States Supreme Court held that while Section 605 forbade such state action, the state courts were nevertheless not constitutionally compelled to exclude such illegally gathered evidence. Five years later this decision was modified slightly in *Benanti v. United States,*[22] when Chief Justice Warren held that the federal courts must exclude wiretap evidence illegally gathered by state agents, even if there was no collusion between the two sets of law enforcement officials. (Left undecided was the question of whether such evidence could be used in state courts.)

In a very real sense, however, the *Nardone, Benanti,* and *Schwartz* decisions were irrelevant, since both the United States Department of Justice and most of the states continued their operations in total disregard of what the United States Supreme Court had to say. The United States Department of Justice has ordered wiretaps from 1931 to the present time, with the exception of a brief interval in 1941, and has justified this practice by the idiosyncratic interpretation of Section 605 cited above. To criticisms that the Department ought not to be doing what the Supreme Court has so plainly said was illegal, the Departmental response has been a bland statement that it wiretaps only when "national security" is involved. The United States Supreme Court has been so ineffective in curbing wiretapping that some states passed laws specifically permitting what the federal law prohibits.

> The best known of these state laws is that of New York, which authorizes the state courts to issue orders which permit the tapping of wires for a specified length of time. . . . The Supreme Court of the United States held in 1957 that every New York policeman who taps a wire under one of these orders and

subsequently repeats what he has heard is guilty of a federal crime. But, despite the Supreme Court's clear statement that this is a federal crime, New York courts continue to issue wiretap orders, New York police continue to tap wires and to testify in court and the Department of Justice continues to look the other way.[23]

No one knows how many illegal wiretaps are ordered by state and federal officials every year. It is clear that the occasional official figures issued far understate the real numbers, and there is some evidence that many thousands of wiretaps are authorized annually by law enforcement officials, in addition to the thousands of unauthorized, totally illegal wiretaps placed by private individuals. Complicating matters still further is the fact that eavesdropping today is probably more commonly and more effectively done by electronic devices such as hidden microphones ("bugs") and parabolic receivers than by wiretapping. Electronic eavesdropping is not covered by Section 605 and, until recently, the United States Supreme Court held that the Fourth Amendment did not cover electronic eavesdropping abuses unless a physical trespass was involved.[24] As a result, eavesdropping by anyone, including private persons, was legal under federal law and in all but seven states until 1968. In six of these seven states, moreover, eavesdropping was legal if done by authorized persons on court order.

In an attempt to remedy the more obvious abuses inherent in this state of statutory and constitutional anarchy, the United States Supreme Court struggled for years to restrict electronic eavesdropping practices without going back to the ultimate constitutional question which had been decided so unsatisfactorily in *Olmstead:* was eavesdropping by a government official on a private individual's conversation a prohibited search within the meaning of the Fourth Amendment? To avoid upsetting the *Olmstead* decision the Court went so far (in *Silverman v. United States*)[25] as to assert that sticking a spike microphone into a party wall a short distance until it made contact with a heating duct in a house was a physical trespass forbidden by the Fourth Amendment, even though the physical penetration of the

187

microphone into the defendant's premises was miniscule.

The Court also developed the principle that an unauthorized disclosure of a confidential communication is permissible if the disclosure is made by or with the consent of one of the parties to the conversation. In *On Lee v. United States*,[26] an undercover agent of the Federal Narcotics Bureau entered the defendant's premises with the latter's consent and, while conversing with him, elicited several incriminating statements. The narcotics agent had on his person an electronic transmitter which conveyed On Lee's statements to another agent outside the premises. Similarly, in *Lopez v. United States*,[27] an Internal Revenue agent who falsely represented himself as willing to accept a bribe, instead recorded Lopez's illegal offer on a pocket tape recorder. In both cases the Court reasoned that when the defendants made their incriminating statements to parties who subsequently turned out to be undercover agents, they assumed a risk that the other party to the conversation might not be trustworthy. The rationale was a kind of caveat emptor policy with relation to conversations. Thus, when James Hoffa made incriminating statements to an undercover government informer who had entered Hoffa's hotel suite under false pretenses, the Court held that Hoffa should not have been so naive as to trust the informer. The majority of the Court felt that the evidence had been obtained not by an invasion of Hoffa's privacy, but rather because of Hoffa's misplaced confidence in the undercover agent.

> The argument is that Partin's failure to disclose his role as a government informer vitiated the consent that the petitioner gave to Partin's repeated entries into [Hoffa's hotel] suite, and that by listening to the petitioner's statements Partin conducted an illegal "search" for verbal evidence. . . .

> Where the argument falls is in its misapprehension of the fundamental nature and scope of Fourth Amendment protection. What the Fourth Amendment protects is the security a man relies upon when he places himself or his property within a constitutionally protected area, be it his home or his office or his automobile. . . .

> Partin was in the suite by invitation, and every conversation which he heard was either directed to him or knowingly carried

on in his presence. The petitioner, in a word, was not relying on the security of the hotel room: he was relying upon his misplaced confidence that Partin would not reveal his wrongdoing. . . .

Neither this Court or any member of it has ever expressed the view that the Fourth Amendment protects a wrongdoer's misplaced belief that a person to whom he voluntarily confides his wrongdoing will not reveal it.[28]

Despite the earnest efforts of the Court to avoid reevaluating *Olmstead,* the question of whether information obtained by eavesdropping or wiretapping was therefore obtained by an unconstitutional search simply would not go away. Finally, in 1967, in *Berger v. New York,*[29] the Court overruled *Olmstead* by holding that conversations are protected by the Fourth Amendment, and an eavesdrop is a constitutionally impermissible search. Berger was convicted of conspiracy to bribe the chairman of the New York State Liquor Authority on evidence obtained by a series of wiretaps placed by the district attorney of New York County. The wiretaps were placed pursuant to a New York State law, which authorized certain administrative officials to request a court order for a wiretap if there were reasonable ground to believe that evidence of a crime might thus be obtained. The persons to be eavesdropped on and the telephone number involved had to be specified, and the order was effective for only two months unless renewed. Berger appealed his conviction by challenging the constitutionality of the New York State statute under the Fourth Amendment. The Court reversed Berger's conviction on the ground that the sweep of the New York statute was far too broad. To pass constitutional muster, reasonable ground would have to be the equivalent of probable cause, and the crime, the place to be searched, and the conversations to be seized would also have to be specified.

The *Berger* decision freed Berger, at least temporarily, but it clearly opened the door to the legalization of wiretapping and electronic eavesdropping. While the decision did much to end the absurdities and strained interpretations forced on the Court by the *Olmstead* decision, nevertheless, by bringing conversations under the protection of the Fourth Amendment, the Court paradoxically opened the door to legalized electronic surveillance. The Court defined its position even more clearly in *Katz v. United States,*[30] decided shortly after *Berger.* Katz was convicted of transmitting betting information in violation of federal law, on the basis of evidence obtained from an FBI bug of a public telephone. Once again, the conviction of the defendant was reversed because of procedural irregularities. (In this case, although the FBI had had sufficient grounds for the search, and had carefully limited the scope of its surveillance, no proper warrant had been obtained.) At the same time, the Court clearly indicated that electronic eavesdropping is constitutionally permissible under restrictions similar to those required for traditional searches.

In 1968, Congress, taking advantage of the broad hints dropped by the Court in *Berger* and *Katz,* enacted, as Title III of the Omnibus Crime Control and Safe Streets Act, a series of regulations establishing guidelines for legal wiretapping and eavesdropping. The Act is quite complex, but the substance of it tries to create as close a parallel as possible with the traditional restrictions on the usual kinds of physical searches and seizures; that is, the person and place to be searched must be specified, the application must be made by an administrative official to a judge, and the evidence procured may be used only for specific purposes.

Although *Berger, Katz,* and Title III have made contributions towards bringing order into the chaos of the wiretapping and eavesdropping field, confusion, constitutional and otherwise, is still the order of the day. The establishment of legal guidelines has probably not ended the prevalent police custom of illegally tapping and snooping electronically, nor has it ended the totally unauthorized, completely illegal use of eavesdropping by private individuals. Worse yet, the legal guidelines established in Title III have so many loopholes that it is questionable whether any effective control over law enforcement officials has been established at all. For one thing, there cannot be any advance notice to the subject that his premises are about to be searched, as there is when the warrant is produced in a conventional search. For another, although Title III requires the termination of a tap after thirty days (unless an extension is obtained from the court), how can such termination be enforced and/or verified? Is overhearing a conversation a search or a seizure, or both? If a conversation is heard, but not used, is it a seizure, or merely a search? Can there be such a thing as an overheard conversation that is not used? How can a defendant protect himself against a tape that has been tampered with? What controls are there over the police to ensure that the tape recording introduced into evidence is accurate and intact? Is a tap which is conducted over a period of time a single intrusion into the suspect's privacy, or a series of intrusions? If it is a series of intrusions, can it be legally justified on the basis of only one showing of cause? What about the rights of innocent third persons who may be party to the conversations under surveillance? Are not the rights of such persons infringed far more than would be the case in a traditional search? Title III also provides for eavesdropping without a warrant in cases involving either national security or organized crime. Such searches may be conducted for forty-eight hours before a warrant must be obtained from the court. Who defines "national security" and "organized crime," and how can the duration of the warrantless search period be verified?

Wiretapping, as Justice Holmes said so long ago, is a dirty business. It is probably impossible to conduct a wiretap without violating the civil liberties of the defendant, and the opportunities for lawless police work, harassment, and invasion of privacy are almost unlimited. It is a procedure which raises the hackles of every civil libertarian. *But, it is a very efficacious tool in law enforcement which police and prosecutors cannot and will not give up regardless of the state of the law.* Perhaps the police should not be asked to give up such an effective weapon in the war against crime. Presumably, this would account for the support given to

Title III by liberals such as the late Senator Robert Kennedy. No happy solution to the problems raised by wiretapping suggests itself at this point. Perhaps the best that can be hoped for is a political culture and climate that frowns upon police harassment of individuals and unnecessary intrusions into their private lives. Technology is not an unmixed blessing.

Confessions and the Right to Counsel

In 1649, John Lilburn, on trial for treason, refused to answer questions, saying, "I am upon Christ's terms, when Pilate asked him whether he was the Son of God, and adjured him to tell him whether he was or no; he replied, 'Thou sayest it.' So say I: thou, Mr. Prideaux, sayest it, they are my books. But prove it." The right not to be forced to testify against oneself is historically very old. Talmudic law, a compilation of ancient Hebrew legal dicta, practices, and precedents predating the Christian Era, records the maxim *ein adam meissim atsmo rasha,* a man cannot represent himself as evil.[31] The same notion appears in the Common Law a thousand years later as *nemo tenetur seipsum accusare,* no one is obliged to testify against himself. The principle reappears in the Canon Law of the Catholic Church, and in the Fifth Amendment of the United States Constitution.

The idea that a man should not be forced to incriminate himself in a criminal investigation no doubt arose in reaction to the inquisitorial practices of governmental authorities seeking to root out treason, heresy, subversion, or whatever offense or mode of thought seemed most threatening to the status quo of the time. Whether the issue involved Catholics rooting out apostate Protestants, Protestants searching for heretical Catholics, the Spanish Inquisition looking for Jews and disbelievers, or the Stuart kings investigating political opponents—whatever the issue historically, investigators and prosecutors have used physical torture to elicit confessions from hapless defendants. It was in reaction to this type of proceeding that the notion of a right against self-incrimination developed. It was the memory of what had gone before that led the founding fathers to incorporate into the Fifth Amendment the phrase "nor shall any person be compelled in any criminal case to be a witness against himself." As Chief Judge Calvert Magruder once said, "Our forefathers, when they wrote this provision into the Fifth Amendment of the Constitution, had in mind a lot of history which has been largely forgotten today."[32]

Traditionally, the U.S. Supreme Court has excluded physically coerced confessions on the ground that such confessions might very well be unreliable or untrue because of the duress used against defendants to produce them. *Brown v. Mississippi*,[33] in 1936, was the first Fourteenth Amendment due process confession case decided by the United States Supreme Court. The conviction of the defendant was reversed when the record was found to indicate that the deputy who had presided over the beating of the defendants conceded that one of them had been whipped, but "not too much for a Negro; not as much as I would have done if it were left to me." The Court, rejecting the law officer's evaluation of Negro psychology, decided that even a slipshod whipping might make the resulting confession unreliable, and therefore inadmissible. In 1944 the Court rejected a confession obtained after thirty-six hours of continuous interrogation of the defendant by the police.[34] The exclusion of such confessions was, at least in part, an attempt by the Court to discipline lawless police officers by refusing them the conviction they had worked to obtain.

As the quality of police work improved in the years after World War II, the use of severe physical torture by the police declined, at least insofar as cases seeking Supreme Court review were concerned. More recent cases have concerned the use of psychological, rather than physical, pressure on defendants. In *Spano v. New York*[35] the accused was questioned for eight hours by six police officers in relays and was told falsely that the job and welfare of a friend who was a rookie cop depended on his confession. He was also refused

193

contact with his lawyer. The Court reversed Spano's conviction by holding his confession inadmissible because involuntary, but a reading of the majority opinion shows that the Court was moving away from the old unreliability rationale to a new rationale of fairness. There was not sufficient physical force used against Spano to warrant the conclusion that his confession was untrue; but the use of such a confession was repugnant to the Court because it was obviously not a voluntary statement.

> The abhorrence of society to the use of involuntary confessions does not turn alone on their inherent untrustworthiness. It also turns on the deep-rooted feeling that the police must obey the law while enforcing the law; that in the end life and liberty can be as much endangered from illegal methods used to convict those thought to be criminals as from the actual criminals themselves.[36]

In *Spano* the Court was adding a new dimension to the old unreliability standard: the importance of the state and its agents observing the decencies of civilized behavior. Even if a defendant's confession is reliable and can be independently verified, it must not be used if the defendant was coerced, psychologically or otherwise, into making it. Though this fairness rationale may be new in terms of Supreme Court jurisprudence, it probably hews more closely to the thinking of the old Talmudists than does the unreliability standard, in that the purpose of the old Talmudic law was primarily the preservation of the dignity and integrity of the defendant as a human being. As Dean Erwin Griswold of Harvard (now solicitor general of the United States) has said,

> We do not make even the most hardened criminal sign his own death warrant, or dig his own grave, or pull the lever that springs the trap on which he stands. We have through the course of history developed a considerable feeling of the dignity and intrinsic importance of the individual man. Even the evil man is a human being.[37]

The state, in short, may convict and punish a defendant, but it must not force him to condemn himself out of his own mouth. The current interpretation of the self-incrimination clause of the Fifth Amendment thus enhances a constellation of values: lawful law enforcement, the reliability of evidence used for conviction, and the preservation of the dignity of the accused.

The exclusion of coerced confessions, like the exclusion of illegally seized evidence, is an only partly effective sanction against undesirable police and prosecutorial practices. Unless all confessions are to be eliminated, there is no means of excluding the confession which results from the fear induced in the defendant by the very circumstances surrounding the process of arrest and arraignment. Only the most experienced and hardened criminal can fail to be terrified when surrounded by armed policemen in a strange and forbidding environment, cut off from communication with friends and family, and faced with an accusation which, if proved, may lead to severe punishment. Even the most secure defendant feels panic and bewilderment. Under these circumstances, any questioning by the police is threatening, and any statement by the accused, especially if he is not completely aware of his legal rights, is not really a voluntary statement given with consent based on knowledge. An example of this is the case of Danny Escobedo.[38]

On the night of January 19, 1960, Escobedo's brother-in-law was fatally shot. At 2:30 A.M., Danny was arrested without a warrant and questioned. He made no statement to the police, and was released fourteen and one-half hours later, after a lawyer retained by his family had secured a writ of *habeas corpus*. Because of the testimony of one DiGerlando, another suspect who had fingered Danny for the murder, Danny and his sister, the widow of the deceased, were arrested and taken to police headquarters. With his hands handcuffed behind his back, as Danny later testified without contradiction, the "detectives said they had us pretty well, up pretty tight, and we might as well admit to this crime," to which Danny replied, "I'm sorry but I would like to have advice from my lawyer." His request was denied, even after the lawyer arrived and requested permission to see his client.

Escobedo was questioned for several hours, handcuffed

and standing up. Finally, a Spanish-speaking police officer suggested to him that, if he pinned the murder on DiGerlando, he could be released. Escobedo, in a face-to-face confrontation with DiGerlando, accused the latter, saying, "I didn't shoot Manuel, you did it." By his statement, Escobedo for the first time admitted some knowledge of the crime, and also acknowledged complicity, an admission which, under Illinois law, is as damaging as firing the fatal shot. On the basis of this and other statements made by Escobedo, he was ultimately convicted. At no point during his questioning had anyone advised him of his right to remain silent, and it was apparent that he was unaware of the legal implications of his statement accusing DiGerlando. His conviction was appealed to the United States Supreme Court on the ground that the police denial of his request to speak to his lawyer made the statements elicited in the subsequent statement inadmissible, because the defendant had, in effect, been denied his right not to incriminate himself. The United States Supreme Court agreed, saying that where

the investigation is no longer a general inquiry into an unsolved crime but has begun to focus on a particular suspect, the suspect has been taken into police custody, the police carry out a process of interrogations that lends itself to eliciting incriminating statements, the suspect has requested and been denied an opportunity to consult with his lawyer, and the police have not effectively warned him of his absolute constitutional right to remain silent, the accused has been denied "the Assistance of Counsel" in violation of the Sixth Amendment to the Constitution as "made obligatory upon the States by the Fourteenth Amendment," *Gideon v. Wainright,* and that no statement elicited by the police during the interrogation may be used against him at a criminal trial.[39]

While the Court based its decision on Escobedo's Sixth Amendment right to counsel, the real thrust of the decision was to protect the defendant's *Fifth Amendment right not to incriminate himself.* What the Court was saying, in effect, was that to make the right against self-incrimination a reality for a suspect detained in police custody, the services of an attorney are essential; that most accused persons are too scared, too ignorant, too flustered, and too bewildered to utilize effectively the protection offered by the Fifth Amendment without the support and advice of an attorney trained in the law. The decisions rendered in *Miranda* and its companion cases* two years later add very little conceptually to Escobedo. They simply set down in fairly explicit form the guidelines for lawful police procedure: that a suspect must be warned of his right to remain silent; that he must be told of his right to consult with a lawyer, and have his lawyer with him during interrogation; that if the suspect indicates that he wishes counsel, questioning must stop until counsel is present; and that if the accused is without funds to obtain a lawyer, a lawyer will be appointed for him.

Very few people aware of the realities of police procedure will disagree with the Court on the need for counsel if the accused is to be effectively protected in his right to silence.** The *Escobedo* and *Miranda* decisions have nevertheless created a tremendous furor in law enforcement circles, largely on the ground that the presence of counsel

---

Miranda v. Arizona, Vignera v. New York, Westover v. United States, and *California v. Stewart,* 384 U.S. 436. Miranda was charged with rape, Vignera, Westover, and Stewart with robbery. In each case, the accused was questioned for several hours while in custody. While some of the defendants had been informed of some of their legal rights, none had been effectively informed of either his right to remain silent, or his right to have a lawyer present during questioning. No evidence of physical coercion was introduced, but in *Miranda,* there was some evidence that the "confession" was in police language rather than Miranda's own words. In each case, there was probably sufficient independent evidence for conviction without the use of a confession.

**John Griffiths and Richard E. Ayres, "A Postscript to the Miranda Project: Interrogation of Draft Protesters," *Yale Law Journal* 77 (1967): 300. The authors report the results of a study of twenty-one Yale faculty, staff members, and students who were interviewed in their homes by FBI agents in connection with their having turned in their draft cards as a gesture of protest against the Viet Nam War. The authors found that even where the suspects were highly educated, articulate, reasonably mature, and strongly motivated individuals who were questioned *in their own homes* by experienced, professional FBI men, the suspects were unable to understand and make effective use of their constitutional rights. The authors found that nervousness "decidedly impaired their judgment and behavior, and that questioning did not cease even when they stated that they did not wish to answer any further questions."

will so inhibit the responses of the accused as to virtually forestall any possibility of a confession or even of information helpful to the police in their investigation. The police, in short, are afraid that if suspects are protected from having to answer questions relating to the crime, investigations will be so hamstrung that the solution of crimes will become impossible.

While it is impossible to determine accurately how damaging *Miranda* and *Escobedo* have been to the police and prosecutorial processes, such evidence as has been gathered by studies of police practices in the four years since *Miranda* (1966) indicates that there is not too much factual basis for these fears.[40] For one thing, suspects frequently feel a strong need to talk to the police, either as a form of emotional catharsis, or because of a desire to explain away seemingly incriminating evidence or circumstances. Many suspects, even when warned, could not grasp the significance of what they were told, or in any event could not apply what they were told to the situation at hand. Furthermore the police, even when they gave the required warnings, implied by their tone of voice, or by the selection of the words used, that the warnings were a routine formality and of no great consequence. They encouraged suspects to disregard the warnings and proceed with their statements. In a fair number of cases the police simply ignored the *Miranda* requirements entirely and failed to issue any warning to the suspects. Several conclusions can be drawn from these studies. One could argue that the statistics showing little change in the pre- and post-*Miranda* rate of convictions in selected precincts were due to the non-implementation of *Miranda* by the police, but there is also considerable data to suggest that: first, suspects talk even when warned (and possibly even after consultation with counsel); and second, that confessions are not always crucial in obtaining convictions.[41]

Because of the lack of data confirming the hypothesis that *Miranda* warnings are adversely affecting the police and prosecutorial functions, there is little likelihood that the

entire *Miranda* decision will be reversed in the United States
Supreme Court, even with the advent of conservative Nixon
appointees such as Burger and Blackmun.* Congressional
attempts to modify *Miranda* through legislation, such as
Title II of the Omnibus Crime Control and Safe Streets Act
of 1968, will also probably have little serious impact on
either police procedure or the effective rights of suspects.**
Miranda, however, has already been modified and probably
will be further redefined by the United States Supreme Court
to establish the scope of its impact.

On February 24, 1971, in *Harris v. New York*,[42] the Court,
in a 5 to 4 decision, held that a statement given to the police
by an unwarned suspect, while not admissible as part of the
prosecution's case, might be brought in as part of the cross-
examination of the defendant, should he take the stand in
his own defense. (The defense, however, presumably could
then introduce the circumstances under which the statement was obtained.) How restrictive of the original *Miranda*
standards this decision will be remains to be seen. Another
question to be decided concerns the rights of suspects not
yet in custody, that is, on the street or in a police car. Also
to be decided is the question of when a suspect becomes a
suspect, that is, at what point the general investigation ends
and the investigation of a specific individual begins. Suppose, for example, that a complaining witness, two days after
an assault, picks out an individual in a crowd and identifies
him to a police officer as her assailant. Must the police
officer, when he questions the suspect, give him *Miranda*
warnings before interrogation? Is the suspect already a suspect in the *Miranda* sense before the policeman has spoken
a word? It is questions like these, relating to the amplitude
of the *Miranda* decision, that remain to be decided, and it
is in these future decisions that *Miranda* may be modified

---

*Assuming that new appointees achieve levels of legal respectability and
competence equal to that of Blackmun and Burger.

**Title II attempts to "repeal" *Miranda* by setting standards of volun-
tariness for confessions which do not necessarily include warning the
suspect of his right to remain silent and his right to counsel.

in an attempt to make it more palatable to critics of the U.S. Supreme Court.

Fair Trial and the Right to Counsel

The right to counsel, as enunciated in *Miranda* and *Escobedo*, is an adjunct of the right to silence specified in the Fifth Amendment. This is a recent and innovative use of the right to counsel. Traditionally, this right concerned efforts to ensure counsel for the accused *at the time of the trial.* The Sixth Amendment to the United States Constitution provides that an accused shall "have the assistance of counsel for his defense." It is quite clear that this clause means, at the very least, that in a federal trial a defendant who wishes to provide himself with counsel may not be denied the privilege. What is not clear, however, is the degree of obligation on the part of the federal government to provide counsel for an accused too poor to pay for his own lawyer.

As early as 1790, in the Federal Crimes Act, Congress ordered the courts to assign counsel for the defendant in all capital cases. The obligation was not considered to extend to non-capital cases, however, and until 1938, if a defendant charged in federal court with a non-capital crime could not or would not retain a lawyer for his trial, the federal government made no attempt to rectify the situation. In that year, in *Johnson v. Zerbst*,[43] the United States Supreme Court declared that the Sixth Amendment deprives the federal courts of the power to convict a defendant unrepresented by counsel, unless the defendant knowingly and intelligently waives the right. Since the *Johnson* case, counsel has been provided for all accused persons in federal courts.

The right to counsel in the state courts was initially established as a *federal* right in the first Scottsboro case, *Powell v. Alabama*.[44] The case involved seven Negro boys charged with the rape of two white girls while all were travelling on a freight train through northern Alabama. The boys were charged in an atmosphere so hostile that it was widely understood that only the certainty that the defendants would be convicted and hanged prevented the local residents from lynching the defendants on the spot. The case first came to trial without counsel. A small group of interested Negroes attempted to procure counsel for the defendants, who were terrified and virtually illiterate. When the attempt proved unsuccessful, the trial judge appointed all the members of the local bar to act as counsel for the defendants.

In fact, the boys were unassisted by counsel when they went to trial on the capital charge of rape. News of the trial began to appear in the New York press, and the case became somewhat of a political cause celèbre when the defendants were quickly found guilty and sentenced to death despite the very weak case presented by the prosecution. The NAACP, the Communist party, and other interested groups raised funds on behalf of the Scottsboro boys which were used to retain Samuel S. Leibowitz (later appointed to the New York State Supreme Court) to defend the boys. Leibowitz appealed the verdict of the first trial on the ground that Powell had been denied due process of law when he was convicted of a capital crime without the assistance of counsel. The United States Supreme Court agreed that "the failure of the trial court to give [the defendants] . . . reasonable time and opportunity to secure counsel was a clear denial of due process."[45] Furthermore, the Court added, if the defendants were unable through their own efforts to procure counsel, it was incumbent upon the state to provide counsel for them. The Court refused to consider whether this obligation applied to all criminal trials or only to those involving capital offenses, but simply decided, on the basis of the facts of the *Powell* case, that the conviction could not stand.

> Whether this would be so in other criminal prosecutions, or under other circumstances, we need not determine. All that it is necessary to decide, as we do decide, is that in a capital case, where the defendant is unable to employ counsel, and is incapable adequately of making his own defense because of ignorance, feeble mindedness, illiteracy, or the like, it is the

duty of the court, whether requested or not, to assign counsel for him as a necessary requisite of due process of law.[46]

The *Powell* decision was too closely tied to the facts of that case to permit a substantial broadening of the right to counsel in state courts. Left unanswered were the issues of whether the right applied in non-capital cases as well as in capital cases, and whether it applied to defendants less helpless than the Scottsboro boys. Ten years later, in *Betts v. Brady,*[47] a Maryland case, an indigent defendant was convicted of robbery without benefit of counsel despite his request for legal representation at the trial. The Maryland law provided counsel for poor defendants in capital cases only. The United States Supreme Court held that Betts had not been denied due process of law by the failure of the state to provide him with counsel. The Sixth Amendment, the Court declared, was not automatically incorporated into the concept of due process of the Fourteenth Amendment, and therefore, counsel could be denied at the discretion of the state where it was felt that the trial on the whole had been fundamentally fair.

Although the majority of the Court, in considering the *Betts* case, seemed to think that Betts was reasonably capable of defending himself in court, the facts when more closely examined do not support this conclusion. Although Betts was a man of normal intelligence, and grasped the principles of cross-examination, he was obviously incapable of analyzing the state's case against him, and pointing out its weaknesses.

For example, the robbery victim testified: The robber "had on a dark overcoat and a handkerchief around his chin and a pair of dark amber glasses. . . . I told the police that I wasn't sure I could identify him without the glasses and the handkerchief, after seeing him when it was almost dark that evening." The *only* man in the line-up the day the victim came to the jail to identify the robber was Betts. And he could only be identified when he put on the dark coat, the smoked glasses and the handkerchief. . . .

No coat or dark glasses or handkerchief was ever offered in evidence. . . . Although the matter is not entirely free from doubt—because neither trial judge nor prosecutor seemed to care much and Betts evidently failed to realize how this would weaken the State's case—a careful study of the record warrants the conclusion that the following occurred: The victim described to the police the various items the robber was supposed to have worn; the police obtained the requisite coat, glasses, and handkerchief and placed them on Betts; the victim then made his identification, based largely on the coat, glasses, and handkerchief the police had put on Betts.[48]

The realities of the criminal justice process are such that very few open-minded observers could accept the Court's reasoning in *Betts*. It was obvious then, and became even more so with the passing years, that no one could receive a fair trial without the presence of his own attorney. Certainly, no one suggested that middle-class or upper-class defendants would be likely to go voluntarily to trial without benefit of counsel. After years of unhappiness with the *Betts* decision, and several decisions modifying the dictum therein, the Court finally seized upon an appeal *in forma pauperis* by one Clarence Gideon, from his conviction on a breaking and entering charge in Florida, as a vehicle for reconsideration of the *Betts* rationale. Gideon had requested counsel at his trial and had been denied an attorney because Florida, like Maryland, provided counsel for indigents in capital cases only. When his appeal reached the United States Supreme Court, the Court appointed Abe Fortas to argue the case for Gideon. In deciding the case, the Court finally overruled *Betts*, holding that the right to counsel is a fundamental right, and therefore an integral part of the concept of due process. By implication the Court also held that the Sixth Amendment right to counsel is subsumed and made applicable to the states through the due process clause of the Fourteenth Amendment.

Thus, as of the present moment, every defendant in every felony case in every court, state and federal, in the United States is entitled to the assistance of counsel at the trial stage of his case, and also at such times prior to the trial as are necessary for the effective preparation for the trial. Still to be fully clarified are several post-trial rights to counsel. For example, is an indigent defendant entitled to counsel and free transcript so that he may appeal the verdict of the trial court? If so, must the counsel be the counsel of his choice, or may the state simply provide him with the services of a public defender? If the public defender finds no merit in his claim, does he have the right to seek the assistance of another lawyer not connected with the legal defender's office? Does an indigent defendant have the right to be represented by counsel in a misdemeanor case? Does an indigent defendant have the right to be furnished with assistance other than that of counsel at the trial, such as expert witnesses and investigators? Does an indigent defendant, in short, have the right to have the state provide for him all the assistance that the well-to-do defendant could purchase for himself with his private means? The answers to these questions are not clear, but the tendency of the past decade has been for the United States Supreme Court to attempt to equalize the impact of the criminal justice system on rich and poor defendants, through the provision of legal services to indigent defendants paid for by the state.*

The presence of an attorney is not the only requisite for a fair trial for the defendant, of course. As important, if not more so, is the right of the defendant to be judged by a jury unprejudiced against him. The problem of prejudice in regard to juries stems basically from two sources: either the jury may be biased by the race, religion, sex, or socioeconomic status of the jurors; or its prejudice may stem from jurors' having fixed or relatively fixed opinions with regard to the guilt of the accused prior to the trial. Regarding bias which stems from race or class considerations, the most thorny problem of the American criminal justice system has been the persistent, widespread discrimination against Negroes in the selection of juries.

Following the Civil War, state laws that specifically

---

*The ACLU, the NAACP and its Legal Defense Fund, and the Legal Aid Society, are private or quasi-private legal defender groups which provide many of these services for at least some indigent criminal defendants in various parts of the country.

restricted jury rolls to white males were struck down by the
United States Supreme Court as violating the Fourteenth
Amendment.[49] The southern states then retreated to a policy
of unofficial discrimination against Negroes, whereby Negroes were excluded from juries in practice though not in
law. Thus, in the second Scottsboro case, *Norris v. Alabama*,[50] Attorney Leibowitz was able to show through questioning hundreds of witnesses that no Negro had served on
a jury in the Alabama county involved within the memory
of the oldest living residents, white or black, and no such
service by Negroes appeared in any of the court records.
He was also able to demonstrate that there were in the
county a sizeable number of fully qualified Negroes who
had never been called for service. On appeal, the United
States Supreme Court upheld Leibowitz's contention that
discrimination against Negroes could be established by
inference from established practice, even though no expressed statutory prohibition existed.

Since the *Norris* case, it is clear that some Negroes
must appear on the jury rolls in every jurisdiction in which
Negroes reside. How many, of course, is another question,
and there is considerable evidence that in some areas
tokenism has replaced the earlier policy of unofficial total
exclusion; that is, one, or a handful of Negroes will be added
to the jury rolls in areas where the Negro population warrants far greater representation. The courts have thus far
been unable effectively to cope with this kind of discrimination. They have been able to assure each defendant the
right to be tried before a jury on which it was *possible* for
Negroes to sit. No defendant, however, has a right at this
point to a jury on which one or more Negroes *does* sit. From
the point of view of black defendants (or conceivably even
white defendants), it is probably unfair to be tried before a
jury whose racial composition is not representative of the
racial composition of the population at large. It is not clear,
however, how the courts can remedy this situation, and most
likely such conditions cannot be rectified in the absence of
willingness on the part of administrative officials to do so.

Not only Negroes are discriminated against by the jury

205

selection system. Poor people are probably vastly under-represented on all juries throughout the United States. The degree to which this is true depends on the particular jury system used, and systems vary not only from state to state, but from federal district to federal district. For many years, for example, federal jurors were chosen under the "key man" system, whereby a prominent member of the community recommended other outstanding citizens as venire-men. Another widely used method for both state and federal jury selection is the use of tax rolls, voting lists, telephone subscriber lists, and the like, all of which tend to represent propertied, employed, home-owning citizens at the expense of poorer people.

In 1949, during the prosecution of Eugene Dennis and his fellow leaders of the American Communist party, the defense attorneys tried to challenge the validity of the jury by establishing that poor people, women, Negroes, Jews, blue-collar workers, and members of the American Labor party had been excluded from the jury rolls. The judge rejected their contention that the jury selection was invalid; nevertheless, the defense contention that the jury was un-representative was probably true. In March 1968, a federal jury reform act was passed, which requires a random selection of jurors from a "fair cross-section of the community," and forbids discrimination on the basis of race, color, sex, national origin, or economic status. How this is to be accomplished, however, is not altogether clear, and as in the case of racial discrimination, the courts find it difficult to cope with the problem of socioeconomic discrimination in jury selection.

Women present a somewhat special problem in terms of jury selection. In many states women cannot be compelled to serve on juries, and in some others will not even be called for jury service unless they voluntarily enter their names on the jury rolls. The purpose of such regulations undoubtedly stems from concern for women's domestic responsibilities, especially in regard to the care of young children. Nevertheless, such practices undoubtedly create juries which by their very nature are unrepresentative. Similarly, the tendency of judges to excuse from service those for whom such service is an economic hardship, or a matter of great inconvenience, tends to make juries over-representative of such groups as government employees and those employed by large corporations willing to continue salary payments during the period of jury service. Self-employed people, teachers, and manual laborers, among others, are found on juries far less frequently than public utility employees, white-collar workers, and corporation officials.

Juries may also be prejudiced by the jurors having formed opinions as to the guilt or innocence of the accused before the trial. Prejudice on the part of individual jurors is normally handled reasonably effectively through the device of challenging, either for cause or peremptorily. Much more serious, however, is the problem which arises when the entire panel of veniremen may have attitudes antagonistic toward the accused, because of either strong local pre-trial sentiment stemming from the status of the defendant or excessive ill-considered pre-trial publicity relating to the crime and the defendant. Some trials, such as the Scottsboro trial or the *Frank* trial in Georgia[51] in 1915, are conducted in an atmosphere so filled with hostility to the defendants as to be virtually legal lynchings. In the *Frank* trial, for example, the defendant was a New York–born Jewish manager of the local textile mill, accused of raping a girl employee. The judge gave tacit recognition to the rampant xenophobia and anti-Semitism of the local population by requesting the defendant and his attorney to remain away from the courtroom when the verdict was brought in, lest there be a lynching if a verdict other than guilty as charged were returned. Frank was convicted, and appealed unsuccessfully to the United States Supreme Court on the ground that the atmosphere surrounding the trial had prevented him from receiving a fair trial. Some months later, while in prison awaiting execution, Frank was taken from the state prison farm by a mob and lynched. His perception of the atmosphere in which his trial was conducted was apparently accurate.

207

It is unlikely that the United States Supreme Court today would be as insensitive to the claims of a defendant in circumstances similar to Frank's as it was in 1915. Eight years later, in *Moore v. Dempsey*,[52] a case involving Negro sharecroppers accused of murdering white men who had terrorized the Negro community, the Court substantially agreed with Holmes's comment in the earlier *Frank* case that "lynch law [is] as little valid when practiced by a regularly drawn jury as when administered by one elected by a mob intent on death."[53]

More troublesome today are cases involving juries inflamed, not by the mere status of the defendant, but by extensive pre-trial publicity unfavorable to him as a person and as a defendant. The ultimate in situations of this kind was the publicity given to the arrest of Lee Harvey Oswald for the assassination of President John F. Kennedy in 1963, in Dallas, Texas. It is highly questionable whether, had Oswald lived and gone to trial, an unprejudiced jury could have been impanelled anywhere in the United States, much less in Texas. The quantity and quality of mass media coverage of the crime and the subsequent search for and arrest of the suspect had such enormous, almost universally felt impact that it is doubtful there existed twelve adult Americans of normal intelligence who had open minds as to the guilt or innocence of Oswald. The issue was not joined, of course, because of the assassination of Oswald himself, an act stemming in part, at least, from the self-same publicity.

Oswald's case, fortunately, is unique, but the problem of pre-trial prejudicial publicity is not. More typical are cases such as *Irvin v. Dowd*,[54] where reports that the defendant offered to plead guilty if promised a ninety-nine year sentence were widely circulated. Local newspapers also described the accused as the "confessed slayer of six," a parole violator, and a fraudulent check artist. Some 90 percent of the veniremen, when questioned, admitted to some opinion as to his guilt. In *Rideau v. Louisiana*,[55] shortly before the defendant's arraignment and trial, a local TV station broadcast, at three different times, a twenty-minute film of the accused in the presence of the sheriff and two state troopers, admitting in detail, in response to leading questions by the sheriff, the commission of various offenses. Most widely publicized of all was the case of Dr. Samuel Sheppard, a wealthy young osteopath accused of murdering his wife.[56]

Sheppard's family lived in a suburb of Cleveland and operated an osteopathic hospital in the vicinity. The Cleveland press quite early took the position that Sheppard was guilty, and that any investigatory action on the part of law enforcement officials pointing in any direction other than Sheppard's guilt was an attempt to shield wealthy and influential people from the processes of the law, and thus was evidence of corruption. The pre-trial publicity given the investigation was intense and virulent.

> Charges and countercharges were aired in the news media besides those for which Sheppard was called to trial. In addition, only three months before trial, Sheppard was examined for more than five hours without counsel during a three-day inquest which ended in a public brawl. The inquest was televised live from a high school gymnasium seating hundreds of people. Furthermore, the trial began two weeks before a hotly contested election at which both Chief Prosecutor Mahon and Judge Blythin were candidates for judgeships.[57]

Not only was pre-trial publicity extensive and detrimental to the accused, but the trial was run in the atmosphere of a Roman circus. Reporters were permitted to sit inside the bar, and the goings and comings of the representatives of the mass media created so much confusion that not only could the testimony of witnesses not be heard, but Sheppard was forced to leave the courtroom to consult with his attorney.

> The fact is that bedlam reigned at the courthouse during the trial and newsmen took over practically the entire courtroom, hounding most of the participants of the trial especially Sheppard. . . . The erection of a press table for reporters inside the bar is unprecedented. The bar of the court is reserved for counsel, providing them a safe place in which to keep papers and exhibits, and to confer privately with client and co-counsel. . . . Moreover, the judge gave the throng of newsmen gathered

in the corridors of the courthouse absolute free rein. Participants in the trial, including the jury, were forced to run a gauntlet
of reporters and photographers each time they entered or left
the courtroom.[58]

The names of the jurors, with their addresses and their
pictures, appeared in the newspapers both before and during
the trial, and the jury itself, although sequestered in the
course of the trial, was permitted to make telephone calls
freely to friends and relatives outside.

Sheppard was convicted of his wife's murder and, after
ten years of motions and appeals (made possible, in part, by
his personal wealth), finally succeeded in obtaining from
the United States Supreme Court a reversal of his conviction
on the grounds that he had not received a fair trial because
of the uncontrolled prejudicial publicity surrounding his trial.
He was re-tried by the state of Ohio and acquitted.

In reaction to the Sheppard, Ruby, and Oswald cases,
and to the potential for a miscarriage of justice inherent in
the mass media coverage of each of them, a good deal of
public discussion was engendered as to how such coverage
could be restricted to best protect the rights of defendants.
In 1967, the Reardon Committee of the American Bar Association made a series of recommendations which would
severely restrict statements to the press by law enforcement
officials, including police, prosecutors, and court attachés,
as well as defense counsel. Such matters as the defendant's
prior criminal record, statements including confessions which he might have made, the identity of witnesses,
their potential testimony, and speculations as to the guilt
or innocence of the accused would all be prohibited. In
general, only such details as might be necessary for the
apprehension of a fugitive or for the protection of the community would be released. The obvious feeling of the committee was that the less publicity surrounding any trial the
better. The proposed restrictions would be enforced either
by internal departmental disciplinary procedures against
law enforcement officials, by bar association proceedings
against private attorneys, or by the use of the contempt
power of the judge against reporters and others.

Representatives of the mass media, understandably, disagreed with many of the suggestions of the Reardon Committee. For one thing, the use of the contempt powers of the courts against reporters, while in line with British practice, runs counter to American tradition. On the whole the United States Supreme Court has been reluctant to sustain convictions of reporters for contempt, that is, publication that does not actually obstruct the business of the court. "A judge of the United States," as Justice Holmes once remarked, "is expected to be a man of ordinary firmness of character,"[59] and presumably, therefore, able to shield his courtroom from unwarranted interference or influence by the press.

More important, however, the representatives feel that publicity is not only not necessarily evil, but is an essential good in a democratic society. While willing to concede that excesses and abuses frequently occur in the coverage of trials, they feel that to virtually do away with press coverage of police investigations and trials is to throw out the baby with the bathwater.

Public discussion of major problems in the court of public opinion has proved historically to be a far more potent method of correction of inbred evil or advocating needed change than legal processes limited to the courtroom alone. We should go slowly about adopting rules that would have prevented Attorney General Richmond Flowers of Alabama from commenting on the hand-picked Liuzzo murder jury, Estes Kefauver from exposing the violent crimes and corrupting influence of the Mafia, or Senator Walsh from denouncing the Teapot Dome Scandal. Nor do I think that Clarence Darrow's great debate on freedom of education in the period preceding the *Scopes trial* should have been stricken from our history.[60]

The critics of the ABA Report correctly point out that the press is a watchdog against official corruption, and while harm may befall an individual defendant through improper press coverage, far greater harm may befall all defendants should public surveillance of police and prosecutorial practices be relaxed.

The point may be illustrated by a consideration of pretrial confessions. . . . If a confession is truly voluntary, it will be

211

admitted at trial, and the damage that the press may bring about by prior publication will be inflicted against principle but not practicality. If, however, the confession is coerced and is *not* admitted at trial, then pretrial news of the confession may hurt the defendant's chances of getting an impartial jury. But it also constitutes a highly necessary and perhaps the only notice to the public of police misfeasance. There has been harm to the defendant, perhaps avoidable. But which was the greater harm to him, the coercion of a confession, or the publication that a confession was made?[61]

On balance, it would appear that excessive restriction of press coverage may well be a greater social evil than totally unrestricted press coverage. There seems no need, however, to select between two such dire alternatives. Recognition of the problem by attorneys, reporters, and law enforcement officials and willingness to set reasonable voluntary standards for restraints should do much to eliminate the worst excesses of the type in evidence at the Sheppard trial. Trial judges, moreover, have sufficient power, if they care to use it, to sequester and insulate the proceedings in their courtrooms from the adverse effects of prejudicial press coverage. Certainly, the circuses that were permitted to take place under the appellation of trials in the cases cited above have had a salutary effect in alerting all concerned to the dangers of improperly influencing the judicial process through unrestricted publicity. The situation, however, does not appear to be so unmanageable as to warrant officially imposed silence, which may lead to even graver evils.

One last consideration in relation to a fair trial is that the right to a jury trial inheres in the seriousness of the punishment for the charged offense rather than the appellation given that offense within a particular penal code. The constitutional provisions regarding jury trial are clearly intended to protect accused persons from serious punishment until after adjudication by *juries*. Traditionally, this has been taken to mean that those prosecuted for felonies have a right to a trial by jury. Recently, however, the United States Supreme Court has broadened this concept to include the right of jury trials in misdemeanor cases where the permissible punishment may be as long as two years. In *Duncan v. Louisiana*,[62] the conviction of a defendant accused of simple battery, a misdemeanor punishable under Louisiana law by two years imprisonment and a three hundred–dollar fine, was reversed because the accused's request for a jury trial had been denied by the trial judge. In reversing the conviction the Court, after some discussion of the relationship of the Fourteenth to the Sixth Amendment, recognized that some crimes are too petty to warrant jury trials, and defined this category as including at least those where the specified punishment was a maximum of six months' imprisonment. The six months standard was later reaffirmed in *Baldwin v. New York*.[63] The *Duncan* and *Baldwin* decisions are regarded with some horror by state and local officials, not so much for the principles they have enunciated as for the practical problems they have created. With court calendars already filled to bursting, the prospect of large numbers of additional cases requiring jury trial is unattractive, to say the least. Should the situtation become sufficiently desperate, there is some likelihood that certain misdemeanor punishments may be revised downward to remove them from the required jury trial category.

Double Jeopardy

The notion behind the constitutional prohibition against double jeopardy is that the state may not get two bites at the apple. A defendant may be tried only once for a particular crime, and the state must then either convict him or forever hold its peace, so to speak. The principal complication that has arisen in the United States, however, stems from the fact that we live in a federal system where there is not one sovereign, but two; not merely federal law, but state law as well.

The Fifth Amendment says, "Nor shall any person be subject for the same offense to be twice put in jeopardy of life or limb." This means quite clearly that if John Robber holds up a federally insured bank in New York State, New

York State may try him only once for the crime of bank robbery. The difficulty is, however, that such a robbery is also a federal crime. The federal government may also try Mr. Robber only once. Neither sovereignty has had "two bites of the apple"; nevertheless, Mr. Robber has been tried twice for the same offense. Thus far the United States Supreme Court has upheld the practice of double prosecutions by different sovereignties as not violative of the Fifth and Fourteenth Amendments, although in *Benton v. Maryland*[64] the Court ruled that the double jeopardy clause of the Fifth Amendment is applicable to the states through the Fourteenth Amendment. Double prosecutions are a very real problem and violate the spirit, if not the letter, of the Constitution. The federal government, for its part, has attempted administratively to remedy the situation by a voluntary decision on the part of all attorneys general since 1959 not to try federal cases where there has already been a state prosecution for substantially the same act. The states, however, have not reciprocated, and continue double prosecutions not only where a federal prosecution has taken place, but even where local or municipal prosecution has taken place for an act that is simultaneously violative of a local or municipal code. Challenges to these practices are expected to reach the U.S. Supreme Court, and there are some indications in recently rendered decisions involving parallel state and federal jurisdictions that the court may strike down this form of double jeopardy.*

Another type of multiple prosecution sometimes occurs when the criminal act committed can actually be thought of as more than one act; for example, if while robbing the bank, Mr. Robber takes money first from the teller and then from each of three customers standing on line, his bank robbery can be thought of as four separate criminal acts. If the state

---

*In *State v. Fletcher,* decided by the Ohio Court of Appeals for the Eighth District on October 23, 1970, the Court held that the *Benton* ruling (that the double jeopardy clause of the Fifth Amendment applies to the states) precludes Ohio prosecution of a defendant already tried in federal court for the same criminal act.

were to prosecute him for the robbery of the teller and fail to convict him, should they have an opportunity to try him subsequently for the robbery of each customer? Again, from the point of view of the state, Mr. Robber, in knowingly taking property from four separate persons, committed four different offenses. From the point of Mr. Robber, however, the transaction was a single one. If the intent of the Constitution is to prevent harassment of an accused person through multiple prosecutions, cases such as that of Mr. Robber certainly offer a potential for harassment. On the other hand, there is sometimes much factual justification for considering such crimes multiple rather than single offenses. The general rule is that separate offenses require separate evidence for conviction; that is, if the evidence for all offenses is identical, only one conviction can be obtained.

Jeopardy normally attaches with the swearing in of the first juror at the beginning of the trial. When a person has been acquitted or convicted by a court of competent jurisdiction he may not be re-tried for the same offense. If, however, the jury fails to reach a verdict, or a mistrial is declared, the accused is not considered to have been placed in jeopardy, and trial proceedings may be reinstituted. (The prosecution may not, of course, for tactical reasons, interrupt the trial and ask for a mistrial if things are going badly for the state. Otherwise, any district attorney who detected an unfavorable response on the part of the jury could throw in the sponge and hope for better things with a subsequent jury.) If the court is later determined not to have had proper jurisdiction, or to have been improperly constituted in some way, the accused may also be re-tried.

Conclusion

In the last decade, the U.S. Supreme Court has made more changes in criminal procedure than had been made by the Court in the previous 170 years of its existence. Critics of the Court have charged bitterly that these changes have "coddled criminals" and have reflected an undesirable attitude of permissiveness toward bad conduct. A fair-minded review of what the Court has actually done will show that these contentions are not true. The Court has not created any new rights for the criminals; it therefore cannot have coddled criminals or been permissive of their evil ways. *What the Court has done is to equalize the rights of rich suspects and poor suspects.* The Court has not created any new rights, but it has extended to the poor, illiterate, and ignorant accused those rights which have long been known and enjoyed by the middle- or upper-class defendant. The *Miranda* decision created not one right or privilege that was not known and used by defendants who were either experienced or sufficiently affluent to hire good counsel promptly.*

Nevertheless, the critics are right in accusing the Warren Court of having created a revolution in the field of criminal procedure. By extending the rights of the rich to the poor, enormous *practical* problems have been created. *Poor people commit more, and more serious crimes, than rich people,* and by giving the poor the treatment that has traditionally been reserved for the rich, the Court is overloading to the point of breakdown our criminal justice system. It is also forcing our society to declare whether it really believes in equality before the law. Many citizens and public officials who are appalled at crowded court calendars, lengthy appellate proceedings, overcrowded prisons, and the need for more and better police work—all of which are to some extent the results of the higher standards enunciated by the Court—have evaded the fundamental issue through rather mindless criticisms of the Court as being soft on criminals. If, however, the criminal justice system is in difficulty today,

---

*The criminal procedure decisions which have most outraged the public have had surprisingly little effect on the fate of the defendants involved. Miranda, Escobedo, and Mrs. Mapp were all subsequently sentenced to prison. Miranda was convicted of possession of stolen goods in 1967, and sentenced to twenty to thirty years in prison; Escobedo was convicted in federal court of narcotics law violations in 1968 and given a twenty-two year sentence; and Mrs. Mapp was convicted in New York City of possession of narcotics found in her home after a police search with a valid search warrant, and was sentenced to twenty years to life.

and it is, the causes are far more basic than weak minds and bleeding hearts on the United States Supreme Court. Either we must abandon the notion of equality before the law without regard to race, color, or socioeconomic status, or we must find another way to *stop creating so many criminals.* While it is true that each individual in a free society has a personal responsibility to obey the law (as a corollary to society's obligation to respect each individual's personal rights), it is only realistic to recognize that, in a statistically predictable number of cases, this responsibility will be evaded or ignored. Either we must improve the socialization process so that fewer young people and adults turn to crime, or we have to restructure our criminal codes so that fewer kinds of actions may be deemed criminal. We must return to the realization that the basic purpose of a criminal code is not to legislate morality, but to legislate against only those forms of immorality which are seriously and objectively known to be socially disruptive. Every society everywhere protects itself against murderers and rapists; not every society must protect itself against gamblers, prostitutes, and drug users.

In fact, in many areas relating to criminal procedure, the United States Supreme Court has taken away rights that suspects previously enjoyed. The standards for legal searches and seizures have been lowered and made more flexible; the rules for the admission of evidence in criminal cases (outside of statements by the accused) have been made less rigid; and wiretapping and eavesdropping have been legalized.

In any case, what the Court has done is only a beginning. Many decisions made by the Court in the last decade have raised as many problems as they settled: the scope of the *Miranda* and Stop and Frisk cases; the extent to which indigent appellants are entitled to legal assistance and services; how far the courts may go in regulating mass media coverage of criminal investigations and trials are examples. On the solution to some of these problems there is as yet little consensus or even organized thought; in

217

other areas remedies may suggest themselves but the Court is not a suitable instrument for reform. It is difficult to see, for example, how the Court can effectively guard against selection of non-representative juries, or against the abuse of permissive wiretapping legislation by administrative officials hostile to official standards of fairness.

In the meantime, the record of the Warren Court with regard to criminal procedure is, on the whole, one of the high-water marks of American history. Despite the legitimacy of much of the criticism of the United States as a violent, machine-dominated, materialistic, inhuman society, the attempt to protect the rights of the most despised members of society—criminals—is surely an indication that we are more decent, more civilized, and more truly libertarian than many critics, on both the Right and the Left, are willing to admit. After all, the point about *Miranda* is not what the decision did for Ernesto Miranda, but what it did for the rest of us.

Selected Readings

Abraham, Henry J. *The Judicial Process: An Introductory Analysis of the Courts of the United States, England, and France.* 2nd ed. New York: Oxford University Press, 1968.

Friendly, Alfred, and Goldfarb, Ronald L. *Crime and Publicity.* New York: Twentieth Century Fund, 1967.

Hall, Livingston; Kamisar, Yale; LaFave, Wayne; and Israel, Jerold H. *Modern Criminal Procedure.* 3rd ed. St. Paul, Minn.: West Publishing Co., 1969.

Lewis, Anthony. *Gideon's Trumpet.* New York: Random House, 1964.

Lockhart, William B.; Kamisar, Yale; and Choper, Jesse H. *Constitutional Rights and Liberties.* 2nd ed. St. Paul, Minn.: West Publishing Company, 1967.

Niederhoffer, Arthur, and Blumberg, Abraham S., eds. *The Ambivalent Force: Perspectives on the Police.* Waltham, Mass.: Ginn and Company, 1970.

Pritchett, C. Herman, and Westin, Alan F., eds. *The Third Branch of Government.* New York: Harcourt, Brace, and World, 1963.

Skolnick, Jerome H. *Justice Without Trial: Law Enforcement in Democratic Society.* New York: Wiley, 1966.

Tiffany, Lawrence P.; McIntyre, Donald M., Jr.; and Rotenberg, David L. *Detection of Crime: Stopping and Questioning, Search and Seizure, Encouragement and Entrapment.* Boston: Little, Brown, 1967.

Williams, Edward Bennett. *One Man's Freedom.* New York: Atheneum, 1962.

Notes

[1] For a good discussion of the rules of jurisdiction and procedure of the United States Supreme Court, see Henry J. Abraham, *The Judicial Process* (New York: Oxford University Press, 1968), pp. 171–245. See also Chapter 1.

[2] *Uveges v. Pennsylvania,* 335 U.S. 437 (1948), at 449–450.

[3] *Gideon v. Wainright,* 372 U.S. 335 (1963).

[4] Anthony Lewis, *Gideon's Trumpet* (New York: Random House, 1964). Although written by a journalist rather than a lawyer or constitutional scholar, this is probably one of the best constitutional case studies ever written. Several interesting, though shorter, case studies can be found in Pritchett and Westin.

[5] *Wolf v. Colorado,* 338 U.S. 25 (1949).

[6] *Rochin v. California,* 342 U.S. 165 (1952).

[7] *Irvine v. California,* 347 U.S. 128 (1954).

[8] *Mapp v. Ohio,* 367 U.S. 643 (1961).

[9] *Terry v. Ohio,* 392 U.S. 1 (1968).

[10] *Sibron v. New York,* 392 U.S. 40 (1968).

[11] *Peters v. New York,* 392 U.S. 40 (1968).

[12] *Terry v. Ohio,* at 13–14.

[13] For further discussion of this point, see Jerome H. Skolnick, *Justice Without Trial* (New York: John Wiley and Sons, 1966), Chap. 10.

[14] *Davis v. Mississippi,* 394 U.S. 721 (1969).

[15] *Warden v. Hayden,* 387 U.S. 294 (1967).

[16] For an analysis of the Stop and Frisk cases in relation to search and seizure problems, see Ruth G. Weintraub and Harriet Pollack, "Acquitting the *De Facto* Guilty: Some 'Stop and Frisk' Problems," in Arthur Niederhoffer and Abraham S. Blumberg, eds., *The Ambivalent Force: Perspectives on the Police* (Waltham, Mass.: Ginn and Company, 1970), pp. 256–265.

[17] *Olmstead v. United States,* 277 U.S. 438 (1928).

[18] *Olmstead v. United States,* at 470.

[19] *Nardone v. United States,* 302 U.S. 379 (1937).

[20] *Nardone v. United States,* 308 U.S. 388 (1939).

[21] *Schwartz v. Texas,* 344 U.S. 199 (1952).

[22] *Benanti v. United States,* 355 U.S. 96 (1957).

[23] Edward Bennett Williams, *One Man's Freedom* (New York: Atheneum, 1962), pp. 113–114.

[24] *Goldman v. United States,* 316 U.S. 129 (1942).

[25] *Silverman v. United States,* 365 U.S. 505 (1961).

[26] *On Lee v. United States,* 343 U.S. 747 (1952).

[27] *Lopez v. United States,* 373 U.S. 427 (1963).

[28] *Hoffa v. United States,* 385 U.S. 293 (1966), at 300–302. There was vigorous dissent from Justices Warren and Douglas who felt it was basically unfair for the government to use a paid informer as a stool pigeon, especially when, as was true of Partin, he was in prison facing indictment for serious crimes. Douglas remarked that a man may have to assume the risk that a friend will turn against him, but the planting of an undercover agent constituted an unlawful breach of privacy by the government.

[29] *Berger v. New York,* 388 U.S. 41 (1967).

[30] *Katz v. United States,* 389 U.S. 347 (1967).

[31] For an excellent discussion of the origins of the right against self-incrimination, see Leonard W. Levy, *Origins of the Fifth Amendment* (New York: Oxford University Press, 1968).

[32] Levy, p. viii.

[33] *Brown v. Mississippi,* 297 U.S. 278 (1936).

[34] *Ashcraft v. Tennessee,* 322 U.S. 143 (1944).

[35] *Spano v. New York,* 360 U.S. 315 (1959).

[36] *Spano v. New York,* at 320–321.

[37] As quoted in Williams, p. 127.

[38] *Escobedo v. Illinois,* 378 U.S. 478 (1964).

[39] *Escobedo v. Illinois,* at 490–491.

[40] For an excellent brief discussion of the effect of Miranda on police practice, see "The Impact of *Miranda* in Practice," in Livingston Hall, Yale Kamisar, Wayne R. LaFave, and Jerold H. Israel, *Modern Criminal Procedure,* 3rd ed. (St. Paul, Minn.: West Publishing Co., 1969), pp. 552–555.

[41] Nathan R. Sobel, *New York Times,* November 20, 1965, p. 1. Also note "Interrogations in New Haven: The Impact of Miranda," *Yale Law Journal* 76 (July 1967): 1521–1648.

[42] *Harris v. New York,* 401 U.S. 222 (1971).

[43] *Johnson v. Zerbst,* 304 U.S. 458 (1938).

[44] *Powell v. Alabama,* 287 U.S. 45 (1932).

[45] *Powell v. Alabama,* at 71.

[46] *Powell v. Alabama,* at 71.

[47] *Betts v. Brady,* 316 U.S. 455 (1942).

[48] William B. Lockhart, Yale Kamisar, and Jesse H. Choper, *Constitutional Rights and Liberties,* 2nd ed. (St. Paul, Minn.: West Publishing Co., 1967), p. 225.

[49] *Strauder v. West Virginia,* 100 U.S. 303 (1879).

[50] *Norris v. Alabama,* 294 U.S. 587 (1935).

[51] *Frank v. Mangum,* 237 U.S. 309 (1915).

[52] *Moore v. Dempsey,* 261 U.S. 86 (1923).

[53] *Frank v. Mangum,* at 350.

[54] *Irvin v. Dowd,* 366 U.S. 717 (1961).

[55] *Rideau v. Louisiana,* 373 U.S. 723 (1963).

[56] *Sheppard v. Maxwell.*

[57] *Sheppard v. Maxwell,* at 354.

[58] *Sheppard v. Maxwell,* at 355.

[59] *Toledo Newspaper Co. v. United States,* 247 U.S. 402 (1918), at 424.

[60] Judge George C. Edwards, as quoted in Hall, Kamisar, LaFave, and Israel, p. 1180, fn.

[61] Alfred Friendly and Ronald L. Goldfarb, *Crime and Publicity* (New York: Twentieth Century Fund, Inc., 1967), p. 240.

[62] *Duncan v. Louisiana,* 391 U.S. 145 (1968).

[63] *Baldwin v. New York,* 399 U.S. 66 (1970).

[64] *Benton v. Maryland,* 395 U.S. 784 (1969).

After Conviction:
Probation, Parole, and Imprisonment

y

"He (the convicted felon) has as a consequence of his crime, not only forfeited his liberty but all of his personal rights except those which the law in its humanity accords to him. He is for the time being the slave of the State."

Ruffin v. Commonwealth (1871)

"I suspect that all the crimes committed by all the jailed criminals do not equal in total social damage that of the crimes committed against them."

Karl Menninger, *The Crime of Punishment*

The criminal procedure decisions rendered by the U.S. Supreme Court have thus far covered only one part of the criminal justice system. With very few exceptions all of the decisions in this area relate to the rights of the accused up to the time of sentence; virtually no decisions relate to the post-adjudicatory rights of defendants.

The criminal justice process does not end when the defendant is convicted or pleads guilty. He must be sentenced; he may be considered for probation; he may be given a suspended sentence; he may be fined or made to pay restitution; or, he may be imprisoned. If he is imprisoned his welfare is utterly and totally in the hands of the state.

When a sheriff or a marshall takes a man from a courthouse in a prison van and transports him to confinement for two or three or 10 years, this is our act. We have tolled the bell for him. And whether we like it or not, we have made him our collective responsibility. We are free to do something about him; he is not.[1]

While in prison a prisoner may need rehabilitative treatment, medical treatment, education, or vocational training. He may desire to keep up his contacts with friends, family, and associates in the outside world and to prepare for his life after prison. He may even wish to hasten the day of his release through the study of legal literature and the perfecting of his appeal. He may seek early release through parole or the earning of "good time."

In determining how each prisoner is to be treated, vast areas of administrative discretion are involved. When a defendant is convicted of a crime, society has a right to punish him but to punish him only according to due process of law. This due process, that is, that which relates to the entire gamut of post-adjudicatory rights, has been left almost totally undefined by the courts. It has not yet even been clearly and unequivocally established that a prisoner has *any* rights that the courts are bound to respect. For many years it was accepted legal dogma that the prisoner, for the duration of his sentence, was in effect the slave of the state, a mere chattel to be handled at the discretion of administrative officials. It seems inevitable that this older attitude will be supplanted by the recognition that even a convict is a human being, and by virtue of his humanity still retains many fundamental protections against the power of the state.

PUNISHMENT

Anthropologically and historically, ours is a society that demands punishment for the commission of a crime. In primitive society, at the level of the tribe, village, or other small social system, conformity is relatively easily achieved. When society expands, personal relationships no longer effectively control human interactive behavior, law develops, and the power of punishment shifts from the kinship group to the state. Primitive law is essentially private in nature and is basically nothing more than custom enforced by cohesive kinship groups. Law, as we know it, is a product of societal growth and urbanization, and emerges whenever

223

intimate personal relationships no longer effectively control human behavior. In societies whose cultures are relatively simple, the meting out of punishment is usually left to the kinfolk of the injured individual; in complex societies and cultures, the administration of justice becomes the concern of impersonal agencies and non-relatives. The aggrieved person or his relatives no longer attempt to obtain vengeance or restitution. Society itself takes on this function and delegates it to the police and the courts. Thus, when Jones assaults Smith, the title of the resulting criminal litigation is not *Smith v. Jones* but *The People v. Jones.* The people have become the plaintiffs.

In the past, social scientists have been concerned mainly with analyzing causes of crime and understanding the criminal. Very little research has been done on societal reactions to law-breaking. Anthropological and sociological studies indicate, however, that reactions of societies to crime vary with differences in culture, and that while all societies disapprove of criminal behavior, not all societies react with the same degree of punitiveness. Punishment must thus be considered in relation to its function in a social system.

As our political, economic, and social institutions have changed through time, our attitudes toward the punishment of crime have changed also. Some of these changes were reflected by the growth of schools of philosophy relating to crime and corrections: the classical school, the neo-classical school, and the positive school.

The classical school held that an individual calculates the possible pains and pleasures of an act before embarking on any course of action. Punishment, therefore, must be designed to make the pain exceed the pleasure, and should be uniform no matter what the mitigating circumstances or background of the criminal.

The neo-classical school, less rigid than the classical school, made exception not only for children and the mentally incompetent who were unable to calculate pleasure and pain, but also for mitigating circumstances. This approach, during the nineteenth century, was less exclusively punitive than the classical approach.

The positive school held that crime may be unconsciously or physiologically motivated, and criminals, therefore, should not be held responsible for their acts and punished but should be treated. If, however, a criminal were dangerous, he should be put to death or imprisoned, not as punishment, but to protect society.

These traditional schools of criminology were in the past the most widely accepted modes of thought on the subject. None of them, however, is whole-heartedly or uncritically accepted today, as those concerned with the criminal justice system tend to be far more eclectic in their conceptual approaches. We still have not decided, even theoretically, whether punishment (as opposed to other dispositions such as therapy or rehabilitation) is necessary. Has our attitude toward crime undergone a real change, which has done away with the need for punishment? Is punishment a true latency in a system of jurisprudence which was functionally effective in the past but no longer has validity in our present social system? Or, is there still, in our system of criminal law, a real need for punishment (a milder type of punishment perhaps, but punishment nevertheless), such that without it we cannot effectively operate within the parameters of our philosophy of administering justice? Has the element of treatment completely taken over the implementation of our criminal laws?

What is our philosophy of punishment? Do we punish for vengeance? Do we punish for retribution, because every crime must be balanced by a suitable punishment? Do we punish in the hope that others will be deterred from future crime? Do we punish to protect society by removing a dangerous criminal from our midst? Do we punish in the hope that the criminal will be rehabilitated and turned from his evil ways? Or, do we punish because, when punishment is imposed on the transgressor, the societal bonds are made stronger?

We do not have a clear-cut or consistent philosophy of

punishment. Our penal codes generally provide judges with a number of alternative methods for disposing of convicted criminals. Felons may be sentenced to death for serious crimes or imprisoned for periods ranging from a year to life. At the other end of the spectrum, minor transgressors may receive suspended sentences or fines, or may be made to pay reparations or make restitution to victims. Judges also have the option of placing a convicted person on probation, where he will be supervised for a period of time fixed by the court. Criminals who are serving prison sentences may also become eligible for parole after serving their minimum sentences. These judicial options however, are frequently not exercised with any consistent pattern. Consider for example, the following five cases which, though the defendants' names are fictionalized, are taken from the records of a criminal court of a major American city:

Case 1. Adams, a dull nineteen-year-old youth of a working-class family, was arrested minutes after he accepted a ride from a friend who was driving a stolen car. Adams had had one previous appearance in juvenile court, and had adjusted well after that incident. Indeed his parents, in an effort to improve the boy's situation, had moved from their old high-delinquency neighborhood to a better residential district. Adams was made to plead guilty to a felony and was committed to a reformatory with a five-year maximum sentence.

Case 2. Baker, an eighteen-year-old boy, while practicing a quick draw with a pistol, accidently killed his sweetheart. He had no previous court record but was committed to a reformatory with a maximum sentence of five years.

Case 3. Chavez, a twenty-one-year-old man recently arrived from Puerto Rico, impregnated a fifteen-year-old girl who had willingly cohabitated with him, evidently with the thought of future marriage. Chavez had no prior record, but his school record was poor, and his work history spotty. He was sentenced to three years in prison for statutory rape.

Case 4. Downs, in a paroxysm of rage, killed his drunken wife who had nagged and irritated him beyond endurance. Downs had an excellent employment record and was the father of several young children. Following his plea of guilty to manslaughter, he was placed on probation.

Case 5. Edwards, an eighteen-year-old boy with a poor school and work record, participated in the armed robbery of a supermarket. Despite his unpromising previous behavior, he was placed on probation.

The sentences imposed in the first three cases, whatever else may be said about them, can hardly be thought rehabilitative. In Case 1, the defendant and his family had already made substantial efforts toward his rehabilitation; in Case 2, the defendant had no criminal record at all, and seemed at worst to have been guilty of poor judgment; in Case 3, the defendant apparently had no sense of moral wrong in connection with his offense since he was acculturated in a different social setting. Considering the realities of treatment of offenders in reformatories, it is far more likely that antisocial tendencies would be encouraged in the defendants rather than the opposite by the sentences imposed. The judge in Case 4, on the other hand, avoided committing the defendant to prison, even though he had admittedly killed a person in a fit of rage. In Case 5 the judge was also apparently willing to risk repeated antisocial conduct by the defendant in hopes of achieving some other goal. One can only speculate on the motives of the judges involved in these cases, but certainly the judges of Cases 1, 2, and 3 seem to have been primarily oriented toward vengeance and retribution, whereas the judges of Cases 4 and 5 seem to have been influenced by a desire to rehabilitate the criminals.

From the defendant's point of view, the severity of the punishment he can expect will vary not only with the offense he has committed, but with the judge by whom he is sentenced. When the sentences imposed within the federal and the various state court systems are reviewed, an absence of objectivity and a marked disparity in the severity of punishment is apparent. While the legal framework of these court systems usually provides for minimum and maximum limits for sentences to penal institutions as well

227

as other options such as probation or restitution, at least three variables will influence the actual sentence imposed.

The most obvious variable is the underlying philosophy of punishment. It is currently fashionable to protest that modern society has eschewed the desire for vengeance that underlay so many earlier social systems. We profess to abhor the *lex talionis*—an eye-for-an-eye, tooth-for-a-tooth approach. We claim to be interested in punishment only as a deterrent to others, or for the purpose of removing the dangerous individual from society, or for the purposes of rehabilitation. Our practices do not bear out our alleged intentions. Any student of a criminal justice system, after even a cursory examination of sentencing procedures, must realize that vengeance and retribution still play important roles in the disposition of cases.

In addition to the general philosophy of punishment, the expectations of a particular community are another major variable in sentencing procedures. An area as large as the United States, or indeed as large as many of the larger states, is heterogeneous both geographically and culturally. What is an appropriate sentence for holding up a drugstore in Chicago may be totally inappropriate for the same offense in Cornwall Bridge, Connecticut. Forcible rape sentences vary considerably from community to community, depending on the section of the country and on the race of the victim as compared to that of the criminal. In small towns where informal social controls over the individual tend to be quite strong and effective, sentences for the offender who flouts those controls tend to be more severe. Conversely, the anonymity, or even anomia, of the big city tends to soften the sharpness of social disapproval of the criminal, which reflects itself in shorter, less severe sentences. Racial, ethnic, and other class prejudices that are idiosyncratic to particular communities will also affect the severity of punishment.

The third major variable in sentencing is the personality of the judge himself. Very little has been written about how the judge as a person influences the judge as a judge.

Criminologists Winick, Blumberg, and Gerver, in a study of judicial psychology, list some of the personal variables that affect the decision-making process: age, sex, ethnic background, nationality, religion, race, marital status, socioeconomic status, law school, and background of legal practice. In another study, Smith and Blumberg relate judicial personality factors to the context in which judicial decisions are made, that is, the socio-legal courtroom milieu.[2]

Personality variables are particularly significant in the area of sentencing, since there are very few formal guidelines or standards to narrow the range of alternatives available to the judge. Unless he comes to his position in the criminal court with a background of experience in sentencing, there are few places where he can seek guidance aside from the wide limits defined in the statutes and the specific precedents established in reported judicial decisions. An American judge, unlike some of his continental counterparts, receives training only as a lawyer, not as a judge. Certainly the law school curricula do not focus on the special needs of judges sitting in criminal court. There is, in short, no specific preparation for this highly important position in our society, and an intuitive understanding of the requirements of sentencing is as much as can be expected or hoped for from any newly appointed sitting judge.

Personality factors probably act to determine the perception of the judge, especially as to what is right. Within the limits set by the statutes and the hindsight judgments of the appellate courts, judges are encumbered with few restrictions in sentencing except their own feelings of what a proper sentence should be. In few cases does the proper sentence result in justice, if one defines justice in the *lex talionis* sense of equalizing the crime and the punishment, as, for example, where the death sentence is imposed for murder. This type of justice cannot be extended to all crimes. Can an auto joy-ride theft lend itself to the same type of disposition as the theft of an auto for resale? We probably do not want the justice of the *lex talionis* in all cases, and do want some kind of discrimination in applying

229

sentences. Certainly, in the case of murder where "Cain kills Abel, [and] the very earth cries out for vengeance," a severe penalty (although not necessarily execution) agrees with the culturally defined demands of our public—as well as with the culturally determined sentences of our judges— but the disposition of other offenders is not so clear. In the vast majority of cases, however, the "right sentence" (a "fair" sentence in Justice Warren's terminology) is not necessarily the one that is just.

For viciously executed crimes, or, on the other end of the continuum, crimes which only incidentally arouse public sentiment, dispositions may be fairly uniform. It is in the middle range of crimes that the right sentence is difficult to arrive at. What is the proper sentence for a confirmed criminal who has behaved and has been steadily employed for more than a dozen years? What is the proper sentence for a serious crime committed impetuously by an individual who previously has lived a constructive, conforming, law-abiding existence? In these cases, the judge cannot poll public opinion, and indeed should not do so. There are many instances where the proper sentence will initially provoke severe censure from the public and the mass media, but with the passage of time will be accepted readily as having been appropriate not only for the crime but for the criminal.

In recent years the judiciary has exhibited concern with the task of achieving some measure of uniformity in sentencing. In the law schools, as in the practice of law, no formal provision has been made to assist judges and lawyers in analyzing their own motivations in dealing with people. It is doubtful, moreover, whether such training in the law schools would be of any value to the handful of students who, many years in the future, might become judges. A more promising approach appears to be the establishment in various judicial systems of institutes and other in-service training programs. Such programs are extremely valuable in that they at least make judges aware of the extent and difficulty of the problems of sentencing. They cannot of course, replace a thorough grounding in the behavioral sciences—

psychology, sociology, and anthropology—which ideally should be part of the background of every criminal court judge, but some of this knowledge can be made available during the course of in-service or sentencing institute training. The essential dilemma in sentencing, however, is that while uniformity is obviously highly desirable, the cultural and regional factors which shape community attitudes toward punishment for the offense charged, as well as toward the defendant himself, make uniformity not only unattainable, but, at least in some cases, undesirable. Judges, after all, do not operate in a vacuum. They must and should respond to some extent to community pressures, and the judge sitting in a county court in a rural area cannot operate in the same way as the judge who sits in one part of a large metropolitan criminal court. The best that can be achieved, probably, is that disparities of sentences within a particular cultural and regional setting can be eliminated, and inequalities of sentencing between one region and another can be reduced as much as possible. This is especially important not only in the interest of the defendant but because grossly unequal sentences for the same offense create serious problems for state and federal prison administrators who must deal with a prison population committed from diverse kinds of communities.[3]

PROBATION AND PAROLE

Probation work is social service carried on in a court setting. The probation officer has two main functions. He prepares a pre-sentence investigation designed to give the judge sufficient social and legal background concerning an adjudicated guilty defendant to enable the judge to impose a sentence which reflects both the severity of the crime and the potential behavior of the defendant in light of his past. If the judge places the defendant on probation, the probation officer is then charged with the responsibility of supervising the defendant (probationer) while he remains at liberty in the community. Supervision entails assisting

231

the defendant in adjusting to his home and his community; helping him get employment; counselling in resolving psychological or other problems; making referrals to other agencies when needed; and supervising the activities of the probationer so that he will refrain from violating the conditions of probation or committing new crimes. The conditions of probation generally involve keeping regular hours, maintaining steady employment, supporting dependents, refraining from frequenting bars, remaining sober, and reporting to the probation office when required to do so. Some jurisdictions have more and some have fewer conditions. A judge may also impose specific conditions such as refraining from particular employment; paying fines, reparations, or restitutions; or other specific directives.

Although the historical backgrounds of probation and parole are dissimilar, in function, on a day-to-day basis, the jobs of probation and parole officers cannot be distinguished.[4] Parole, according to one definition, is

> conditional release, usually by a board of parole or a board of managers, of an inmate from a penal or reformative institution after he has served a part of the sentence imposed upon him.[5]

Probation is a judicial function, presided over by a judge, while parole is an administrative function performed by an independent board of parole, board of managers, or some other body. (While the rights of both probationers and parolees are still to be determined, the courts have recognized probationers' rights more frequently than those of parolees.) The parole officer prepares pre-parole reports designed to assist parole boards in making decisions concerning the release of inmates prior to the maximum expiration of their sentences. The material in the probation and parole reports is similar, although in probation more emphasis is given to a discussion of the crime, while in the parole reports relatively greater attention is paid to an inmate's home and employment programs. The parolee on release is met with conditions similar to that faced by the probationer, and the casework and counselling services are the same for probation and parole.

Probation in the United States and England dates from 1841, and parole had its beginnings some years later. Despite their well-established character however, probation and parole practices are being reshaped by the same ferment that is affecting so much of the criminal justice system. Increasingly, defendants are questioning procedures never challenged before. Does a defendant, for example, have a right to counsel at probation or parole revocation hearings? Does a defendant have a right to see the pre-sentence investigation report which was used by the judge in sentencing? Does an inmate have a right to see the pre-parole report prepared for the use of the parole board? Is there a right to cross-examine the witnesses who gave testimony in a probation violation hearing? May an offender present witnesses on his own behalf, or rebut the testimony offered in probation or parole hearings? On what grounds may probation or parole be revoked? Most basic of all, does an individual have a right to probation or parole at all?

Whether one is entitled to probation or parole depends on whether probation and parole are considered to be privileges extended to those worthy of them at the mercy and discretion of the state; or, on the other hand, whether probation and parole are considered merely available alternative forms of punishment subject to the same due process requirements as any other form of punishment. Is the granting of probation or parole an act of grace comparable to the commutation of a sentence, or does it have only the same procedural significance as the levying of a fine or the commitment to a penal institution? The traditional view of the courts has been that a defendant has no rights after conviction other than the right to the maximum sentence prescribed by law for the offense for which he was convicted. This view is slowly changing.

In *Mempa v. Rhay,*[6] two petitioners challenged the right of the State of Washington to revoke their probation at hearings at which the defendants were not assisted by legal counsel. Mempa, aged seventeen, after having pleaded guilty to joy-riding, had been placed on probation with a deferred sentence. Some months later, the prosecutor moved to revoke probation on the ground that Mempa had been involved in a burglary. At the hearing, to which Mempa was accompanied by his stepfather, the state made no offer of counsel for the probationer.

> At the hearing Mempa was asked if it was true that he had been involved in the alleged burglary and he answered in the affirmative. A probation officer testified without cross-examination that according to his information petitioner had been involved in the burglary and had previously denied participation in it. Without asking petitioner if he had anything to say or any evidence to supply, the court immediately entered an order revoking petitioner's probation and then sentenced him to 10 years in the penitentiary.[7]

The other petitioner, Walkling, had been convicted of burglary and placed on probation for three years. Two years later he was arrested, charged with forgery and grand larceny, and brought before the court for a hearing on a petition by the prosecuting attorney to revoke his probation. Walkling requested and received a short continuance so that he might obtain a lawyer. When the hearing was called, however, the attorney did not appear and the proceedings continued with Walkling unrepresented by counsel.

> A probation officer presented hearsay testimony to the effect that petitioner had committed the acts alleged in the 14 separate counts of forgery and 14 separate counts of grand larceny that had been charged against petitioner previously at the time of his arrest. The court thereupon revoked probation and imposed the maximum sentence of 15 years on Walkling. . . . Because of the failure of the State to keep a record of the proceedings, nothing is known as to whether Walkling was advised of his right to appeal. He did not, however, take an appeal.[8]

On appeal the U.S. Supreme Court reversed the petitioners' convictions and remanded the cases to the Washington courts for further hearings. The basis for the reversal was largely that an accused person is entitled to counsel at every stage of a criminal proceeding. The decision, thus, may be nothing more than an extension of the *Gideon* decision, but it may be, on the other hand, an important first

step in broadening the post-adjudicatory rights of probationers, prisoners, and parolees. This view is based not so
much on the content of the *Mempa* decision as on the context in which it arose.

The Court, for ten years, has been assiduous in protecting the rights of accused persons. The only important
segment of the criminal justice system that has not yet been
reached is post-adjudicatory processes: probation, parole,
and penal confinement. This area is characterized, moreover, by both broad legislative delegations of power to
relevant officials and an almost total absence of formal
constitutional safeguards. With the exception of the prohibition against cruel and unusual punishment, no section
of the U.S. Constitution relates to post-adjudicatory rights.[9]
The courts in general have been loath to review the decisions made in probation, parole, and corrections cases,
primarily because probation and parole have been looked
upon as privileges extended to the convicted defendant,
and imprisonment has frequently been considered to have
effectively nullified all of the prisoner's personal rights for
the duration of his sentence. The result is that decisions in
this area have been made by a variety of officials, virtually
uncontrolled either by previously established legislative or
constitutional standards, or by post hoc judicial review.

> A combination of extremely broad legislation, narrow judicial
> review, and the consignment of most of the legally relevant
> issues to matters of privilege rather than of right has created a
> situation of virtually uncontrolled, unreviewable discretion in
> the administration of the correctional process. . . .
> There is no area of law, except perhaps the civil commitments
> of the mentally ill, where the lives of so many people are so
> drastically affected by officials who exercise a virtually absolute,
> unreviewed discretion. As the Court becomes increasingly
> aware of this situation, through a steady increase in the number
> of appeals that raise peno-correctional issues, the discretion
> factor alone could stimulate the Court's reformative energy.[10]

It will be difficult however, for the Court to extend the
procedural protections of accused persons to probationers
and parolees, without evaluating the impact of the system

on the individuals concerned. Are our probation and parole programs punitive or rehabilitative? Is the probation or parole hearing an adversary proceeding, or is there an identity of interest between the probationer or parolee and the officials charged with overseeing their lives? These questions are precisely analogous to the questions the Court has not yet resolved in the extension of procedural rights to juveniles. In the *Gault, Kent,* and *Winship* cases, the Court extended some of the procedural rights of adult defenders to children at a juvenile court hearing, but the Court has not yet made up its mind whether the juvenile hearing is essentially rehabilitative or punitive in its impact on the child. The basic contradiction in juvenile cases is obvious: children are in fact punished in the name of rehabilitation, but to view the process as purely punitive and extend to it all the procedural safeguards associated with adult true adversary proceedings would be to eliminate the rehabilitative ideal completely— to throw out the baby with the bathwater. The same contradiction applies to parole and probation programs. While rehabilitative in intent, many of the conditions, including provisions for automatic revocation of probation or parole without procedural safeguards, are punitive in fact. However, to extend to probation revocation hearings the same range of procedural safeguards applicable to the original trial of the accused is to remove some of the flexibility which is desirable in a rehabilitative program. At the same time, to make such revocation possible almost at the whim of administrative officials is to punish, not rehabilitate, without due process.

The underlying conceptual difficulties are admirably illustrated by a response in the *Georgetown Law Journal* to an opinion of Judge Burger (now Chief Justice Burger) of the U.S. Court of Appeals for the District of Columbia. The issue, in *Hyser v. Reed,*[11] was whether a parolee was entitled to assigned counsel at a parole revocation hearing. Justice Burger, for the majority, argued that,

> The Bureau of Prisons and the Parole Board operate from the
> basic premise that prisoners placed in their custody are to be

rehabilitated and restored to useful lives as soon as . . . that transition can be safely made. . . . Thus there is a genuine identity of interest . . . in the prisoner's desire to be released and the Board's policy to grant release as soon as possible. Here there is not the attitude of adverse, conflicting objectives as between the parolee and Board inherent between prosecution and defense in a criminal case. Here we do not have pursuer and quarry but a relationship partaking of *parens patriae*. In a real sense the Parole Board in revoking parole occupies the role of parent withdrawing a privilege from an errant child not as a punishment but for misuse of the privilege.[12]

to which the *Georgetown Law Journal* responded,

It is submitted that the view that parole revocation proceedings do not involve adversary interests is invalid. When the Board maintains that a parolee has done a specific act for which his parole may be revoked and he denies it, there are undeniable adverse objectives; this falls far short of a genuine identity of interests. . . . Furthermore, the revocation process presents basic similarities to the consequences of a criminal trial. The possibility of a parolee losing his conditional liberty is the most obvious similarity. . . . In the analogous area of juvenile courts, the Supreme Court, rejecting an argument that *ex parte* juvenile proceedings are totally non-adversary in their determinations of delinquency, recently recognized that adverse interests do in fact lurk beneath the *parens patriae* surface.[13]

At present, the procedural rights of probationers and parolees are largely undefined, at least by the U.S. Supreme Court. They are emerging from limbo into a state of chaos. The Court, if it chooses to enter this field, has its work cut out for it. The rights of probationers (such as they are) are different from those of parolees, and for both groups many challenges to established procedures have yet to be mounted. As in the problem of the juvenile court, there are no obvious simple answers. The almost unlimited discretion in the hands of judges and parole boards must undoubtedly be limited in the interests of fairness; at the same time, to fully equate probation and parole with punishment rather than rehabilitation probably is to destroy the only part of the criminal justice system whose avowed aim is the restoration of the offender to useful life in the community.

PENAL CONFINEMENT

Like probationers and parolees, prisoners are attempting increasingly to use the courts to define and to enlarge their personal rights. The traditional view of the courts has been that an individual, once legally consigned to prison, has no rights and that he is, for the duration of his sentence, in effect "the slave of the state." This view is currently under attack, and the pressure to modify it will undoubtedly grow more intense in the near future. Reformers, civil libertarians, and others concerned with the rights of inmates hold that only those rights necessary to effectuate the sentence of the court are lost to the prisoner, and that he retains all others. The inmate, in other words, must be restrained to the extent necessary to keep him in a penal institution, but beyond that he should retain control over his personal life. Dozens of questions concerning the extent to which prisoner administrators may restrict the activities of their charges can be raised, since prison is, after all, probably the most total of total institutions.

> Enormous discretion is left to correctional administrators to define the conditions of imprisonment. They determine the way in which the offender will live for the term of imprisonment; how he is fed and clothed; whether he sleeps in a cell or a dormitory; whether he spends his days locked up or in relative freedom; what opportunity he has for work, education, or recreation. They regulate his access to the outside world by defining mailing and visiting privileges. They define rules of conduct and the penalties for violation of such rules. And increasingly, they make classification decisions—assigning different prisoners to different kinds of correctional programs. This may involve decisions to place prisoners in different institutions or to grant certain prisoners relative freedom in the community, as for example, on educational or work-release programs.[14]

Whether a prisoner has a right to receive unlimited quantities of uncensored mail; whether he has a right to give legal advice to other inmates; whether he has a right to practice actively any religion he chooses; whether he has a right to advance and support political opinions while in prison—the answers to all these questions depend not so much on the letter or even the spirit of the Constitution and the laws as on society's view of the purpose of imprisonment. Is an offender sentenced to prison to punish him, to keep him out of circulation, or to rehabilitate him? When he is sent to prison, is the imprisonment itself the punishment, or is the prison simply the locus of further punishment?* As previously indicated, we do not have a simple, clear-cut philosophy of corrections. When pushed, most people will assert that rehabilitation is probably the most important goal to be achieved, but the reality of our corrections system is such that vengeance and possibly a desire to quarantine dangerous offenders are obviously far more important goals. Not only does society permit prisoners to be housed and fed in inhuman and degrading conditions, but underneath the seeming apathy which accounts for the slowness of prison reform is a seldom expressed, though widely prevalent feeling that whatever inmates suffer, it is probably no more than what they deserve. One cannot read any of the massive literature relating to prison conditions without becoming aware that the public probably does not wish things to be any different. Dr. Karl Menninger called his recent book on corrections *The Crime of Punishment* and states that the crimes committed by society against prisoners in the name of corrections are greater than the crimes these prisoners had committed against society.[15]

If the purpose of prison is punishment, prisoners should have very few rights, since after all, the purpose of confining them is to make them suffer, and there is little point in mitigating that suffering by defining personal rights. Prison personnel, to be sure, should not be degraded by having to administer punishments too barbarous or grisly, but according to this philosophy prisoners who have been sent away to suffer should be permitted to do so. On the other hand,

---

*The distinction between being committed to prison as punishment or for punishment is the difference between Sing Sing, where prisoners are simply held in custody, and certain southern prison systems where inmates are forced to work on a chain gang.

if the purpose of the prison sentence is to keep the offender out of circulation and away from the public for a given period of time, there is no reason why the inmate should not enjoy all personal rights except those which would permit him to leave his place of confinement at will. If the purpose of imprisonment is rehabilitation, however, then it is *essential* that the inmate not be deprived of his personal rights more than is absolutely necessary, since the primary goal of rehabilitation is to restore a sense of dignity and integrity to one who is already degraded in the eyes of society. As Menninger points out, if one hopes that on release a prisoner will re-enter society as a decent man living with other decent men, he must be treated in the way that we expect him to treat others on his release. Humiliating or degrading programs and punishments are thus entirely counterproductive since they confirm in the inmate his own sense of lack of self-worth and make him even more vicious than he already is.

Our prison programs are a reflection of our lack of focus and direction in terms of a philosophy of corrections. Most prison programs, though described in rehabilitative terms, are in fact highly punitive. Their success in rehabilitation has been minimal, as attested by the high recidivism rate. Menninger suggests an interesting and unorthodox approach to the problem of the disposition of convicted criminals. He recommends the establishment of diagnostic centers in which social scientists, including psychiatrists, psychologists, social workers, and others, will make an examination of the offender and of the situation in which his offense was committed, appraising the assets and liabilities of both the offender's personality and his social environment. After such an appraisal, disposition can be recommended in terms of what is best for both the offender and society. If the offender is treatable, then he should be treated in some appropriate manner and released as soon as he is adjudged rehabilitated. If, on the other hand, he is both dangerous and not treatable, he should be given custodial care for an indefinite period — possibly for life. Between these two extremes varying combinations of custodial care and rehabilitation treatment might be imposed.[16]

At present, our corrections system suffers not only from ideological confusion but also from bureaucratic apathy. Prisons tend to be understaffed and to attract insufficient numbers of bright, dedicated administrators. There are seldom enough funds or physical facilities for innovative creative programs, and all too often there is a lack of genuine desire on the part of the staff to get such money or to formulate such programs. When all else fails, moreover, an indolent prison administration can always invoke the name of security to justify the status quo and kill at birth any new program which would entail altering prison routine.

The greatest likelihood at this point is that if constructive changes are to take place in our prison systems the impetus will have to come from the outside, that is, the courts or the legislatures, and of the two, considering the lack of political power possessed by inmates, the courts appear to be the most probable source of innovation. Relatively few cases regarding the rights of prisoners have reached the U.S. Supreme Court. Since most prisoners are either poor, ignorant, or both, it is easy to see that without legal defender organizations, very few cases are likely to reach the lower appellate courts, much less the U.S. Supreme Court. Prison officials, moreover, are understandably less than enthusiastic about prisoner attempts to reach the courts and are uncooperative, if not actually obstructive. Indeed, one of the earliest Supreme Court decisions in this area concerns the rights of prisoners to access to the courts.

> The state and its officials may not abridge or impair petitioner's rights to apply to a federal court for a writ of *habeas corpus*. Whether a petition for a writ of *habeas corpus* addressed to a federal court is properly drawn and what allegations it must contain are questions for the court alone to determine.[17]

Prisoners have challenged in the lower state and federal courts the right of prison officials to limit mail that they may wish to send or receive. At the present moment mail privileges are still firmly in control of prison administrators, with the exception of letters from inmates to the courts, which may not be delayed, censored, or not delivered. Mail to and from a prisoner's attorney is not so privileged however, and such correspondence may be opened, inspected, and even delayed, thus vitiating the confidential lawyer-client relationship. Prisoners may indeed have virtually no opportunity to consult in private with their attorneys, since, although electronic eavesdropping has been condemned, a guard may be stationed close enough to overhear any conversation.

Another obstacle in the path of a prisoner seeking access to the courts is the lack of legal materials available to him. Since so many prisoners do not have funds to obtain counsel, many would attempt to do at least the preliminary legal work in regard to an appeal if law books were available. Until now the courts have held that the state has no obligation to provide prisoners with legal materials, nor does a prisoner have the right to use such materials even if he can obtain them on his own. For many inmates the most accessible type of counsel is the "jailhouse lawyer," another inmate with usually self-taught knowledge of the law. Prison administrators generally forbid this type of legal assistance because they feel that jailhouse lawyers are inimical to discipline in that they focus the attention of inmates on faults in the prison or in the criminal justice system and encourage false hopes of release. In two federal court cases however, it was held that jailhouse lawyers may extend assistance to any inmate in need of such help.[18]

Another right which prisoners have recently sought to assert is the right to practice their religion while they are in prison. Most prisons make chaplains, church services, and the like available to inmates, at least for those of the locally dominant religious persuasions. Little or no provision is made for prisoners who have special religious needs such as dietary laws or specially scheduled masses. Currently, however, the most thorny problem in this area relates to the right of the Black Muslims to practice their religion while in prison. The lower federal courts are beginning to

extend to the Muslims the right to hold services, to possess
religious medals, and carry on other religious activities. The
problem with the Muslims stems largely from the belief held
by prison administrators that certain Muslim beliefs and
practices are sufficiently militant as to lead to disorder, and
on this ground many Muslims have been placed in solitary or
denied "good time" because of their beliefs. Another problem in regard to religion has been posed by the Berrigan
brothers, two radical Catholic priests, confined in federal
prison in connection with the destruction of Selective Service records. The Berrigans have insisted on not only their
right to say mass and perform other priestly religious duties
but their right to write and deliver sermons which doubtless
will express the same radical political views which motivated the actions for which they were jailed in the first
place.

Recent challenges have also been mounted as to the
kinds of discipline and punishment prison administrators can
impose on inmates. The definition of a "cruel and unusual
punishment" is of course culturally determined, and many
practices such as whipping, iron yokes, and hanging by the
wrists, which were once permissible, are no longer acceptable. It is the use of solitary confinement, either with or
without dietary restrictions, removal of clothing, and removal
of furniture and sanitary facilities, that is most commonly
challenged today. The courts are beginning to apply federal
correctional standards and those determined by the American Correctional Association in defining cruel and unusual
punishment. These standards forbid corporal punishment as
well as denial of normal clothing, bedding, hygienic materials, and standard rations.

Another successful legal challenge against prevailing
prison administrative practices was mounted by an inmate
who claimed that New York State statutes regulating the
transfer of prisoners to an institution for the criminally insane
provided for fewer procedural safeguards than is afforded
those who are not prisoners facing involuntary confinement
in a mental hospital, thus denying prisoners equal protection

of the laws.[19] The Federal Circuit Court agreed that the prisoner was entitled to an examination by independent, outside physicians, and a hearing at which he could produce witnesses and evidence. He was entitled moreover to judicial review of the proceedings before his transfer and to a periodic administrative review of the need for his continued confinement in the mental institution.

One of the most significant recent court decisions in the area of prisoners' rights was made by Federal District Court Judge Constance Baker Motley in *Sostre v. Rockefeller.*[20] Sostre was a Black Muslim who had been held in solitary confinement for some twelve months because of the legal and Black Muslim activities he carried on in prison, in the course of which he expressed militant and politically radical ideas. The Court not only upheld Sostre's claim that he should not have been so confined, but awarded him thirteen thousand dollars in damages. Prison officials, moreover, were enjoined from placing Sostre in solitary again without a formal hearing at which Sostre would have right to counsel, the right to call witnesses, and the right to introduce evidence. The most significant aspect of the *Sostre* decision, however, is not the unprecedented award of damages to an inmate, but the fact that it clearly rejected the old "slave of the state" approach and embodied the newer approach — that a prisoner carries with him to prison all of his personal rights, losing only those necessary to effectuate his imprisonment.*

Sostre's force as law for the future is still questionable, but it points in the direction our courts must take if prison reform is to be achieved. Prison reform, moreover, must be achieved, unless we plan to lock up every offender for life and throw away the key, because at present our prisons are

---

*On February 24, 1971, in a rather confusing opinion, the U.S. Court of Appeals for the Second Circuit affirmed in part and reversed in part Judge Motley's decision. While the Court of Appeals refused to uphold the precise procedural requirements for notice, counsel, and hearing imposed on prison officials by the District Court, it unequivocally declared that the time was long past when a prisoner could be treated "as temporarily a slave of the state."

in many cases turning out men more hardened, more vicious, more knowledgeable in the ways of crime than when they went in. They go in as individuals already defeated and degraded by society; they often come out as either snarling animals or misfits unable to live in the outside world.

It is easy to say that prison reform is necessary and that the courts must point the way. One must recognize, on the other hand, that the most basic challenges to the prison system have not yet been made. What will happen, for example, when and if inmates of the Tombs in New York City challenge the right of the city to confine them, three to a cell, in living quarters designed to hold one man? What will happen if the courts declare that all prisoners have a right to decent living conditions, clean bedding, good food, and rehabilitative treatment? Only disaster can ensue at that point unless the legislature and the administrative agencies have kept pace with the social movements that are impelling the courts to take the lead in penal institutional change. Obviously the courts alone cannot do the whole job, and we may be worse off than ever if they attempt to do so without cooperation from other branches of government. The legislature and administrative officials however, cannot be expected to act without some prodding from the public itself, which must become aware of the needs for intelligent handling of prisoners. The hope is, as Dr. Menninger has put it, that

> The public will grow increasingly ashamed of its cry for retaliation, its persistent demand to punish. This is its crime, *our* crime against criminals—and incidentally our crime against ourselves. For before we can diminish our sufferings from the ill-controlled aggressive assaults of fellow citizens, we must renounce the philosophy of punishment, the obsolete, vengeful penal attitude. In its place we would seek a comprehensive, constructive social attitude—therapeutic in some instances, restraining, but preventive in its total social impact.[21]

Can we? Will we?

Selected Readings

Cohen, Fred. *The Legal Challenge to Corrections.* Washington, D.C.: Joint Commissions on Correctional Manpower and Training, 1969.

Dressler, David. *Practice and Theory of Probation and Parole.* 2nd ed. New York: Columbia University Press, 1969.

Hart, H. L. A. *Punishment and Responsibility: Essays in the Philosophy of Law.* New York: Oxford University Press, 1967.

Menninger, Karl. *The Crime of Punishment.* New York: Viking, 1968.

Newman, Charles L. *Sourcebook on Probation, Parole and Pardons.* 3rd ed. Springfield, Ill.: Charles C. Thomas, 1968.

Sellin, Thorsten. *Capital Punishment.* New York: Harper and Row, 1967.

President's Commission on Law Enforcement and Administration of Justice. *Task Force Report: Corrections.* Washington, D.C.: U.S. Government Printing Office, 1967.

Toch, Hans, ed. *Legal and Criminal Psychology.* New York: Holt, Rinehart and Winston, 1961.

Notes

[1] Chief Justice Warren E. Burger, Address to the 100th Anniversary Convocation of the Association of the Bar of the City of New York, February 18, 1970.

[2] Charles Winick, Israel Gerver, and Abraham Blumberg, "The Psychology of Judges," in Hans Toch, ed., *Legal and Criminal Psychology* (New York: Holt, Rinehart and Winston, 1961), pp. 141–145; Alexander B. Smith and Abraham Blumberg, "The Problems of Objectivity in Judicial Decision-Making," *Social Forces* 46, no. 1 (September 1967): 96–105.

[3] For a discussion of the relation of disparate sentences to prison problems, see James V. Bennett (Director of U.S. Bureau of Prisons), "Of Prisons and Justice," an unpublished article inserted for distribution in the September 1961 issue of *Federal Probation.*

[4] For a complete and full description of probation and parole, including their historical backgrounds, see David Dressler, *Practice and Theory of Probation and Parole,* 2nd ed. (New York: Columbia University Press, 1969).

[5] *Manual for Probation Officers in New York State,* 6th ed. (New York State Great Meadow Correctional Institution, 1960), p. 1308.

[6] *Mempa v. Rhay,* 389 U.S. 128 (1967).

[7] *Mempa v. Rhay,* at 131.

[8] *Mempa v. Rhay,* at 132–133.

[9] See Heinz R. Hink, "The Application of Constitutional Standards of Protection to Probation," *University of Chicago Law Review* 29 (1962): 483–497.

[10] Fred Cohen, "Sentencing, Probation, and the Re-Habilitating Ideal: The View from *Mempa v. Rhay,*" *Texas Law Review* 47 (1968): 1.

[11] *Hyser v. Reed,* 318 F. 2nd 225 (D.C. Cir., 1963).

[12] *Hyser v. Reed,* at 237.

[13] Note, "Parole Revocation in the Federal System," 56 *Georgetown Law Journal* 705 (1968): 721–723.

[14] President's Commission on Law Enforcement and Administration of Justice, *Task Force Report: Corrections* (Washington, D.C.: U.S. Government Printing Office, 1967), p. 84.

[15] Karl Menninger, *The Crime of Punishment* (New York: The Viking Press, 1968).

[16] Menninger, pp. 228–231.

[17] *Ex parte Hull,* 312 U.S. 546 (1941), at 549.

[18] *Johnson v. Avery,* 393 U.S. 483 (1969); *Wainwright v. Coonts,* 409 F 2nd 1337 (1969).

[19] *Schuster v. Herold,* 410 F 2nd 1071, 2nd Cir. (1969); *cert. denied,* 396 U.S. 847 (1969).

[20] *Sostre v. Rockefeller,* 312 F. Supp. 863 (S.D.N.Y.) 1970.

[21] Menninger, p. 280.

247

Index

254

A B C D E F G H I J   9 8 7 6 5 4 3 2 1